SOCIA

REV

Edited by

Hartley Dean
Professor of Social Policy
The University of Luton

Roberta Woods
Staff Tutor in Social Sciences
The Open University

SPA
SOCIAL POLICY
ASSOCIATION

SOCIAL POLICY REVIEW 11

Published by the Social Policy Association
University of Luton
Luton LU1 3JU

First published 1999

British Library Cataloguing in Publication Data
Social Policy Review - (No. 11) -
1. Great Britain. Social Policies
361.6'1'0941

ISBN 0 9518895 8 3

Typeset and produced by the University Printing Unit, University of Kent at Canterbury

Contents

International developments

Contributors

John Benington	Director of the Local Government Centre The Warwick Business School, University of Warwick
Tim Blackman	Deputy Head of the School of Social Sciences and Law Oxford Brookes University
Michael Cahill	Principal Lecturer in Social Policy The University of Brighton
John Clarke	Professor of Social Policy The Open University
Dee Cook	Professor of Social Policy The University of Wolverhampton
David Donnison	Professor of Social Policy, The University of Glasgow
Sharon Gewirtz	Lecturer in Social Policy The Open University
Howard Glennerster	Professor of Social Policy The London School of Economics
Bob Hudson	Senior Research Fellow Nuffield Institute for Health, University of Leeds
Peter Kemp	Professor of Housing The University of Glasgow
Hilary Land	Professor of Family Policy and Child Welfare The University of Bristol

Robert Lerman   Director of the Human
                      Resources Policy Centre,
                      The Urban Institute, American University,
                      Washington DC

Mike O'Brien   Senior Lecturer in Social Policy
                      and Social Work
                      Massey University, Aukland

Jacqueline   Senior Research Fellow
O'Reilly   WZB – Social Science Research Centre
                      The Free University, Berlin

Amanda Palmer   Senior Lecturer in Sociology
                      Oxford Brookes University

Günter Schmid   Director of Labour Market Policy and
                      Employment Group
                      WZB – Social Science Research Centre
                      The Free University, Berlin

1 Introduction

Hartley Dean and Roberta Woods

Students of social policy are characteristically warned from the outset that not only should they concern themselves with the processes which secure or deny human well-being, they must also recognise 'the normative and contested nature of social policy' (Erskine, 1998, p19). This remains as true as it ever was. Social policy currently finds itself at the eye of a storm of reform and intellectual controversy. The last two editions of *Social Policy Review* (*SPR*) have addressed the consequences in Britain of the social policy reforms portended by or resulting from the election of a New Labour government in 1997. The scale of change has been at least as dramatic as that which followed the election of the first Thatcher government in 1979, and the pace, if anything, has been more rapid. The emerging significance of the reforms continues therefore to preoccupy the academic social policy community and this is reflected in the chapters which follow. Additionally, however, as the new millennium approaches, controversies over the future of social policy are increasingly debated in a global context and the editors have endeavoured to ensure that this too is reflected in the current edition.

It is in the nature of *SPR* that each edition contains a fairly eclectic selection of chapters. Not only do the authors address a range of different subjects, but they do so from a variety of different theoretical or ideological perspectives; this should be regarded as a strength rather than a weakness of the publication. Additionally, it will never be possible for any one edition of *SPR* to address every salient contemporary issue. Nonetheless, it is possible to distil from the chapters in this year's SPR two broad sets of intersecting themes. The first of these is concerned with the changing nature of the global orthodoxy that appears increasingly to influence the development of social welfare policy. The second relates to emergent debates within the traditions of critical analysis that constitute social policy as an academic subject. Before outlining the substance of the particular chapters which make up the edition, we shall briefly introduce and engage with these two sets of themes.

New orthodoxies

It is widely acknowledged that during the last quarter of the twentieth century social welfare provision has become 'unsettled' (Hughes and Lewis, 1998). In the 1970s, it is often claimed, the welfare state confronted a 'crisis' (e.g. Mishra, 1984), and while some argue that it weathered that crisis tolerably well (e.g. LeGrand, 1990), others say it has been transformed, restructured, reconstructed, dismantled or even ended (for a summary account see Powell and Hewitt, 1998). There have nonetheless been several attempts to define that which is distinctive or essential about the programme of welfare reform that is being advanced in the UK by the New Labour government. This has been variously conceptualised as:

- 'The Third Way' (Giddens, 1998), a consolidating compromise between the destabilising tendencies of the New Right and the Old Left.

- 'Post-Thatcherism' (Driver and Martell, 1998), a political agenda that was defined by the neo-liberal/neo-conservative synthesis that characterised Thatcherism, but which has departed from it.

- 'The Blair/Clinton orthodoxy' (Jordan, 1998), a reflection of a broader political consensus dictated by the subordination of social justice to global markets.

To the extent that the government itself repeatedly describes its approach on a variety of issues as a 'Third Way' (though not always in the sense ascribed to the term by Giddens), it is the term which has tended to stick. Several of the chapters that follow attempt critically to unpick what constitutes the 'Third Way' or, to put it less grandly, what is new about New Labour? What emerges is a number of issues, some of which are very much concerned with the *style* of governance under New Labour (cf. Bochell and Bochell, 1998), while others are concerned with the *substance* of New Labour policy.

Questions of style

The more facile critiques of New Labour, by focusing on its preoccupation with policy presentation, imply that it has style without substance. This is to miss the point. The style and discourse of New Labour's presentation are intimately bound up with the substantive effects of its approach to government. New Labour enjoins us to believe on the one hand that the reins of government must be held in the iron grip of fiscal 'prudence', but on the other that all the institutions and processes of politics and government must be relentlessly 'modernised'. Prudence and modernisation are the new political imperatives that can brook no argument: to suggest that taxes might be increased to pay for improved services is 'imprudent'; to suggest the retention of established policy mechanisms is to be Luddite and reactionary. This is the first of two ways in which we may be witnessing a certain foreclosure of political debate.

The second way in which this occurs is perhaps more subtle. It is the pragmatic insistence that 'what counts is what works' (Labour Party, 1997, p4). By eschewing 'outdated ideology' New Labour aims to achieve new forms of 'joined-up government'. At one level this is a call to enhanced coordination and 'partnership' between different arms of government, and between government (central and local) and the voluntary and private sectors. In itself, such an objective is beyond reproach. At another level, however, it is clear that 'joined-up thinking' is to be addressed to processes, not theories of welfare. The implication is that there is something carping and immature about analytical approaches which seek merely to understand or explain the barriers to effectiveness as opposed to practical-outcome-oriented approaches which will drive the necessary measures through. There is a risk that 'joined-up government' may in fact entail a greater centralisation of political power, a diminution of professional autonomy and the further encroachment of managerialism. Passing responsibility for policy implementation to local actors is one thing, but to require them by an effort of will to 'join up' policy elements which may

ultimately prove to be systemically incompatible is a recipe for
disempowerment. The implications require an analysis rooted in
objective theory, not political pragmatism.

Questions of substance

Turning to the substance of New Labour's approach to social
policy, at least three major themes emerge in the chapters that
follow. These may be identified as work, community and social
exclusion.

During its 1997 general election campaign New Labour
famously declared that work is the best form of welfare. Initially
this was demonstrated through the New Deal for unemployed
people (Finn, 1998). However, the government's welfare reform
green paper has now made it explicit that New Labour's objective
is nothing less than 'rebuilding welfare around the work ethic'
(Department of Social Security, 1998, p3). Work here means
paid employment. To the extent that the government has
expressed a range of other objectives, about supporting families
and helping those in poverty, these are subordinate to ensuring
that those who are capable of participating in the labour market
should do so. Work is in one sense New Labour's definitive value.
It is through work that its notions of equality and social justice are
derived. In this, the government has drawn on the proposals of
the Commission for Social Justice (CSJ, 1994) which had
recommended the goal of an 'investors' Britain'. Governments, it
is now believed, cannot and should not aim to secure complete
equality of outcome for their citizens. What matters more is
equality of opportunity in relation to the labour market. Social
justice is achievable through investment in opportunity: in
education, lifelong learning, welfare-to-work and training. To
promote opportunity instead of dependency on benefits, it is also
important to ensure that work should pay, or be seen to pay; and
so the government has legislated for a national minimum wage
and will legislate for new systems of tax credits rather than welfare
benefits – a working families tax credit, childcare tax credit and
even, it seems, a tax credit for housing costs – to ensure that
income is more directly associated with waged employment.
Underpinning the centrality of work as a policy objective is an
insistence – now written into the Labour Party's constitution –
that the rights we enjoy should reflect the duties we owe. The
primary social duty it would seem is paid work, and it is upon our
capacity and willingness to work that our social entitlements will
depend (e.g. Lister, 1998).

The 'investors' Britain' envisaged by the Commission for Social Justice sought also 'to combine the ethics of community with the dynamics of a market economy' (CSJ, 1994, p4). If the work ethic is the key to accommodating social justice with market forces, then the ethic of community is the key to addressing society's social ills. In taking up this challenge from the Commission for Social Justice, New Labour has added yet another layer of meaning to that most slippery of terms – 'community'. One thing that is clear is that, as Driver and Martell put it, 'When Blair talks of community . . . he does not mean the working class community, but the whole nation, all included, with a common purpose' (1998, p163). New Labour's brand of communitarianism, to the extent that it is shared with that of Clinton's New Democrats, is not socialist but, some would argue, inherently conservative (Jordan, 1998). It embodies a set of moral assumptions that are concerned, as we have seen, with the responsibilities of individuals, but also with the nature of families and local communities. In its willingness to support families, New Labour more or less explicitly lends support to a 'traditional' family model. In its bid to enhance local communities – through, for example, the New Deal for communities, and Action Zone initiatives for Health, Education and Employment – the focus is on failing communities and the measures necessary to secure the participation of the members of those communities with the 'joined-up' interventions of the government and its local partners. Whereas the New Right blamed poverty and deprivation on their victims and the Old Left blamed them on capitalism, the Third Way is ambiguous. In some instances it appears to blame them on a failure of community – or of particular communities – although at other times this implication is conflated with allusions more redolent of a social democratic analysis, as when Tony Blair declares that the modern welfare state should tackle community decay by tackling the 'fundamental causes', among which he numbers 'structural unemployment, poor education, poor housing, the crime and drugs culture' (Blair, 1999).

Closely bound up with these particular conceptions of work and community is a preoccupation with concepts of social exclusion and inclusion. Unlike its New Right predecessors, New Labour does profess concern about growing social inequality and poverty. It has even promised an annual audit of poverty indicators by which 'to be judged on its progress in tackling the causes of poverty' (*The Guardian*, 12 February 1999). The clear and insistent message of the government, however, is that its aim is to attack social exclusion, and it is to this end that it has created its cross-departmental Social Exclusion Unit. The 'causes of poverty' lie in the failure of the means to social inclusion and not, as the Old Left believed, in the failures of the market economy: the solution lies not in the redistribution of incomes, but in the promotion of the means to ensure that individuals are included in the labour market and/or the wider community. It is through the concept of social exclusion – or rather its obverse, social inclusion – that New Labour redefines equality. According to Giddens, the Third Way defines equality, not just in terms of equality of opportunity, but 'as inclusion' (1998, pp70 and 105 [*emphasis added*]).

New Labour's analysis of course is not unique. It signifies the growing consensus that the 'golden age' (Esping-Andersen, 1996; Pierson, 1998) of the protectionist welfare state has now passed. Elements of the analysis are to a greater or lesser extent reflected in (if they have not been borrowed from) processes of welfare reform that are occurring in other parts of the world. It can incidentally be argued that, as an instance of an emerging orthodoxy, New Labour's project represents not a new political discourse, but the product of a subtle recombination of established but potentially contradictory discursive repertoires (Dean with Melrose, 1999). However, the salient point that emerges in this edition of *SPR* is that, beneath political rhetoric and in spite of significant national differences, the bare bones of an internally consistent orthodoxy are beginning to take on a detectable shape.

Critical traditions

How, then, has academic social policy reacted to substantive social policy change? Social policy as an academic subject area or discipline has a relatively short, but nonetheless complex, history (e.g. Bulmer *et al.*, 1989). At the risk of oversimplification, it is possible to identify two dominant traditions that are alive and well within the contemporary discipline: these may be characterised (or, perhaps, caricatured) as the Fabian Social Administration tradition and the Critical Social Policy tradition. The former is concerned broadly with the efficacy of welfare, the latter with its underlying function or meaning. Not only are these labels potentially misleading, but it is no more than a limited ideal-typical distinction: neither tradition is necessarily 'Fabian' or otherwise ideologically driven; both traditions can be equally intellectually 'critical'; and most social policy commentators draw freely on both traditions. However, the distinction retains some heuristic value and can be applied to further our understanding of the chapters which follow. It is not only debates between these traditions but also debates within them that are currently contributing to the development of the discipline.

The efficacy of reform

There are debates which engage with the efficacy of current welfare reforms. There is scope here both for optimistic and pessimistic constructions of the present situation. In any process of reform it is possible to trace historical and conceptual continuities, and there are debates to be had about what constitutes continuity and what might constitute points of departure and change. For good or for ill, most commentators accept as reality a shift towards welfare pluralism, and that social policy is and will be less concerned with the extent of the welfare state than with the nature of the welfare mix. It is possible, for example, to embrace the role of market provision insofar that, up to a point, markets may be able to deliver some welfare services better than the state, while other services require some level of collective coordination. The question for debate, therefore, is – up to which point? Similarly, when government insists that 'what counts is what works', this inevitably provokes debate about what indeed will work. For example, on the available evidence, would the current approach to active labour market policy withstand the effects of a recession? How effective have managerially inspired approaches been in securing collaboration between welfare services? Is it feasible for the commercial sector to provide social care insurance?

In spite of the above-mentioned tendency on New Labour's part to foreclose debate, there have been attempts on the part of some social policy academics in the UK to challenge the Third Way, most notably after the last annual conference of the Social Policy Association when an open letter was sent on behalf of some 150 delegates to the government's Secretary of State for Social Security. Published in *The Guardian* (29 July 1998), the letter responded to the government's welfare reform Green Paper with five main concerns:

- That the duty which the government seeks to impose on benefit claimants to take up work and training opportunities is not reciprocated by the acceptance on the government's part of a duty to provide such opportunities.

- That the emphasis on *paid* work by implication devalues other forms of work, including and especially care work.

- That, in spite of assurances of security for those who cannot work, the government is not committed to ensuring the adequacy of benefits for all who cannot work.

- That, for all its talk of 'modernising' the system, the government has not reviewed the structure of social security nor, in particular, the role of social insurance.

- That the reforms entirely neglect the specific needs of minority ethnic groups.

Some of these points are echoed and some are contradicted in the contributions which follow. It is important to stress, on the one hand, that many aspects of the UK government's welfare reforms have also been publicly welcomed by members of the academic social policy community as real gains and, on the other, that New Labour's project remains incomplete (though further developments are being announced – almost on a weekly basis).

The meaning of reform
What of the other tradition in social policy? How are we to deconstruct the immanent logic and interior discourses of the welfare reform agenda? It is possible to look beyond the pronouncements of governments and the declared intentions of political leaders to detect the inherent function of a policy regime. There is a certain tendency to preoccupation with Tony Blair and 'Blairism' – as once there was a preoccupation with Margaret Thatcher and 'Thatcherism' – at the expense of an analysis of the historical moment. It might be argued that:

> the logic is perfectly clear, the aims decipherable, and yet . . . no one is there to have invented [those aims], and few can be said to have formulated them: an implicit characteristic of the great anonymous, almost unspoken strategies which co-ordinate the loquacious tactics whose 'inventors' or decisionmakers are often without hypocrisy. (Foucault, 1981 p95)

It is as futile to blame the leaders of welfare capitalist states for surrendering to the logic of global economic forces as it is to suppose that they necessarily have a fully coherent or effective plan by way of response. It is more important to understand the changes that are occurring within the material relations of power. In this way, we can see that governments are indeed effecting an accommodation with international capital and flexible labour markets, by becoming risk-managing states rather than welfare states (e.g. Beck, 1992). Even within these parameters, however, it is possible to predict a range of alternative outcomes and indeed to theorise alternative strategies.

By paying attention to the discourses through which justifications for welfare reform are framed it is also possible to understand more about the strategies by which individual 'welfare subjects' (e.g. Leonard, 1997) are constructed and regulated. Underpinning the approaches we have outlined above to work, community and social exclusion are discourses that supposedly define 'cultures' of low expectation, dependency and crime, and which set out to change those cultures and the behaviour for which they are allegedly responsible. In some instances, therefore, the object of policy, if it is not explicitly authoritarian, is to introduce an implicit disciplinary effect. Through the extension of managerial doctrine this extends to the regulation of service providers and professionals, as well as to their 'customers'. In the event, it must be noted that this specific reconstitution of subjects as customers or consumers (a discursive device inherited in the case of the New Labour government from its predecessors, but which has never been disclaimed) has a significance of its own. Government may seek to manage risk as has been suggested, but it does so without inhibiting the consumerism which fuels the production of risk; on the contrary, it promotes the identity of the citizen or subject, both as a worker and as a consumer (Bauman, 1998). These kinds of issues and contradictions are pursued in various ways by some of our contributors, offering alternative frameworks through which to make sense of the present and speculate about the future development of social policy.

Outline

This edition of *SPR* is arranged in three sections: the first is concerned with new thinking in the field of social policy; the second with current welfare reforms in the UK; and the third with international developments.

New thinking

Our first section opens fittingly with a critical account of 'Third Way' thinking provided by Howard Glennerster (Chapter 2). Glennerster expresses his mistrust of big ideas and his scepticism about the term 'The Third Way'. Nonetheless, he is broadly supportive of New Labour's approach and acclaims Tony Blair for bringing a 'blessed sense of honesty' to the welfare debate. For

Glennerster, the so-called 'Third Way' correctly interprets the will of 'the taxpaying public' and the incentives which 'ordinary people' require in order to work and save. There are, of course, other views on this point (e.g. Dean with Melrose, 1999). The chapter stands in striking contrast to our opening chapter last year (Fitzpatrick, 1998), but interestingly shares several key elements of Fitzpatrick's theoretical analysis (note, for example, the similarity between what Glennerster says about 'required saving' and what Fitzpatrick defines as 'surrogate taxation'). Glennerster, however, endorses what he calls New Labour's 'retreat to the core': the government should increase spending on universal schooling and health care, but reduce social security spending by concentrating 'scarce tax pounds on the poor'. To this extent, he believes, New Labour's pension proposals are a bold move in the right direction. Declaring his opposition to criticisms made by other members of the social policy academic community (see above), he similarly demonstrates the logic of New Labour's welfare-to-work strategy, arguing that it represents an ideal and distinctive compromise between US workfare and Swedish active labour market policies. He suggests that the net effect of tax and spending under New Labour has already been mildly redistributive, but he strikes a more critical note when he points up contradictions between New Labour's centralising and democratising tendencies.

The next contribution, by John Benington and David Donnison (Chapter 3), hones in on the thinking behind New Labour's strategy to combat social exclusion. Benington and Donnison appear to take more seriously the proposition that what New Labour is seeking is indeed a 'Third Way', though they are more critical than Glennerster of its adequacy. They argue that, whereas old Labour represented an alliance between an industrial working class and the public service professions, fundamental socio-economic changes mean that any party bidding for power must now speak to the needs of what is widely characterised as 'Middle England'; a stratum, rather than a class, that is socially included yet chronically insecure (cf. Hutton, 1995). New Labour's task is to shore up Middle England against the risks of exclusion, but at the same time to enhance the mobility of those who are excluded from that stratum. By implication, Benington and Donnison embrace a concept of social exclusion that is wider than that which is usually applied by the government. Nonetheless they are broadly supportive of the idea that social problems may be addressed through strategies of neighbourhood renewal. They point out that we have in Britain a thirty-year history of largely ineffectual pilot projects aimed at neighbourhood renewal, but they acknowledge that New Labour's approach appears to be more strategic and better integrated with mainstream government policies and programmes. It is in the wider context of New Labour policy that they see pitfalls. The emphasis upon promoting the work ethic and 'networks of opportunity' as the basis for routes into inclusion – and into the Middle England stratum – will only succeed where appropriate jobs exist; when networks provide effective opportunities for the excluded to equip themselves for those jobs; and if the whole process is sufficiently inclusive and supportive to ensure that it does not exacerbate the isolation of those for whom paid employment is not a viable solution.

A very different kind of new thinking is presented in John Clarke's contribution (Chapter 4), which exemplifies an approach that is squarely within the second of the traditions of analysis we have outlined above. Clarke addresses the ambiguous concept of 'culture' and its relevance for social policy. He distinguishes various usages of the term. First, he addresses culture as a 'field of difference' and the important part the concept has played, on the one hand, in the construction of 'multicultural' approaches to social policy but, on the other, in fostering traditionalist and essentialist critiques. Second, he addresses culture as 'not-structure', and the debates that have surrounded such notions as the 'culture of poverty' and 'dependency culture' theses; these, as has been discussed above, represent a critical feature of current political discourse. Third, he argues nonetheless that culture has a place in social policy as a 'mode of analysis' that accommodates the part played by human agency. Boldly embracing an entire swathe of critical theory – theories of ideology and of discourse, symbolic interactionism, social constructionism, post-structuralism and postmodernism – as part and parcel of a 'cultural turn' in the social sciences, Clarke argues that social policy can confidently engage with culture as 'a practice of producing meaning'; as the constructed, changeable, contradictory and contested realm of discourse and meaning that bears upon the production of human welfare. Culture is the practice by which social differences and problems are constructed, by which social roles and expectations are constituted. From within this perspective, Clarke argues against a prevailing tendency to *desocialise* social policy; to reduce social policy to moralistic prescription, economistic calculation or managerialistic fiat.

The final contribution to the section on new thinking is by Michael Cahill (Chapter 5), who introduces an ecological perspective and invites us to enlarge our understanding of what constitutes social policy. Whereas New Labour's commitment to the objective of global sustainability is ostensibly less tokenistic than its predecessors, Cahill argues that any attempt to link environmental and social policy must contend with the dominant ideology of consumerism. In the current era, Cahill contends, social identity is constituted through consumption: poverty – or social exclusion – is to be understood as a failure to consume, and the 'me first' ethos which this engenders militates against electorally popular reforms. He illustrates this with reference to transport policy and the failure of New Labour to go so far as seriously to threaten Middle England's dependency on the motor car, with all the implications this has both for the environment and for the social exclusion of those without access to cars. Cahill explores the measures which the government has begun to pursue or could realistically countenance in order to make environmental restructuring – including the environmental modernisation in the economy – a reality. He discusses the possibilities presented by the extension of valuable initiatives begun under Local Agenda 21; the enlargement of our understanding of what constitutes quality of life, including the use of quality-of-life indicators; and the development of the social economy, including the parts played by local economic trading schemes and credit unions. He also addresses how impetus for change might be generated, through the application of sustainability indices, environmental space and environmental 'footprint' measures, and the development of associated taxation measures. While underlining the scale of the task to be addressed, Cahill's claim is that environmental sustainability *is* a credible policy objective, with clear social policy implications.

Current welfare reforms in the UK

The section on current 'domestic' welfare reform starts with a contribution by Tim Blackman and Amanda Palmer (Chapter 6), who provide a broad overview of the changes that have occurred since May 1997. The chapter offers a somewhat different perspective to that by Howard Glennerster's and a more detailed treatment of substantive policy developments. Blackman and Palmer set out to contrast the rhetoric of 'modernisation' under New Labour with the reality that many of their initiatives demonstrate continuity with Conservative policies. The shift begun under the Conservatives towards greater selectivity, privatisation, managerialism and support for 'family life' all prepared the ground for New Labour's modernisation project. To changes which had been set in motion upon ideological grounds, New Labour has applied a pragmatic emphasis on 'fairness' and 'effectiveness'. This is illustrated with reference to health and social care policy on the one hand and welfare-to-work policies on the other. For example, the primary care strategy that underpins current changes in the National Health Service (NHS) in fact builds on foundations laid down during the construction of the Conservatives' internal market. While New Labour has still to resolve the Conservatives' legacy with regard to the funding of long-term social care, it has already proposed a centralised standard-setting regime for the regulation of local social services premised on the kind of managerialist principles pioneered by the Conservatives. The unfolding New Deals for unemployed people, lone parents and disabled people – culminating in the introduction of the 'single gateway' claims process – were in many vital respects prefigured by changes tested or mooted by the Conservatives. Blackman and Palmer argue that New Labour's declared 'one nation' objective *is* distinctively different from that espoused by the New Right, but that its realisation may be jeopardised by a continued retreat from universalism.

Hilary Land's contribution (Chapter 7) focuses more closely on the barrage of New Labour policies which purport to support families with children and which will certainly redistribute income to such families. However, Land detects underlying ambiguities about the family model that is being supported. The classic 'male breadwinner model' upon which the Beveridgian welfare state was founded has long since been undermined by both employment and social trends: the former have contributed to the rise in the number of dual-earner families on the one hand and non-earning families on the other; the latter have contributed to the rise in the number of lone-parent families, which tend to be predominantly female headed and benefit dependent. This had been recognised in policies that provided compensatory levels of support to lone-parent families through the benefit system and, more recently, through the (albeit 'spectacularly unsuccessful') Child Support Act (CSA). The conundrum for New Labour – in the context of its desire to promote work *and* family life – was that, if it wished to support marriage, it would have to relatively disadvantage lone parents; it would have to redress the chronic shortage of childcare provision; and it would have to tackle the particular educational disadvantages which characteristically face lone parents wishing to enter the labour market. The response has included cuts in benefits for lone parents, tempered by across-the-board improvements in child benefit, the New Deal for lone parents, the working families tax credit and the additional childcare credit, a national childcare strategy, policies to promote 'family friendly employment', and simplification of the CSA. Land drives home three main points. First, the resources devoted to the

New Deal for lone parents (predominantly women) – who have particular training and educational needs – are far less than those devoted, for example, to the young unemployed (predominantly men). Second, the operation of the working families tax credit is likely – in practice and for the majority of families receiving it – to reinforce incentives for men to become or remain the principal breadwinner, so reinstating the male breadwinner model for low-income families: and at the very least it will accentuate the distinction between families with working parents and those with none. Third, close attention to the details of how the new tax credit and childcare proposals will work suggests they will convey or reinforce the message that providing care within families is no longer to be counted as work: Beveridge acknowledged women carers as second-class citizens, but New Labour, according to Land, barely recognises them as citizens at all.

The next contribution to bear upon the current UK reforms is by Sharon Gewirtz (Chapter 8), who focuses upon New Labour's proposal for the introduction of Education Action Zones (EAZs). EAZs epitomise New Labour's approach to community and social exclusion. They are intended to focus relatively small sums of additional money on groups of schools in areas of social and economic disadvantage. Gewirtz identifies nine explicit or implicit elements of the EAZ policy: it is to function in the context of a 'marketised' education system, driven by parental choice and formula funding; it is 'managerialist' in nature and will impose upon existing league table and inspection regimes a process driven by a tendering exercise, flexible staffing, target setting and performance monitoring; it requires an element of 'privatisation' and some degree of involvement or participation from the private sector; it is 'pedagogically traditionalist' and explicitly linked to criteria stipulating specified teaching methods; it aims, nonetheless, to encourage 'experimentation' with a view to improving school performance; it is 'redistributive', insofar as it transfers resources to deprived areas; it aims to secure 'integration of separate welfare domains' – or 'joined-up government' – at the local level, so as to address, for example, the part which poverty and housing deprivation might play in depressing educational performance; it urges 'responsibilities' upon all participants, including self-monitoring and the use, for example, of home–school contracts and family learning schemes; and finally, it requires an element of 'associationalisation', since an array of representatives are required to participate as 'partners'. Gewirtz analyses the contradictions between several of these elements with regard both to their provenance and their likely effects. She concludes that, notwithstanding the inclusion within this Third Way approach of some relatively progressive elements, the prospects of the policy functioning in practice are probably poor.

From education we move to housing and a contribution by Peter Kemp (Chapter 9), who contends that the 'landscape of debate' in relation to housing policy has been completely changed since Labour last held office. For most of the present century, governments of various persuasions have been concerned with the issues relating to the 'quantity, quality and price' of housing provision. That changed after 1979 under Conservative governments committed to 'reprivatisation': they promoted owner-occupation, deregulated private rented housing and reduced public housing expenditure, while subjecting public housing to 'demunicipalisation' and the doctrines of new public management. New Labour, according to Kemp, has adopted a 'modified reprivatisation' discourse. Notwithstanding some notable silences, the shape of its approach to housing is beginning to emerge. It constitutes, once again, a pragmatic espousal of 'what counts is what works'. In particular, the declared aim is to make the market work, although specific initiatives relating to owner-occupiers and private tenants have so far been relatively minor. What is clear is that, though not as ideologically opposed to public housing as the New Right, New Labour *has* 'lost faith' in it. The government appears to favour the transfer of housing management (though not necessarily housing stock) from the public to the private sector and wishes to subject it to a further tranche of managerialist controls, including the new Best Value performance regime (that is to be applied in place of compulsory competitive tendering across local government) and the institution of an 'Ofsted style' Housing Inspectorate. Accompanying these changes are new proposals for tenant empowerment, placing a certain responsibility on tenants to participate in management. However, housing is also a key focus in the government's urban regeneration strategy and the New Deal for communities. The government entrusted its Social Exclusion Unit with the task of devising 'joined-up' approaches to rough sleeping on the one hand and the problems of the 'worst neighbourhoods' on the other. Kemp shows that central to New Labour's approach is an accommodation of housing policy to its objectives of strengthening communities and combating social exclusion.

Bob Hudson's contribution (Chapter 10) is focused on New Labour's response to the enduring problems associated with coordination at the interface between health care and social care. Hudson traces the origins of the problem to the creation of the NHS as a central government institution, its separation from elected local government, and the boundaries established during subsequent reorganisations between local health care agencies and local social services departments. The introduction by Conservative governments of internal or quasi-markets into both health and social care has compounded the problem, since local purchasing authorities and provider agencies are required to compete rather than cooperate. In spite of the introduction of joint commissioning and joint planning arrangements to facilitate the development of the Conservatives' community care strategy, effective collaboration has seldom been forthcoming. In particular, disputes between health and social services about which is responsible for the costs of providing long-term care for elderly and/or disabled people have often defied satisfactory resolution. This represents a classic test for New Labour's aim of 'joined-up government'. To this end an array of proposals based on 'partnership' between health and social services has been presented: the proposed new NHS primary care groups are to work closely with local social services departments; health authorities and social services are to collaborate in the production of Health Improvement Plans for their areas; there is provision for Health Action Zones which, like EAZs, are intended to focus resources on coordinated intervention in chosen areas; and a regime of new incentives and sanctions is proposed – coupled with stern warnings from the government – to encourage health and social services to collaborate on strategic planning, service commissioning and provision. The government has elected to try and impose collaboration rather than unification and appears to have set its face against the possibility that health services should be brought under local government control. Hudson detects a new air of realism in Labour's approach to the issue, but questions whether it will be enough to establish trust between the various agencies involved.

The final contribution in this section is by Dee Cook (Chapter 11), who discusses New Labour's approach to crime reduction. New Labour has made much of its determination to tackle crime and its causes. To this end it has invested substantially in *criminal* justice reforms dealing with offenders, but, argues Cook, its commitment to *social* justice as a means to crime prevention is more ambiguous. The most specific measure is the community safety provisions contained in the Crime and Disorder Act. These require all local authorities, in partnership with the police and other agencies, to conduct crime audits and devise Community Safety Strategies. Many of the problems which beset inter-agency working in other contexts (see above) can be seen to apply, and little in the way of resources has been committed to the initiative. More generally, crime reduction has been set by the government in the context of its wider approach to issues of social exclusion and community regeneration. The problem of crime, the government believes, is located primarily in poor neighbourhoods and, once again, it is through parallel initiatives in 'joined-up government' – Health and Education Action Zones, New Deal for communities and the Single Regeneration Budget – that its causes will be addressed. Cook points to certain similarities between the government's welfare-to-work and crime reduction strategies as 'discursive projects'. Both are predicated on local solutions and an emphasis on applying decontextualised examples of 'best practice' – in particular, innovations based on experiments in the USA. This, Cook fears, may be addressing the 'politics of crime' rather than its roots. It does not adequately address deeper issues associated with the economic conditions and social inequalities – and the perceived injustices which stem from them – that may be sources of crime; it does not do enough to succeed in accommo-dating social justice to criminal justice.

International developments

Our section on international developments begins with a contri-bution by Robert Lerman (Chapter 12) on recent welfare reforms in the USA, which have been informed by similar thinking to the reforms we are witnessing in the UK. In particular, Lerman concentrates on the implementation of the Personal Responsibility and Work Opportunity Reconciliation Act (PROWRA) of 1996, a piece of legislation condemned by its critics as welfare repeal rather than welfare reform. Lerman helpfully puts the provisions of PROWRA into context. The new legislation replaced the Aid for Families with Dependent Children (AFDC) scheme with Temporary Assistance for Needy Families (TANF), under which an individual's entitlement to federally funded social assistance is limited to a five-year lifetime limit. TANF also institutionalises variations to the AFDC regime which had previously been tried in some states, including 'family capping' and 'workfare' provisions. However, PROWRA still allowed individual states freedom to supplement federal funding and, for example, to exempt up to 20 per cent of their caseloads from the lifetime limit. In place of a system of matching funding, states now receive an annual block grant, but this has been fixed at the level of 1993–94 allocations, when in fact unemployment and welfare spending was higher than at present. Associated with these changes was the introduction, nationally, of an expanded Employment Income Tax Credit scheme to supplement low wages and an extension of Medicaid for children in low-waged families. The overall intention was to provide a bridge better to support the transition from welfare to work. Critics feared the changes would promote a 'race to the bottom' as states sought to undercut each other's level of welfare spending and, because there would not be jobs for all, some claimants would be left destitute. In the event, some states have actually increased their levels of welfare spending, while increasing numbers of welfare claimants have successfully entered the labour market. Lerman acknowledges, however, that it is early days. The labour market has been buoyant and the first round of lifetime benefit cut-offs is not due until 2000–01. His guarded conclusion, nonetheless, is that the results of the new approach, if potentially damaging for some, is promising for many.

Written from a less optimistic perspective, Michael O'Brien's contribution (Chapter 13) provides an account of welfare reforms in Aotearoa (being the original Maori name for New Zealand) in the 1984–98 period. Once an exemplar of a developed welfare state within the Anglo-Saxon tradition, Aotearoa has lately undergone a period of welfare retrenchment in consequence of which it has suffered a steeper rise in social inequality than any other OECD country, a process that has disproportionately disadvantaged Aotearoa's Maori and Pacific Islands communities. O'Brien demonstrates that rising inequality resulted in part from rising unemployment, but also from the effects of deliberate tax and benefit changes which redistributed resources from poor to rich, reflecting the ascendancy of a neo-liberal belief that inequality is the engine that drives society. While embracing social inequality, the government also embarked on the 'remoralisation' of welfare. On the one hand it increased the 'hassling' and surveillance of state beneficiaries, while on the other it sought to shift responsibility for welfare increasingly to the market, the family and charity. Many of the changes introduced in relation to the work-testing of state benefits are strongly redolent of changes in the UK; however, controversial proposals for a Code of Social and Family Responsibility (that included a suggestion that the parents of school truants should have their benefits cut) went further than any UK government has dared to. The familiar justification for such reforms has focused on the need to target resources on those that need most help, while maximising freedom of choice for others. In Aotearoa, however, targeted welfare provision for needy individuals has been made less rather than more adequate and, to the extent that some resources have been targeted on marginalised groups, such as Maoris and Pacific Islands peoples, these have been limited and there is evidence of an incipient racist backlash which will blame such groups for not taking up the opportunities presented to them. Meanwhile,

O'Brien argues, the language of choice has become an apologia for consumerism rather than an instrument of social justice.

Finally, Jacqueline O'Reilly and Günther Schmid's contribution (Chapter 14) provides a comparative analysis of labour market policy in Germany and the UK. In contrast to the USA and Aotearoa/New Zealand, Germany represents a quite different welfare regime to the UK. Whereas the latter represents a Beveridgian safety-net model with a comparatively low wage–low skill economy, Germany epitomises a Bismarckian social market model with a comparatively high wage–high skill economy. However, both regimes are subject to the same global trends and, exacerbated by the effects of German reunification, unemployment is now higher in Germany – especially among women – than in the UK. O'Reilly and Schmid trace out in some detail the differences in labour participation rates, training systems, wage differentials, non-wage costs and productivity levels between the two countries. While polarisation of the labour market – in terms of pay and working hours – is greater in the UK than in Germany and the concept of 'standard' employment remains much stronger in Germany, there is now an emerging tendency in Germany to the creation of low hour–low pay jobs which, nonetheless, do not necessarily provide stepping stones out of unemployment for men, so much as inherently limited opportunities for non-employed women. Conventional regime theory approaches – whether based on 'decommodification' or 'breadwinner' models – do not adequately capture the complexity of the situation or the contrasts between the two countries at a time when the 'social contract' (governing productive economic relations) and the 'gender contract' (governing reproductive familial relations) are both effectively up for renegotiation. With that prospect in mind, O'Reilly and Schmid conclude by exploring the concept of 'transitional labour markets' as a means to reconceptualise policy in both countries. If 'standard' employment (full-time, lifelong employment – predominantly for men) is no longer a sustainable or acceptable concept, the object of policy should be to provide institutional 'bridges' to facilitate the necessary flexibility across the working lives of both men and women: sustaining workers through cash transfers or tax credits during periods of non-waged activity, reduced working hours or early retirement, while encouraging cooperation over the sharing or rotation of work opportunities.

Conclusion

What may be drawn from the above contributions is not so much a single conclusion as a set of further questions. If 'work' is to become the guiding principle of welfare and if labour market policy is to be the central plank of social policy, what does this mean for such principles as 'need' and 'care', and what will this portend for those whose lives are centred outside the formal labour market? If the promotion of 'community' and 'social inclusion' are to be premised on a one-nation ideal, how is social policy to address social inequalities based on social difference – including differences of gender, ethnicity and class? How will the new symbolic meanings associated with the emerging welfare orthodoxy translate into popular understandings and into struggles over the future of welfare provision? To the extent that we may be beginning to understand the consequences of economic globalisation for social welfare in the Anglo-Saxon and continental European worlds, what have we to learn from and about parallel or contrasting developments in post-Communist Eastern Europe and the 'developing' world? All these questions and more remain to be pursued, perhaps in future editions of *SPR*.

References

Bauman, Z. (1998) *Work, Consumerism and the New Poor,* Buckingham, Open University Press.
Beck, U. (1992) *The Risk Society, Towards a New Modernity,* London, Sage.
Blair, T. (1999) *The Beveridge Lecture on Welfare Reform,* Toynbee Hall, London, 18 March.
Bochell, C. & Bochell, H. (1998) 'The governance of social policy', in E. Brunsdon, H. Dean & R. Woods (eds) *Social Policy Review 10,* London, Social Policy Association.
Bulmer, M., Lewis, J. & Piachaud, D. (1989) *The Goals of Social Policy,* London, Unwin Hyman.
Commission for *Social Justice (1994) Social Justice: Strategies for national renewal,* London, IPPR/Vintage.
Dean, H. with Melrose, M. (1999) *Poverty, Riches and Social Citizenship,* Basingstoke, Macmillan.
Department of Social Security (1998) *New Ambitions for our Country, A New Contract for Welfare,* Cm 3805, London, The Stationery Office.
Driver, S. & Martell, L. (1998) *New Labour, Politics after Thatcherism,* Cambridge, Polity.
Erskine, A. (1998) 'The approaches and methods of social policy', in P. Alcock, A. Erskine & M. May (eds) *The Student's Companion to Social Policy,* London, Blackwell.

Esping-Andersen, G. (ed.) (1996) *Welfare States in Transition,* London, Sage.

Finn, D. (1989) 'Labour's "New Deal" for the unemployed and the stricter benefit regime', in E. Brunsdon, H. Dean & R. Woods (eds) *Social Policy Review 10,* London, Social Policy Association.

Fitzpatrick, T. (1998) ' The rise of market collectivism', in E. Brunsdon, H. Dean & R. Woods (eds) *Social Policy Review 10,* London, Social Policy Association.

Foucault, M. (1981) *The History of Sexuality, An Introduction,* Harmondsworth, Penguin.

Giddens, A. (1998) *The Third Way,* Cambridge, Polity.

Hughes, G. & Lewis, G. (eds) (1998) *Unsettling Welfare, The Reconstruction of Social Policy,* London, Routledge.

Hutton, W. (1995) *The State We're In,* London, Jonathon Cape.

Jordan, B. (1998) *The New Politics of Welfare,* London, Sage.

Labour Party (1997) *New Labour, Because Britain Deserves Better,* London, Labour Party.

LeGrand, J. (1990) 'The state of welfare', in J. Hills (ed.) *The State of Welfare, The Welfare State in Britain since* 1974, Oxford, Clarendon Press.

Leonard, P. (1997) *Postmodern Welfare,* London, Sage.

Lister, R. (1998) 'From inequality to social inclusion, New Labour and the welfare state', *Critical Social Policy,* vol. 18, no. 2, pp215–225.

Mishra, R. (1984) *The Welfare State in Crisis,* Hemel Hempstead, Harvester Wheatsheaf.

Pierson, C. (1998) *Beyond the Welfare State,* 2nd edn, Cambridge, Polity.

Powell, M & Hewitt, M. (1998) 'The end of the welfare state?', *Social Policy and Administration,* vol. 32, pp1–13.

2 A Third Way?

Howard Glennerster

All wind?

A great deal of rather purposeless journalistic ink has been spilt on the subject of the Third Way in the past year. On a rather different level my own director has contributed a social scientist's interpretation of the term (Giddens, 1998). Writers on the Left of politics in the *New Statesman, Prospect, Marxism Today* and *Red Pepper* have poured scorn on the whole notion, and few have defended or sought to define it.

Examining the speeches of Tony Blair before the last election, we find a clear echo of much communitarian writing from the USA. There should be no rights without responsibilities, for example, a strong theme of Laurence Meade's work and the consequent 'paternalistic' flavour to much US welfare reform policy (1986, 1997). There were echoes of the American emphasis on the importance of civil society – 'mediating structures' like churches and local voluntary organisations that stood between the individual and the state (Berger and Neuhouse, 1996). There were echoes of the underclass rhetoric, too, and a focus on single parents, at least at the early stages of debate, reflecting the then social security minister's strong concern with the issue. There was much focus on work expectations, if not requirements, that should be laid on such mothers. Some of the speeches at the 1997 Election sounded like reruns of the US welfare reform debate. All this attracted a wider spectrum of interest and support than the normal audience interested in the welfare state. Yet it made it quite difficult to decide just what welfare reform might mean.

Is New Labour really a pale copy of Newt Gingrich, as journalists on the Continent seem to think? (For an extended discussion of New Labour's debt to American ideas see Deacon (1998).)

In truth, hard policy agendas rarely begin with a clear abstract set of ideals that are then carefully translated into legislative form. Most attempts to do so end in grief. If we think of leading political philosophers in the past, their contributions have been to rationalise and give more abstract theoretical form to events that have already happened – to make sense of the world rather than form it.

John Locke elegantly justified the Glorious Bloodless Revolution of 1688. 'All men are born free' and have the right to choose their own rulers, the theory of the separation of powers, the inherent importance of property rights for liberty – these follow; they do not form the basis of the revolution. Marshall's (1950) theory of the three stages of citizenship and of social rights follows and interprets the spate of social legislation between 1944 and 1948. It does not pre-figure it.

It is thus probably too early to decide if there is a philosophical coherence behind the new Labour Government's first year and a half in office, yet it has been an active period. We now have the main outlines of public spending and tax policy for the whole Parliament. We have a new National Health Service (NHS) organisation, a welfare-to work programme, the basis of a new pensions and social security scheme, a schools policy, and a new system of funding higher education. As I write, the Royal Commission on Long Term Care is about to report and recommend a fundamental shift in the boundary line between health and social care. The majority report will propose an extension of free universal service beyond the old illogical boundaries of the NHS to cover social care too.

Taken as a whole, this is at least as productive a period of action as the first eighteen months of the Attlee government was able to achieve. People may not find the measures as agreeable, but numerous and significant they certainly are (for an insightful brief review see Timmins, 1999). Do they have an internal consistency? If so, what is it? Is it a Third Way?

The role of the state and the market

At its most basic level the Third Way is concerned with an alternative route that is not either pure capitalism or pure socialism. It reflects the need for neither an omnipotent state nor an all-embracing market. However, that sense of the term has

been around at least since the end of the nineteenth century
(Browning; see Halpern and Mikosz, 1998). It was similar to
Macmillan's use of The Middle Way (1938).

It was also the sense in which Clinton used the term in his
State of the Union message: 'We have moved past the sterile
debate between those who say Government is the enemy and
those who say Government is the answer. My fellow Americans
we have found a Third Way. We have the smallest Government
in 35 years, but a more progressive one' (Halpern and Mikosz,
1998, p5). So, in that broad sense, there is nothing new about
the aspiration. It was precisely the claim made for the social
legislation of the Attlee Government by Tom Marshall, to whom I
have already referred. His Cambridge Lectures in 1948 were not
just a neat, if disputed, account of British social history (see
Harris, 1997). More fundamentally he claimed that Britain, and
indeed Western Europe, had an answer to both capitalist and
Marxist interpretations of history. The citizenship state precluded
the necessity of a full-scale takeover of the economy required by
socialist thought. There would always be a tension between
democracy and the market but an accommodation was possible.
Democracy would allocate citizenship goods on the basis of equity
and the market would allocate the rest on the basis of efficiency
and individual choice.

At that level of generalisation there is nothing new the Third
Way is offering, though the dilemmas may be different and the
boundaries drawn in different ways. Indeed, the emphasis Blair
and Field put on responsibilities and duties matching those rights
in the Green Paper (Cm 3805, 1998, ppiv and 80) is also firmly
embedded in Marshall, especially the later Marshall (Rees, 1995)
– even if some superficial readings of his work missed the point.

Nor, if we study the Labour government's comprehensive
spending review (Cm 4011, 1998), do we find a major change
proposed in the share of the gross domestic product (GDP) going
to state expenditure over the next three years. The percentage of
the GDP devoted to public expenditure in the March 1998 budget
(HC 620, 1998) showed a gradual decline from about 40 per cent
to a little below. Subsequently the slower growth in the GDP will
mean that figure rising in the short run and then returning to the
40 per cent level if the economy recovers reasonably quickly.
Even so, this definitely is not a tax-and-spend government. So
what's new?

A shift

There *is* a real and strategic shift that is taking place, it seems to me, both at the level of ideas and of practical policy (Glennerster, 1998a, 1999). Firstly, there has been an explicit acceptance that for most things markets work better than any other known mechanism as a way of allocating resources. There are also ways in which they can be harnessed to social purposes, such as environmental taxes. There are other areas where they work very badly – health and long-term care are examples. This is a view firmly grounded in modern economics, but one which Labour politicians have found it very difficult to be at all open about. I remember sitting through excruciating meetings at which masters of the art, such as Harold Wilson, would speak to one part of the Labour Party membership in terms redolent of contempt for the market. Clever people like him in Whitehall knew better how to run the economy than markets. At some time in the future all would be planned in some socialist way. At the same time, to the rest of the audience, he was reassuring that nothing would really change. To me Blair brought a blessed sense of honesty to the debate. We have learned that command-and-control economic systems do not work except in situations where the economy needs to be run as a war machine. We are simply not clever enough to bring it off.

If old style socialism did not work, neither did the Crosland-type socialism that had been its alternative. Improved levels of public services could be paid for out of growth, we were told, and some of us convinced ourselves it was true. If not, the electorate would be prepared to pay more to support better services. Well neither was true. Growth in the rest of the economy gave rise to higher wages and salaries in the private sector and then in the public sector. The rise in relative costs seeped away most of the extra dividend growth was supposed to deliver. Rising standards of service in the private service sector increased expectations of the state sector. But electors were not prepared to pay more in taxes whatever they told pollsters in the comfort of their sitting rooms or kitchens. The level of taxes raised from the UK public has changed remarkably little over recent decades. Much the same is true in other countries. They may tax at a higher or lower level than we do, but there is a stability in these patterns. Politicians may be remarkably stupid and unable to do the very thing they are there to do – interpret the public's will – but the more plausible explanation is that they have got it about right. Certainly a closer study of the polls leading up to the Labour victory at the last election suggests just that. It was only when voters became convinced Labour was not going to raise taxes that they gave them their support (Heath and Curtice, 1998). That is not how I would have expressed my preferences, but that hardly counts.

New priorities

Now, if that diagnosis is anything like that which New Labour made, and I am sure it was, it called for a big reappraisal of its social policy priorities. That could or should have been the essence of the Third Way. But it would have meant alienating many of its traditional supporters, so we had rhetoric about the need for welfare reform and no substance.

In the past two decades the circle had been partially squared by governments, including those of the Conservatives, devoting more of the total public spending to social policy. In 1974 social policy took about half the share of the public budget. By the time Labour came to power in 1997 the share had risen to over 60 per cent (for the detail see Glennerster and Hills, 1998). This figure is to rise more, to about 62 per cent, by the year 2001–02. But this way out cannot go on for ever. Government has to be about things other than just social policy.

Within that spending review health and education expenditure is to rise faster, especially in the last three years covered by the review up to 2001–02. The real annual rates of increase in those years average about 5 per cent per annum, unheard of since the 1960s. The average is less over the whole five-year period because of the freeze imposed on the first two years of spending. Even so, it will be 3.7 per annum for health and 2.9 for education over the whole Parliament (see Hills, 1998). These services' share of the GDP will rise. The rise may even be more than planned because of the slowing in the economy that seems likely in 1999.

How can this be squared with a fairly constant share of the GDP devoted to public expenditure? The answer is to reduce partly defence and partly social security. To quote John Hills:

A measure of the overall switch in spending allowed by the 'peace dividend' after the end of the Cold War is that in 1993–4 defence spending was £25 billion, compared to NHS spending in England of £32 billion. By 2001–2, defence spending is planned to be £21 billion but health spending to be nearly twice as much, £41 billion all figures at 1997–8 prices. This kind of switch from defence to social spending would have been associated with the Left of the Labour Party in the 1980s and early 1990s. (Hills, 1998, p27)

There is a fundamental problem here. Some services are going to take more of the GDP if they are to remain universal and hence keep the support of the middle class. The government seems to want to keep the tax burden steady. These are not consistent objectives unless something gives. The answer seems to be to shift the cost of pensions onto the individual, where possible, and the same for housing and higher education. This is, at least, a coherent, if not universally acceptable, strategy. But it is not what ministers are saying. If you read the White and Green Papers carefully the strategy emerges.

Reducing the cost of public pensions long term

The Green Paper on pensions (Cm 4179, 1998) is a good illustration. The basic flat rate pension is to be allowed to continue to fade away. The state earnings related pension scheme – on which I laboured in my early years!– is to go. Broadly speaking, providing for your income in old age is to be a personal affair. You will be obliged to save enough to take you above the state minimum income in old age and given tax advantages to encourage you. Private stakeholder pension schemes for the moderately paid will be closely regulated but they will replace the state scheme. Carers and mothers, or fathers, bringing up children will have contributions credited by the state to enable them to acquire their own non-state pensions. Existing SERPS contributors with incomes below £9,000 and up to about £19,000 will have their pensions topped up by the Exchequer. A minimum income guarantee will be raised in line with earnings of those in work.

The net effect will be to reduce the public sector cost of pensions (excluding tax expenditures) from 5.4 per cent of the GDP today to 4.5 per cent in 2050, despite an increase in the size of the elderly population. Tax spending will be concentrated much more directly on the lower income groups. Tax reliefs remain untouched. (If the Le Grand–Agulnic (1998) proposals had been accepted the redistributive effect would have been greater by replacing tax reliefs and targeting tax credits on the poor.)

The logic here is that, with the market carefully regulated, and individuals helped where there is good cause, people can make their own arrangements for old age. If they wish to live it up now and die poor, that is their business so long as they do not free ride on the rest of us. The pensions insurance market works reasonably well. It does not in long-term care. Use the market where it works, not where it does not.

It is certainly true that required saving by those in jobs, which, to some extent, we already have, is like taxation. But it does have the advantage that people do not think of it as taxation and it does not count in the public spending accounts.

If we examine the proposals for widows and the disabled, the same logic prevails. Those that can work should. Those that have reasonable incomes do not need a flat rate pension. Concentrate scarce tax pounds on the poor.

Compared with social security schemes in the rest of the world, Japan and the USA included, this will leave us with a remarkably slimline and thus robust social security budget. By the second quarter of next century the USA will be spending about 8 per cent of its GDP on public sector pensions and most European countries 16–20 per cent, unless they slim them down, as they are doing. The true economic cost of pensions in the UK, public and private, will be about 12 per cent of GDP, but that too will be low compared with other countries.

If from 1945, or even 1965, we had created a generous state pension scheme that won middle-class support we might have persuaded the electorate to pay social security contributions to finance it. Beveridge and later governments of both colours failed in this respect. Hence political support for high state pensions for all is simply not there in the UK.

Muddling along in the middle with private pensions providing for most people and low untargeted state support for all at a mean level was the worst compromise of all. The Labour government's plan is a bold move in what I think is the right direction, bar arguments about detail on which I have reservations. Right or wrong, it will be quite a different path from that being adopted in other European or North American countries. I suspect it will become something of a path-breaker.

Retreating to the core

What this whole strategy amounts to is what I have called 'a retreat to the core' (Glennerster and Hills, 1998). Raise spending in line with rising public expectations on those universal services where the economic case and political support for collective provision is powerful. If we wish to retain health and schooling as universal services we are going to have to increase spending on them faster than the GDP. Expectations of rising quality and the relative price effect require this. Where this does not happen users will opt into the private sector (see Burchardt *et al.* (1999) for evidence and discussion on this). The only place the money can come from in the long run is social security. Target spending on the poor and use regulation and requirements to save for the rest.

This amounts to a way forward quite different from that being followed in other European countries at present. It is also different from the US strategy. It is different from the Swedish strategy of moderating the size of their universal state pension scheme. It is coherent. It is different. Many will not agree with it, but that is a different issue. Since this is the broad strategy I advocated in a plenary lecture to the Social Policy Association in 1993 (Page and Deakin, 1993) I cannot complain!

So, the first way in which there could be said to be a Third Way is that the new social policy embodies a different balance of responsibilities between the state and the individual from that embodied in the old welfare state. It is one that stands by the commitment to high-class universal schooling and health care (and, I would hope, long-term care, where the case is at least as powerful) but it explicitly accepts and indeed pushes forward the role of the dominant private sector in pensions and housing. It sees higher education finance as essentially a shared private and public matter.

Work

The second way in which the New Labour social policy differs from the old is in its stress on paid work and employment and on creating incentives to encourage it. 'Work for those who can; security for those who cannot', to quote from the Prime Minister's Foreword to CM 3805 (1998).

On a very generalised level, again, there is nothing new about this. It was there in Beveridge and Marshall. Full employment was the twin pillar of the post-war settlement. It was the Callaghan government that explicitly recognised that merely pumping more cash into the economy every time unemployment rose was unsustainable. What it did not have was an alternative.

New Labour now does. Whether it will work is another matter. New and coherent it is. It is not American in origin; it is not Scandinavian in origin; it is a mixture of the two with a strong splice of Australian experience and it owes much of its inspiration to an LSE colleague, Richard Layard (1997b).

- Unemployment is deliberately created by governments and central bankers concerned to keep inflation at a politically and economically acceptable level. This is the only weapon available to them in the absence of agreements to limit wages.

- The only way to reduce unemployment is to reduce the level of unemployment at which labour shortages begin to drive up prices. This means raising education and training levels of those on the margins of the labour force and increasing the flow of people into the skilled labour force. It means tackling areas of very high unemployment where people are trapped outside the working economy.

- The UK suffers from a far higher level of long-term unemployment than any other comparable economy (Gregg and Wadsworth, 1996). One reason for this is a geographical mismatch of jobs and people, but another is the series of financial disincentives to work presented by the benefits system. These need to be put right. The longer the duration of unemployment benefits the longer the periods of unemployment (Jackman *et al.*, 1996).

- Once people are trapped outside the employment market for a long time they get trapped there. Job search and job re-entry declines rapidly as people's length of time out of work grows (Layard, 1997b). They need very positive encouragement to re-enter.

- Reducing benefit traps is not enough. Rewards to work need to be increased. Hence the minimum wage and the working families tax credit. Indefinite rights to benefit increase the scale of long-term unemployment. Shorter time limits reduce it.

- Employers need to be given financial inducements to take on the long-term unemployed.

This diagnosis is based on some of the best economic evidence available. The measures introduced by this government to follow through on the diagnosis are a mixture of American style sticks (though very moderate), free labour markets and Swedish-type positive labour market policies. Now this is very definitely not Gingrich-style welfare reform *or* Continental European job protectionism. It is a distinctive way – third or not.

The welfare reform agenda has clearly been affected by the American debate. But the ideas that have proved influential are those of the original liberal Democrat advisors like Ellwood (1988), not the ideas legislated in the Republican legislation of 1996.

- No one in the UK is talking about returning the finance of income security to local authorities.

- No one, or almost no one, in the UK is talking about cutting off families from welfare altogether purely because of the time they have been on welfare.

- Work requirements for single parents in the UK remain remarkably lenient compared with most other countries. In the USA some states are now requiring mothers to return to work when their child is three months old. Most European countries expect return by the time the children are at school or much earlier.

Ellwood argued for more incentives to work, a working families tax credit, a higher minimum wage and more childcare support. Arguably, it is Blair that has implemented his programme, not Clinton.

At the last SPA conference delegates were critical of this emphasis on paid work, claiming that it denigrated unpaid work. I have to say I totally disagree. Paid work brings dignity and respect. That does not preclude us from also giving dignity and worth to caring and non-paid work. But to deny paid work or to encourage people to live without it is to deny a main source of dignity in our Western capitalist industrialised world. To quote Amartya Sen (1997):

> An exclusive focus on income inequality tends to give the impression that West Europe has done very much better in keeping inequality down and in avoiding the kind of increase in income equality that the USA has experienced. In the space of incomes, it does indeed have, on the whole, a better record both in terms of levels and trends of inequality . . . And yet if we shift our gaze from income to employment the picture is very different. Unemployment has dramatically risen in West Europe, whereas there has been no such trend in the USA. . . . If unemployment batters lives, then that must somehow be taken into account in the analysis of income inequality. The comparative trends in income inequality give Europe an excuse to be smug, but that complacency can be deeply questioned if a broader view is taken of inequality. (Sen, 1997, pp8–9)

What then does this new employment policy amount to?

- *Make work pay.* Reduce the dead weight human and economic cost of long-term unemployment that is not even useful in keeping down the level of inflation. Hence the working families tax credit, the childcare tax credit, the minimum wage. Together these will increase the rewards for the lower paid. The enhanced pensions for the lower paid contributors in working life and for those in non-paid work will enhance the long-term rewards for contributing to society in one form or another.

- *Make work available*. Hence the measures to subsidise employers who take on staff from the pool of young and older long-term unemployed.

- *Make voluntary non-work unacceptable*. Hence the no fifth option – not to work or train will bring penalties.

- *Increase employability*. Raise standards of basic literacy and numeracy by concentrating more time on these activities. Research suggests that this works for maths especially and that basic mathematical capacity is one of the most important factors increasing employability (Glennerster, 1998c).

- *Give particular attention to areas of high unemployment*. Hence the work of the Social Exclusion Unit.

While I see a lot of coherence in these measures, I wonder if the seriousness of the problems facing areas of high concentration of worklessness, notably on public housing estates, have really been addressed. General policies like the working families tax credit and the minimum wage may work in the more endowed parts of the country. Whether they can reach the areas of extreme joblessness is less clear. Our work in the ESRC Centre for the Analysis of Social Exclusion (CASE) in some of these very deprived areas shows their limited attachment to labour markets (Glennerster *et al.*, 1999). Improving schools, attracting jobs into the area, helping young people out, especially on job experience schemes outside the area, improving cheap travel and above all tackling the housing benefit trap problem are all needed too. Intensive tailor-made solutions may be needed.

Moreover, the inevitable consequence of smoothing out the intensity of the unemployment trap in the working families tax credit is to extend the numbers of people caught in some kind of high withdrawal 'tax' rate. There is no realistic way out of this dilemma. Time will tell if the strategy will work.

Redistribution and independence

The period from 1977 to 1993 was one of unprecedented growth in inequality, at least as far back as we have any reliable figures (Hills, 1996). Part of this was down to world economic forces – trade and technology – but much of it was down to

Conservative government policy on taxes and benefits. Labour pledged itself to reverse this trend. The New Labour rhetoric here is not that different from old Labour: 'I believe in greater equality. If the next Labour Government has not raised the living standards of the poorest by the end of its term in office, it will have failed' (Blair, 1996, quoted in Oppenheim, 1997).

The government's central theme is 'to make, once more, our national purpose to tackle social division and inequality' (quoted in Hills, 1998). But at the same time the government's first 'Annual Report said it was:

> . . . developing a new approach, moving beyond the old debate between those who say the answer is to increase the level of benefits and those who say the answer is to cut benefits. We believe the key test of most benefits is whether they are helping people to be independent. (Cm 3969, 1998, p50)

This juxtaposition of ideals is again new for a Labour government. The last element of encouraging independence strongly underpins the welfare-to-work schemes and the intensive, almost casework, approach to helping people back into work as the other side of receiving benefit.

Figure 1: Winners and losers by income group

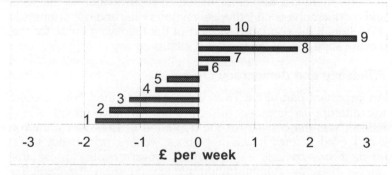

Source: Institute of Fiscal Studies

What of the redistributive side of the coin? If you analyse the redistributive effects of the 1998 budget and compare them with the impact of most of the budgets presented in the past eighteen years the comparison is striking. The Conservative budgets systematically gave more to the top two deciles – the top decile especially – and made the lowest deciles worse off. The Brown Budget of 1998 did the precise opposite (see Figure 1).

In his commentary on the 1998 Budget in the Financial Times Paul Johnson of the Institute of Fiscal Studies said: ' A Budget for lower income families with children. It has been a long time coming, but this is a genuinely redistributive Budget' (*Financial Times,* 18 March 1998).

The working families tax credit helped in three ways. Firstly, as families begin to earn more, the rate at which their tax credit is withdrawn will be much slower than had been the case under the old cash benefit families received. Under the old system the help you received was reduced by 75p for every extra pound you earned. Under the new scheme this falls to 55p. Secondly, it is more generous to young children. Thirdly, it extends support for childcare. On top of this were the increases to child benefit. The tax basis for the benefit has been criticised, but it has two big advantages. It will be more acceptable and likely to reach a wider group of families than social security benefit claimants. It does not count as public expenditure – no mean practical advantage. Mothers will still be able to draw it. On the revenue side the income at which national insurance contributions begin is to be raised and the tax relief owner-occupiers receive is to be cut to a 10 per cent rate. Where these measures fell down in many peoples' eyes was the failure to increase basic benefit levels in line with earnings. That, the green paper on pensions, at least, proposes to do.

So there is a new combination of redistribution to the poor and more emphasis on individual responsibility and opportunity. It is doubtful if the continued support of the taxpaying public for the welfare state can be kept without such a duality.

Efficiency and democracy

An important part of the Third Way agenda in the USA has been the attempt to improve the efficiency of government. That, indeed, was the context for the quotation of President Clinton's that I cited before. It was not about welfare reform but more efficient government – 'reinventing government', to use the phrase that the Administration picked up from the book by Osborne and Gaebler (1992). What that involved was a range of changes – 'introducing the entrepreneurial spirit', to use their phrase. It meant devolving budgets to smaller local units and giving them autonomy, privatising some agencies, introducing competition and giving local citizens more voice. In short, it proposed adopting much of the Thatcher agenda. Local management of schools, separation of purchaser and provider, autonomy for NHS trusts, general practitioner (GP) fundholding, estate based budgets for public housing estates, transfer of estates to tenant coops or housing associations with tenant involvement. This has clearly posed a problem for the new government. The Conservatives had stumbled across a strategy for improving the public sector and indeed implementing what some saw as a form of market socialism. Certainly it was an approach which some research evaluations suggested was working (Glennerster and Turner, 1993; Foster and Hope, 1993; Glennerster, 1998b). But since the Labour Party in opposition had railed against many of these changes, it was not easy to incorporate them into a clear statement of the Middle Way.

The NHS White Paper (Cm 3807, 1997) is a classic example. The first part of the White Paper returns to the pre-election rhetoric and castigates the wickedness of the internal market. Yet what it puts in its place is, on one reading, an improved version of the internal market. The principle of the purchaser and provider split is kept. That separation is pointless unless the 'commissioning' agents have the chance to exit – to switch provider if they are not satisfied with the outcome. Will they have that chance? 'Of course', came the reply from No. 10 when it heard that Julian Le Grand and I might be about to rubbish the White Paper. Primary care groups with GPs as lead actors will stand for nothing less. The 'service agreements' will last for several years instead of the pointless non-legal contracts on a yearly basis. The devolved budgets to primary care groups will cover all of health care, more or less, and all the population eventually. All very sensible, but really a development of the old GP fundholding system if only district health authorities and some GPs let that work. Yet the government cannot say so and is not putting the drive behind the changes the Conservatives did behind their reforms.

Instead the Department of Health is trying to 'drive the NHS' from the top, to use a phrase overheard in the corridors. There is the National Institute for Clinical Excellence and other national driving devices. One may be forgiven for thinking that there is more central driving ambition here than enthusiasm for delegation and autonomy.

The government has accepted local management of schools and school choice. But its most trumpeted contribution is tougher central control of the national curriculum, a powerful inspectorate telling schools what to do. There is a deep contradiction here. It may well come to be played out with painful results in the aftermath of Scottish devolution. In the most thoughtful contribution I have read to the Third Way debate David Marquand (1998) says:

No one can tell what the Scots will make of home rule when they get it. What is certain is that, once a Scottish Parliament exists, there will be an alternative power centre in Britain, speaking for an increasingly self-confident nation, with a political culture and moral economy from those of Thatcherised middle England, where New Labour made its biggest gains. It is whistling in the wind to expect the Edinburgh Government to be an obedient clone of the London one. (Marquand, 1998, p21)

New Labour cannot quite bring itself to embrace competition and budget devolution, it cannot let go. So it misses the chance to be as distinctive as it is, at least potentially.

Overall

In sum, this government is about a changed set of priorities and values compared with both old Labour and the Conservatives. As a leader in the *Financial Times* (11 February 1999) put it, commenting on the new Welfare Bill, 'This is one of those defining moments for British Welfare'. But there is also a lot of pure pragmatism and continuity with the past. 'What is best is what works.' That is what makes it so difficult to come up with a blinding new idea that encapsulates the Third Way. That is fine by me. I distrust blinding new ideas. They become stale news next day or next month.

References

Berger, P. and Neuhouse, J. (1996) *To Empower People: From State to Civil Society*, 20th anniversary edn, Washington DC, American Enterprise Institute.

Burchardt, T., Hills, J. & Propper, C. (1999) *Private Welfare and Public Policy*, York, Joseph Rowntree Foundation.

Cm 3805 (1998) *A New Contract for Welfare*, London, The Stationery Office.

Cm 3969 (1998) *The Government's Annual Report 97/98*, London, The Stationery Office.

Cm 4011 (1998) *Modern Public Services for Britain: Investing in Reform*, London, The Stationery Office.

Cm 4179 (1998) *Partnership in Pensions*, London, The Stationery Office.

Deacon, A. (1998) 'Welfare reform in the 51st state? The influence of US thinking and experience on the welfare debate in Britain', paper given at the Twentieth Annual Research Conference of the Association for Public Policy Analysis and Management, New York.

Ellwood, D. (1988) *Poor Support: Poverty in the American Family*, New York, Basic Books.

Foster, J. & Hope T. (1993) *Housing Community and Crime: The Impact of the Priority Estates Project,* London, The Stationery Office.

Giddens, A. (1998) *The Third Way,* Cambridge, Polity Press/Oxford, Blackwells.

Glennerster, H. (1998a) *Toward a New Philosophy: A Global Reevaluation of Democracy at Century's End, 5. Social Policy in the UK: Creating a New Social Contract,* New York, Carnegie Council on Ethics and International Affairs.

Glennerster, H. (1998b) 'Competition and quality in health care: the UK experience', *International Journal for Quality in Health Care,* vol. 10, no. 5, pp403–410.

Glennerster, H. (1998c) 'Tackling poverty at its roots: education', in C. Oppenheim (ed.) *An Inclusive Society: Strategies for Tackling Poverty,* London, Institute for Public Policy Research.

Glennerster, H. (1999) 'Which welfare states are most likely to survive?', *International Journal of Social Welfare,* vol. 8, no. 1, pp2–13.

Glennerster, H. & Hills, J. (eds) (1998) *The State of Welfare: The Economics of Social Spending,* Oxford, Oxford University Press.

Glennerster, H. & Turner, T. (1993) *Estate-based Housing Management: An Evaluation,* London, The Stationery Office.

Glennerster, H., Lupton, R., Noden, P. & Power, A. (1999) *Poverty, Social Exclusion and Neighbourhood,* CASE paper no. 22, London, ESRC Centre for Analysis of Social Exclusion, London School of Economics.

Gregg, P. & Wadsworth, J. (1996) *It Takes Two· Employment Polarisation in the OECD,* CEP Discussion Paper No. 304, London, London School of Economics.

Halpern, D. & Mikosz, D. (1998) *The Third Way: Summary of the NEXUS On-line Discussion,* London, Nexus.

Harris, J. (forthcoming) *Community and Citizenship: The 1997 Ford Lectures,* Oxford, Oxford University Press.

HC 620 (1998) *New Ambitions for Britain: Financial Statement and Budget Report 1998,* London, The Stationery Office

Heath, A. & Curtice, J. (1998) 'New Labour new voters?' paper presented at the annual conference of the Political Studies Association, April.

Hills, J. (ed.) (1996) *New Inequalities,* Cambridge, Cambridge University Press.

Hills, J. (1998) *Thatcherism, New Labour and the Welfare State,* CASE paper no. 13, London, ESRC Centre for Analysis of Social Exclusion, London School of Economics.

Jackman, R., Layard, R. & Nickell, S. (1996) 'Combating unemployment: is flexibility enough?' in *Macroeconomic Policies and Structural Reform,* Paris, OECD.

Layard, R. (1997a) 'Preventing long term unemployment: an economic analysis', in D. S. Snower and G. de la Dehesa (eds) *Unemployment Policy,* Cambridge, Cambridge University Press.

Layard, R. (1997b) *What Labour Can Do,* London, Warner Books.

Le Grand, J. & Agulnik, P. (1998) *Tax Relief and Partnership Pensions,* CASE paper no. 5, London, ESRC Centre for Analysis of Social Exclusion, London School of Economics.

Macmillan, H. (1938) *The Middle Way,* London, Macmillan.

Marshall, T.H. (1950) *Citizenship and Social Class,* Cambridge, Cambridge University Press.

Marquand, D. (1998) 'Blair's birthday; what is there to celebrate?' *Prospect,* May 1998.

Mead, L. (1986) *Beyond Entitlement: The social obligations of citizenship,* New York, Free Press.

Mead, L. (1997) *From Welfare to Work: Lessons from America,* London, Institute for Economic Affairs.

Oppenheim, C. (1997) 'The growth of poverty and inequality' in A. Walker & C. Walker (eds) *Britain Divided: the Growth of Poverty and Exclusion in the 1980s and 1990s,* London, Child Poverty Action Group.

Osborne, D. & Gaebler, T. (1992) *Reinventing Government: How the Entrepreneurial Spirit is Transforming the Public Sector from Schoolhouse to Statehouse,* City Hall to the Pentagon, Reading, MA, Addison-Wesley.

Page, R. & Deakin, N. (eds) (1993) *The Costs of Welfare,* Aldershot, Avebury.

Rees, A. M. (1995) 'The other Marshall', *Journal of Social Policy,* vol. 24, no. 3, pp341–362.

Sen, A. (1997) *Inequality, Unemployment and Contemporary Europe,* DERP Discussion Paper no. 7, London, STICERD, London School of Economics.

Timmins, N. (1999) 'The death of universalism', *Financial Times,* 10 February, p25.

3 New Labour and Social exclusion: the search for a Third Way – or just gilding the ghetto again?

John Benington and
David Donnison

Introduction

The new Labour government has put social exclusion (or rather inclusion) at the very heart of its agenda for modernisation and reform. In his first speech after the election – from a housing estate in Peckham – the Prime Minister promised that there would be 'no more forgotten people, no one left out'.

This was followed quickly by the setting up of a Social Exclusion Unit (SEU) in the Cabinet Office, with a brief to 'develop integrated and sustainable approaches to the problems of the worst housing estates, including crime, drugs, unemployment, community breakdown, and bad schools etc' (SEU, 1997).

By September 1998 the SEU had already produced reports on school truancy, rough sleepers and, most substantial of all, a new

National Strategy for Neighbourhood Renewal – revealingly entitled 'Bringing Britain Back Together' (SEU, 1998).

The neighbourhood renewal strategy included the setting up of seventeen 'pathfinder' districts to take part in an £800 million, three-year New Deal for communities and eighteen 'policy action teams', each headed by a champion minister, to develop fast-track inter-departmental responses to key issues affecting social exclusion like jobs, skills, neighbourhood management, anti-social behaviour and information technology (with progress reports back to a Cabinet committee within twelve months).

Many in the UK poverty lobby welcomed this indication of direct prime ministerial support for tackling concentrated areas of deprivation and disadvantage, but argued that the work of the SEU would be cosmetic and ineffective if mainstream government policies continued to cut back on welfare spending and services, and to tighten eligibility and control over benefits to poor, sick, unemployed and disabled people.

The Chancellor's Spring 1999 Budget has provoked further debate on this question – whether the government is seriously developing a new approach to social exclusion and poverty, or whether it is just throwing a few scraps from the gourmet tables of the middle classes?

For example, the Chancellor has been criticised for reducing basic tax levels for middle-income earners at a time when there is urgent unmet need for investment in many public services. However, the budget can also be read as a modest redistribution of resources from the better off (with the abolition of mortgage interest relief and the married couple's allowance, and an increase in national insurance contributions for those on higher incomes) towards both families with children and pensioners (with a cut in the basic rate of income tax to 10 per cent, an increase in child benefit, a new children's tax credit, the extension of the New Deal scheme to the over-50s, a minimum income guarantee for pensioners and a fivefold increase in their winter allowance).

Gordon Brown's response to this debate is that the government is trying to find a new way through the traditional tension between the interests of the middle class and those of the poor, and that the Budget is 'built on the central idea that our future depends upon enterprise and fairness together' (*Guardian,* 10 March 1999), and reflects a commitment to combining social justice with economic prudence (*Express,* 10 March 1999).

Though this kind of Third Way talk is in danger of sounding a glib compromise, the subsequent Treasury document *Tackling Poverty and Extending Opportunity* (Treasury, 29 March 1999) demonstrates that the government is under no illusions about the scale or the scope of the challenge they have undertaken. Research commissioned by the the Chancellor shows that two in five children in Britain are born into poor households, that up to 25 per cent of children never escape from poverty and that deprivation is being passed down the generations by unemployment and underachievement in schools. The Treasury data show that while a third of all children at any one time live in households with incomes below half the national average, up to a quarter will live in persistent poverty (*Guardian,* 29 March 1999).

The government's strategy for tackling poverty and social exclusion is bold and wide ranging. The Prime Minister has set a public target of eliminating child poverty within 20 years. The strategy is seen as requiring inter-ministerial and inter-depart-mental action, involving not only social security, but also education and employment, and health. In addition to the budget changes summarised above, it also encompasses the statutory minimum wage, the New Deal for the unemployed, and the special measures introduced for improving education and health for the disadvantaged, including action zones and a range of special projects.

A central plank of New Labour's strategy is to offer many of the excluded routes out of poverty and out of the ghetto, and inclusion in the mainstream of society (alongside the enterprise-driven middle classes), via education, skill training and employment opportunities, rather than support in surviving their poverty through welfare benefits – 'hand-ups rather than hand-outs', as the media spin-doctors have put it.

This article discusses the strengths and weaknesses of this employment-based strategy, and analyses the government's evolving approach to social exclusion. Because the overall strategy has already received extensive commentary (e.g. Oppenheim, 1998), we focus on the SEU's proposals and actions for dealing with neighbourhood deprivation, comparing and contrasting them with previous strategies and programmes to combat poverty. We question whether this adds up to more than merely 'gilding the ghetto' again (Community Development Project, 1977a), or whether it reflects a serious search for a 'Third Way' beyond the previous unsuccessful strategies of both old Labour and the New Right. We will also explore how far it is likely to succeed where previous policies have failed, and who will be the winners and who the losers.

We adopt a broad definition of social exclusion, in terms of the forces and factors which may exclude people from the resources, services and opportunities (e.g. employment, housing, education, participation) enjoyed by those in the political, economic and social mainstream of a given society. Social exclusion in our terms is therefore a dynamic process, not a static condition. It is a relative not an absolute concept. It focuses upon the interrelationships between the poor and those from whom, or by whom, they may be excluded.

We are particularly interested, in this article, in the interrelationships between on the one hand the poor and excluded, and on the other hand the next stratum of those on middle incomes, who are included but insecure. This allows us to examine both ends of the bridge (from welfare to work, from the ghetto to Middle England) which forms a central part of the government's preferred route out of poverty.

We begin by analysing the economic and social changes underlying New Labour's policies for social inclusion, and in particular their preoccupation with 'Middle England'. We go on to look at their specific strategies for tackling social exclusion and neighbourhood deprivation, particularly through the work of the SEU.

The politics of Middle England: included but insecure

It is easier to write an intriguing story about politicians than about the political forces to which they respond. It is not only journalists who present our government's social policies as a tale about Tony Blair and his colleagues. But central features of these policies, such as the reduction of redistributive taxes and benefits, growing reliance on market mechanisms and severe measures against offenders, lone parents and unemployed people – in short, the shift to the Right of once-radical parties – were to be seen in other countries long before they appeared in the New Labour Party. We have followed where Australia, New Zealand (see Chapter 13 below), Canada and the USA (see Chapter 12 below) led the way, and a growing number of European socialist or social-democratic parties are now moving in similar directions. If Tony Blair and his colleagues were lost in some air disaster tomorrow it is unlikely their Labour successors would behave very differently. More fundamental forces than a passing array of politicians must be at work. What are they, and how do they shape the social policies of the Left, and this government's strategy for social exclusion in particular? These are the questions we explore in the first half of this article. In the second half we briefly examine the evolution of the Blair government's social exclusion policies, and ask whether they are likely to provide greater room for manoeuvre in future or to impose even tighter political constraints.

The model of behaviour we use in this analysis is a simple one. It starts with a changing economy on which is built a social structure shaped by the opportunities the economy provides. This society creates in turn a political marketplace in which conflicts can be managed and visions of the future formulated. The economic and social policies that emerge from these processes feed back further influences on the economy, the society and its politics which make an impact on the next round of policy making. We deal very briefly with each stage of these interrelated processes: the economy, social structure, politics and social policies, and – finally and most speculatively – the influences these policies feed back and their likely impact on future policies.

Economy and society

Socialist ideas developed in Europe during the second half of the nineteenth century, the Germans playing a leading role in the movement. The British Labour Party, formed at the end of the century by trade unions to represent the interests of working people, did not adopt a socialist programme until the election of 1918 (Sassoon, 1996). It formed a minority government in 1924 and gained its first parliamentary majority in 1945. Much of the 'classic' or 'old' Labour policies were worked out during the times of these governments and in the intervening years – that is to say, during the second quarter of the twentieth century. Meanwhile the Soviet government, with scant guidance from the Marxist texts, was compelled to make policy on its feet in the chaotic aftermath of the 1917 revolution and the civil war that followed. It, too, played an influential part in shaping the meaning of socialism (Hobsbawm, 1994).

These are some features of the British economy at that time which need to be borne in mind by anyone who wants to understand the society it supported. The country depended heavily on manufacturing industries with large numbers of workers labouring in big factories, mills, pits and shipyards. Construction, transport and communications workers formed other major elements of the labour force, employed in more scattered units. With the exception of textile production, most of these industries had a labour force dominated by men, with a skilled elite trained as apprentices within the plant or on the building and transport sites. Although many of the bigger British companies operated on a worldwide basis at this peak period of the Western empires, their headquarters were in Britain and this country was their main base.

Manual workers and their families, accounting by the Second World War for about two-thirds of the population, lived mainly in rented housing belonging to private landlords – usually small, local landlords. Industrial cities were crowded, smoky and unhealthy; and, by 1945, badly devastated by wartime bombing. For their medical care men depended heavily on state-funded schemes related to their employment while their families depended on medical clubs, private insurance and friendly societies. Their children went to state-funded schools, and usually aimed to leave at the minimum age of fourteen and gain an apprenticeship if they could. Many workers were exposed to dangers of accidents and industrial diseases, and to the risk of unemployment in an economy that lurched through major cyclical fluctuations. A state insurance scheme provided short-term benefits for the unemployed, underpinned by a much-hated poor law system providing an income of last resort based on a household means test.

Alongside the manual workers there was a steadily growing minority of professional and managerial workers who paid for their own medical care and pensions, and much of their children's education. They sought to buy their own homes. Many young people originating from working class families gained entry to the middle and lower middle classes, often after many years of evening study and work-based training.

Politics and social policies

So brief an account is inevitably a bit of a caricature, but it provides some understanding of the politics of the Labour movement. Its policies were first hammered out at a time when many social distinctions cut through society at much the same point: roughly along the line dividing manual from non-manual workers. Above that line were the minority of people who had a career of some sort with an income rising in real value into middle life. Many of them belonged to professions which had secured some control over entry to the occupation. That gave their members greater security, a better income and fringe benefits. These people hoped to buy a house some day, and to have within it a bath, flush toilet and hot water – perhaps a telephone. They hoped to buy a car and take holidays away from home. Expecting to pay for education, medical care and pensions, they had some choice about the doctors, schools and insurance systems they depended on.

Below the line most people had incomes which peaked early in life – in their twenties – and thereafter rose only through collective action taken at times when market forces were favourable. They expected that all their lives they would rent a house, wait in the bus queue or walk or cycle to work, use the public telephone boxes, and depend on the state for most of their education, medical care and retirement incomes.

The Labour Party's main purpose, as its manifestos show (Craig, 1970), was to win for working class people the privileges the middle class already had: safer and more secure jobs and holidays with pay; a good home at a rent they could afford; safer, cleaner streets and towns; medical care with some choice of doctor; an education that would take their children as far as they were capable of going; and an end to means tests and the poor law.

The main instruments reformers relied on in order to achieve these things were the nationalisation of industry, good town planning and public housing, universal social benefits and the growth of a 'welfare state' manned by public service professions whose members formed an unspoken but powerful alliance – still to be seen in many Labour Party meetings – with those who depended most heavily on the services they provided.

There was no bland consensus in the years that followed the Second World War, but there was a recognition that the working class, if it could get its act together in alliance with the public service professions, would always win in the end. They were the majority. And the class war was benign. With full employment and a growing economy, all could win something from it. Thus Conservative governments consolidated, and sometimes extended, the reforms introduced by their Labour predecessors. Neither party had to think much about the poor or to develop systematic policies for preventing social exclusion. It was assumed that they would benefit from the broader development of universal services available to all. Services for the poor, it was believed with good reason, always tended to become poor services.

New times, new politics

That economy has gone and, with it, the society it supported and the politics it generated. Meanwhile the success of the reforms introduced by post-war governments has fed back further changes which help to break up the old alliances. Whole books have been written about these changes and the society they have created – 'late modern', 'global', 'plural', 'post-Fordist': we are still searching for the words to describe it. The old, two-part class system has given way to a more confused set of alignments, described by Will Hutton and many others as a three-part system in which 40 per cent are doing well – the top layers very well indeed – 30 per cent in the middle are employed or reasonably pensioned but often anxious, and 30 per cent at the bottom are increasingly falling behind – the last 10 per cent suffering a real decline in living standards (Hills, 1996).

Manufacturing industry has collapsed in cities which used to be Labour's heartlands, and many of the surviving manual workers are now buying their own homes and fleeing to the suburbs. Meanwhile the greatly enlarged public sector of the housing market – and the schools and other services with local catchment areas – have been sifted out into increasingly stratified social layers that create growing concentrations of poverty at the bottom of the pile (Joseph Rowntree Foundation, 1995). The class war which used to be fought out between employers and workers, landlords and tenants, now increasingly takes place across the counters of the public services and between neighbouring quarters of our cities. People who never talk to residents of our poorest neighbourhoods have no idea of the ferocity of their feelings towards those with power – including the Labour government and almost anyone wearing a suit.

The politically crucial feature of this society, repeated in many other parts of the Western world, is the large group in the middle of it – call them 'Middle England' (and they probably *are* more concentrated in England than in other countries of the UK). With few interests and allegiances which firmly ally them either to those who are poorer or to those who are richer, or even to others in their own stratum of society, they have to fend for themselves. The fact that they are not a social class in traditional terms but only an arbitrarily defined stratum is not a problem; it is a finding, explaining a good deal about their politics. They have great influence because no party can win power or hold it for long without a lot of their votes. They are shaping the politics of Western countries and deserve more serious study than they have yet received from most social scientists. Galbraith (1992) has famously characterised the influence of this middle stratum in terms of a complacent 'culture of contentment', but this thesis is contradicted by other evidence (e.g. Dean with Melrose, 1999) that demonstrates the extent to which anxiety about poverty extends to middle-income groups. In one sense the spectre of poverty or exclusion may have some of its greatest effects within such groups.

Middle England

We can sketch some features of the people who make up Middle England. The middle third of the income distribution is more varied in social character than the outer thirds, including young couples, struggling to gain a foothold on life's ladders; retired people with modest occupational pensions who worry about

Figure 1: Decline in home owner support: Financial assistance to home owners

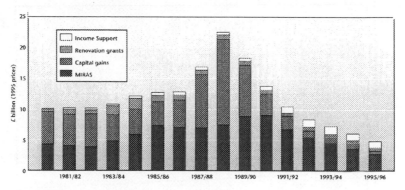

Source: Wilcox 1996, Fig. XXII

inflation; and people in middle life doing a wide range of manual and non-manual jobs for modest rates of pay.

These people have taken on heavier responsibilities and bigger risks than their predecessors in the same social strata. Three-quarters of them are house buyers or home owners (Wilcox, 1997). But public expenditure supporting home ownership has fallen drastically, as Figure 1, prepared by Steve Wilcox, shows. Many are sending, or hope to send, their children to universities at heavy cost to the family. Some must be unsure whether a degree will win their youngsters a job that justifies the sacrifice. Some of them are contributing to private pension schemes which will have little value if they cannot keep up the payments. Many of those in work now find themselves in the occupations most exposed to contracting-out, downsizing, de-layering and all the other processes which shift risks from employers to workers. It is likely to be in Middle England that the sales of dud private pensions and the big increases in mortgage arrears and repossession of homes have taken place. Meanwhile the massive growth in the numbers who are not working but would like to do so means they are aware there is a growing queue of people who would be happy to take their jobs if they had an opportunity to do so.

If things go badly wrong for Middle Englanders, the safety nets their predecessors used to rely on have been weakened or removed. Entitlements to contributory benefits for the sick and unemployed have been drastically reduced, as have payments under income support to cover the interest due on mortgages. The growing percentage of our people depending on means-

Figure 2: Receipt of social assistance in Great Britain, 1948-1991

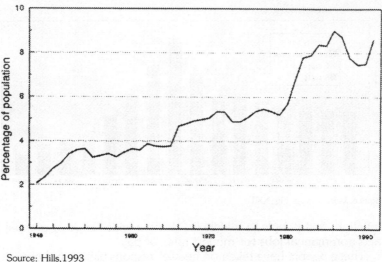

Source: Hills,1993

tested social assistance is shown in Figure 2, prepared by John Hills and his colleagues. The poor laws are back, but decent, privately rented housing at a price that can be afforded by those who have lost their homes is in many cities no longer available. Many must fear, with reason, that if things go wrong they will drop straight into one of the least popular public housing estates.

Meanwhile, opportunities for upward mobility in middle life into professional and technical jobs have been greatly reduced. After years of night school and home study, rent collectors used to become housing managers, draftsmen became architects or engineers, clerks became lawyers, social workers, surveyors, bank managers . . . Their successors need professional qualifications for these jobs, and these, in our full-time, 'front-loaded' system of education, usually have to be taken early in life, immediately after completing school or college. Management is now the only major profession recruiting large numbers of people in middle life (Gershuny, 1993) – and the business schools are working hard to close that route to upward mobility.

Figure 3, prepared by Jay Gershuny, shows, for successive cohorts of men and women entering the labour market at different dates, the proportions who were in professional and technical jobs at various subsequent points in time. It shows that, in each succeeding generation, there were more people in these white-

Figure 3: Percentage of successive cohorts in professional and technical occupations

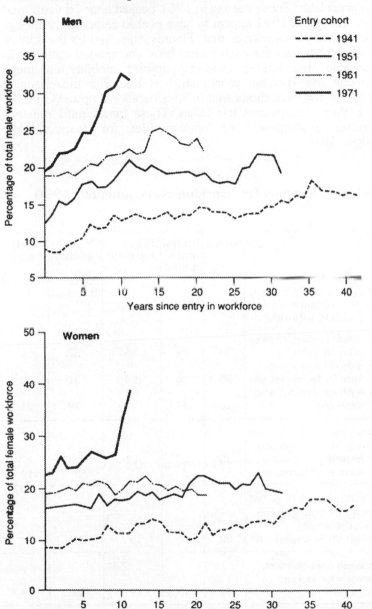

Source: Gershuny,1993

collar jobs but the percentages peaked sooner. Those starting
work in 1941 were still showing a net movement into these jobs
35 years later. Those starting in 1961 peaked after 15 years, and
men starting in 1971 appear to have peaked earlier still, although
we cannot yet be sure of that. Figures expressed by the succes-
sively higher lines for each cohort have encouraged optimists to
conclude that inter-generational upward mobility continued
through the Thatcher years, which is true. But the changing
shape of the lines shows that *intra*-generational upward mobility
into these occupations has fallen. These trends must create a
bleaker environment of opportunities for many Middle
Englanders.

Table 1: Support for 'working class benefits', 1990

	Salariat	Routine non-manual	Petty bougeoisie	Manual foremen	Working class
% saying it should definitely be the government's responsibility to provide:					
● decent housing for those who can't afford it	38	39	36	52	56
● a decent standard of living for the unemployed	25	26	23	31	38
● a job for everyone who wants one	16	14	17	39	31
% nominating as 1st or 2nd priority for extra spending:					
● housing	15	20	23	23	22
● social security benefits	8	9	11	9	19
% nominating as 1st or 2nd priority for extra spending on social benefits:					
● benefits for unemployed	22	20	16	21	24
% saying unemployment benefit is too low and causes hardship	49	45	39	49	57

Source: Jowell et al. 1991, p32.

Implications for social policy

We are not telling a sob story on behalf of those we have described as Middle England: one-third of the population is worse off than they are, and many of them are having a much harder time. We are arguing that changes in the character of those now found in the middle reaches of Western societies mean that they have less reason than their predecessors had for solidarity with those worse off than themselves, and probably greater reason for anxiety about jobs, housing, pensions and much else. For political parties bent on winning the next election, these are the people most likely to be selected for the focus groups and opinion polls which help to shape their policies. What is such research likely to tell them?

Table 1, taken from the 8th British Social Attitudes Report, based on a survey made in 1990, shows that support for spending on the unemployed takes a U-shaped curve when plotted against an occupational breakdown ranking people according to social status. But support for housing and social security benefits in general takes a less clear-cut course, and the 'petit-bourgeoisie' who play an important part in these comparisons are a slightly odd group – not equivalent to the larger numbers we have described as Middle England. So we need better evidence.

Table 2, from the 13th British Social Attitudes Report, based on the 1995 survey, provides firmer data for three equal-sized income groups. When asked whether it would be in the *national* interest to spend more money on each of seven different public services, no clear pattern emerged. But when asked whether it would be in their *own* interests to do so, a clear U-shaped pattern appears for the five 'social' services – although not for the police or defence. The differences may not be large but they are highly consistent.

This is a tantalisingly superficial glimpse of more profound patterns of feeling. One is tempted to expand it with less scientific evidence. Take the most popular 'soaps' broadcast on radio and television: 'The Archers' and 'Eastenders', for example. Their main characters are small business people: farmers, publicans, shop-keepers . . . Middle England in fact. About the only professionals who appear are a doctor, a vet, a parson and a solicitor – all single-handed general practitioners, running what amount to small enterprises. And what do they talk about? Their children, their relations with neighbours and – incessantly – their businesses and their money. Politics, unemployment and poverty (other than their own), the future of the nation or the world – these are never discussed. The continuing popularity of such programmes

Table 2: Support for public expenditure in different income groups, 1995

	Income group		
	Low	Middle	High
% saying that higher spending on each programme is:			
● in their own interests			
Health	67	62	69
Education	55	53	59
Police/law enforcement	44	38	37
Public transport	33	24	28
Environment	30	26	30
Culture and the arts	10	5	9
Defence	17	8	5
● in the national interest			
Health	69	74	79
Education	65	67	82
Police/law enforcement	41	39	39
Public transport	30	26	41
Environment	31	28	34
Culture and the arts	10	6	7
Defence	12	11	5
Base	*406*	*328*	*346*

Source: Jowell et al. 1996, p195.

suggests that their makers may have been consulting the same focus groups as the politicians.

These patterns of opinion, which must be well known to the political parties, help to explain why they all promise to reduce income tax, to restrict expenditure on benefits for the unemployed, lone parents and other less popular claimants, and – more generally – why the Labour Party and its counterparts in other countries have drifted to the Right. The competition to demonstrate that they are toughest on 'law and order' may have the same origins. Owing to the disintegration of older class loyalties, the parties are compelled to compete for the support of the same voters in the centre of the political spectrum. Opposition, it often seems, is left to the churches and the *Guardian* newspaper.

Policies and their feedback

Such a programme may win elections, but once in office a party finds that medical science continues to grow more expensive, more students qualify for entry to the most expensive stages of education, more old people survive to the advanced ages at which they become an increasingly heavy burden on medical and social services, more cars demand more roads, and all these demands outpace the growth of tax revenues. Ministers who have promised that income tax will be reduced still further are compelled to seek new sources of revenue or savings which can be captured for their own services. Education withdraws maintenance grants from students; Health plans to charge insurance companies and their motorist policy holders for treating victims of motor accidents; Housing withdraws mortgage interest tax relief and other benefits from house buyers; Social Security plans to reduce benefits for disabled and sick people and to make child benefit taxable; Transport gets motor license duties and petrol taxes increased . . . and so it goes on.

That is inevitable, and some of it quite creative from an old Labour standpoint. In amongst the tax and benefit changes there is a lot of somewhat surreptitious egalitarian redistribution going on. But what impact will it all make on Middle England? If the increased costs of motoring, community care, house purchase, university education and the rest fall disproportionately heavily on households in these sections of society they may increase the hardships and anxieties they already experience and make them still more resistant to the claims of people poorer than themselves. A clear and fair system of progressive taxes on income might be more acceptable if the reasons for it were frankly explained.

A system of proportional representation may break up the monolithic parties now competing with each other for the middle ground and bring some of the things now said only by clerics and the *Guardian* into franker public debate. But the experience of other countries which already have proportional representation suggests that this will not transform social policies, for they owe more to fundamental features of the economy and the social structure it creates than to voting systems.

It may be necessary to give the people of Middle England greater security in their working lives, greater confidence in the future and a more reliable safety net if things go badly wrong for them before they can be expected to support more generous provisions for the poorest people and a serious attempt to create a more inclusive society. Policies to end social exclusion may have to start with Middle England – the included but insecure people.

New Labour's social exclusion strategy

New Labour's approach to social exclusion and inclusion, while not yet fully articulated, is nevertheless a reflection of the wider attempt by the government (as discussed above) to re-draw social identities and electoral loyalties around a new kind of one-nation consensus – the notion of a broad, encompassing, all inclusive, middle stratum in society.

The attempt to create a new political and economic coalition around this grouping is supported by the attempt to generate a new ideology of the Third (middle?) Way, which goes beyond the state-centred approaches previously adopted by old Labour and the market-centred approaches beloved by the New Right.

In spite of a series of high profile books and international conferences to clarify the meaning and content of the Third Way, it is still not much more than an inspired slogan. However, one element is clearly articulated – a declared intention to shift the centre of gravity of governance away from the bureaucratic state and the private competitive market, and towards civil society and informal communities.

New Labour's policies for tackling poverty therefore challenge both old Labour's reliance upon a universal welfare state and the New Right's romance with unregulated competitive markets. The search is for a middle way, between left and right, and beyond both the state and the market.

The government's modernisation agenda

In order to understand the application of this approach to social exclusion it is necessary to put it in the context of the government's wider commitment to modernisation of public services, but without increasing taxation. Their agenda for modernisation of government and public services has tended so far to focus upon changes in the forms and processes of policy making (e.g. devolution in Scotland, Wales and Northern Ireland; reform of the House of Lords; reform of local government and the civil service) more than upon changes in the policy content or resource-base for public services. Their approach includes the following features:

● A new policy agenda for public services, with policy making and service-delivery starting not from the preoccupations of government departments and the professions (e.g. law, accountancy, teaching) but from the cross-cutting problems and issues facing citizens and communities (e.g. ageing, unemployment, crime and community safety, social exclusion).

- A new style of policy making – involving a shift from detailed regulation of local government through legislation and prescription, towards a more provisional, experimental approach, illustrated by Education Action Zones, Health Action Zones, and a profusion of 'pilot projects' to develop and test new policy initiatives.

- A new culture of central/local relations – which is consultative and collaborative in its initial form, with an invitation to local authorities and other agencies to join in new forms of collaborative partnership and multi-level governance. However, government demands rapid and visible improvements in the quality of public service, and threatens to intervene very directly and forcibly if minimum standards are not met (e.g. education in Hackney).

- A new centre of gravity for governance – which, it is suggested, should be shifted towards the citizen and the grassroots community, so that governance is based not just in the state bureaucracy or the private competitive market, but also in civil society and its informal networks and associations. The Third Way between the state and the market is seen to lie in public/private/voluntary partnerships, and in citizen-centred government.

One of the key themes in the modernisation debate is that joined-up government and citizen-centred services will require a greater degree of both vertical and horizontal integration – that is, closer joint working between

- different tiers of government (local, regional, national and European);

- different spheres of society (public, private, voluntary and the grassroots community).

At the local level this will require much closer collaboration between local authorities, education authorities, health authorities and other agencies, at both the institutional level and the neighbourhood level. This radical agenda for modernisation of public services already finds expression in a series of practical initiatives and programmes from central and local government, and is embodied in the work of the SEU.

Thirty years of pilot projects

The residents of Britain's most disadvantaged neighbourhoods could be forgiven for scepticism about the government's high-profile programme to tackle social exclusion. Many of them have been on the receiving end of a succession of pilot programmes and special projects over their lifetimes, and question what, if anything, has changed in their everyday lives as a result.

At least eight different national pilot programmes to tackle disadvantage have been launched in the UK over the past thirty years, including the Educational Priority Areas in the late 1960s, the Community Development Projects in the 1970s, the Urban Programme, Peter Walker's Six Towns Studies, Keith Joseph's Cycle of Deprivation studies (the story that he approved this programme thinking it was tackling the Cycle of Depravation is possibly apocryphal!), City Challenge, Single Regeneration Budget and so on.

In addition to these UK programmes, the USA has had its own War on Poverty and Model Cities programmes, described in Peter Marris and Martin Rein's classic account of the Dilemmas of Social Reform (Marris and Rein, 1967). The European Union has run three cross-national programmes to combat poverty and social exclusion, and the Irish government has set up a series of programmes and agencies to combat poverty.

New Labour has now added its own profusion of pilot programmes – Education Action Zones, Health Action Zones, Employment Zones, best value pilot projects, pathfinder estates, New Deal for regeneration, New Deal for communities – to this apparently endless flow of area regeneration acronyms and initiatives. (Newham, one of London's poorest boroughs, now has a full pack of all the available zones, pathfinders and pilots, as well as leading partnership arrangements for the New Deal for the unemployed, the Single Regeneration Budget 5, and objective 2 European Regional Development Funding.)

What can be learned from the thirty years of past programmes to combat small area disadvantage and social exclusion, to illuminate the government's current strategy? On the positive side most of these pilot anti-poverty programmes have generated some tangible short-run improvements in the physical and social infrastructure of disadvantaged neighbourhoods. Benefits have included measures:

- To bring about small but practical improvements in the cost and quality of living for the poor – including welfare rights and income support, credit unions, and the socialisation of some costs like community transport.

- To develop opportunities for skill training and re-training, job placements, and work experience for the unemployed.

- To increase the relevance, accessibility, coordination and accountability of government services at neighbourhood level, and their integration with voluntary and community networks.

- To improve the physical condition of housing and of the local environment, through repair and refurbishment of existing facilities, and some new building and provision of community facilities.

- To mobilise and empower the poor to represent their interests more effectively, to claim and gain access to services to which they are entitled, and to strengthen their own networks of cooperation, action and mutual help within the community.

However, most of the previous pilot programmes have tended to suffer from the following limitations:

- They are too brief to achieve significant impacts. Pilots have usually lasted around five years, which has been long enough to identify problems and to introduce a number of short term measures, but not to implement medium- or longer-term strategies and programmes for intervention.

- Their focus on the local and neighbourhood levels has assisted the process of micro-problem identification, but it has been harder to analyse causation or to develop strategic action at national or federal government levels.

- The local focus and the relative brevity of the programmes has tended to lead to a concentration on physical and social dimensions of deprivation, and less on the economic factors which underlie much disadvantage for both individuals and neighbourhoods.

- Most of the pilot programmes have been monitored and evaluated in some way, but the findings have rarely been fed back into the next stage of the decision-making process, or had any major influence upon mainstream policy making by governments.

This is the background against which the government is developing its own latest concerted strategy to combat exclusion. A number of distinguishing features can be noted, some of which try to overcome the above limitations. However, the government's approach contains several crucial contradictions of its own.

The first is the focus on social exclusion rather than poverty per se. This may partly be a matter of fashion (the European Union has adopted and promoted this language since the mid-1980s, when the British government of the time was forbidden by ministers to use the 'p word'!). However, the concept of social exclusion is also used to signify a shift of focus away from the poor and the state of poverty, towards the processes, policies and institutions which cause or reinforce poverty by excluding people. On the other hand, some commentators fear that social exclusion is a dangerously sanitised and abstract discourse, masking the harsh facts of poverty. The emphasis on social exclusion can also divert attention from economic and political exclusion.

Second is the fairly concrete definition of the problem in statistical and practical terms, compared with several previous programmes which have been based less upon evidence than upon ideology or ideal. The Treasury document *Tackling Poverty and Extending Opportunity* is based upon commissioned research (from Steve Machin at University College London) and detailed longitudinal statistical analysis of child poverty. Similarly, the SEU's work on small concentrated areas of multiple deprivation reviews various data about the forty-four local authority districts and the several thousand small neighbourhoods with the highest concentrations of deprivation in England – with high levels of unemployment, lone parent households, underage pregnancy rates, children growing up in families on income support, poor educational records, high mortality ratios, poor housing, vandalism and dereliction, and so on.

While there are questions that could be raised about specific indices, the definition is a broad one, covering not only physical conditions but also personal and family circumstances and quality of life. The data about deprivation are also set in a context of growing inequality, where net incomes after housing costs of the richest tenth of the population grew by 68 per cent between 1979 and 1994/5, while those in the bottom tenth fell by 8 per cent. The report also highlights the change in the geography of poverty, with the widening gap between affluent and poor wards between the 1981 and 1991 censuses, leaving the very poorest becoming more concentrated in small areas of acute need.

The detailed focus on conditions in small areas of disadvantage is to be welcomed as a starting point for evidence-based policy making. However, a small area focus of this kind can run the risk of diverting attention away from the wider political economic forces which cause and maintain the concentrations of poverty and unemployment in these areas. The CDPs in the 1970s showed convincingly that much of the deprivation in these areas was caused and reinforced by wider industrial change, at the city, regional, national and international levels (Community Development Project, 1977b).

Third, there has been some attempt to learn lessons from past experience. The SEU has consulted widely on why more has not been achieved by previous policies and programmes. It has highlighted several key lessons, including: too much departmentalism; too little integration of policy and service delivery; too many short-term initiatives; too many restrictive rules; too exclusive a focus on the neighbourhood in isolation from the wider area; and too much emphasis on buildings and too little upon the people. They have also looked at what can be learned from good initiatives that have worked. They make a cogent critique of the form and processes of previous anti-poverty initiatives, but the most crucial limitations probably lie in the content and the resourcing of these programmes. As the SEU says, there has been too much initiative-itis and 'mainstream policies and spending have rarely been bent towards the needs of poorer areas, and . . . public spending has been focused too much on dealing with the symptoms and not their prevention.' (Social Exclusion Unit, 1998, p38, para. 2.9).

A fourth feature, which follows on from the third, is the clear acceptance of responsibility that government is part of the problem as well as part of the solution. The language is blunt and honest: '. . . for too long governments have simply ignored the needs of many communities. When they have acted the policies haven't worked' (p7); 'Past Government policies have often contributed to the problem' (p9); 'The failure to get to grips with the problems of the poorest neighbourhoods represents a costly policy failure' (p10). The diagnosis is also incisive and familiar: 'Too much has been spent on picking up the pieces, rather than building successful communities or preventing problems from arising in the first place' (p7); 'Problems have fallen through the cracks between Whitehall departments, or between central and local government. And at the neighbourhood level, there has been no one in charge of pulling together all the things that need to go right at the same time' (p9).

This candour is refreshing, but it leaves the government with a clear self-imposed challenge to do (and to be seen to do) very much better than previous programmes. At first sight there does appear to be a risk of replicating the 'initiative-itis' which they correctly identify as part of the problem in the past. The social exclusion strategy includes the coordination or targeting of a plethora of existing projects (New Deals for the unemployed, Employment Zones, Health Action Zones, Education Action Zones, single regeneration budget) as well as a range of new initiatives (e.g the New Deal for communities, which provides £800 million over three years for the intensive regeneration of small neighbourhoods in seventeen pathfinder areas; and Sure Start, with £540 million to support young children in deprived neighbourhoods).

However, a fifth characteristic of this government's approach is the strong commitment to developing a national strategy for social exclusion, rather than just a collection of local projects. The organisational design of this programme holds out greater hope of a serious strategic impact across the whole of government than before. The design of the SEU links central government, local government and local communities into the strategy in an unusually close way. The Unit has direct personal support from the Prime Minister. The Minister for Housing and Local Government, Hilary Armstrong MP, has overall coordinating responsibility; several other senior government ministers have specific responsibilities for championing and chairing policy action teams, to coordinate policy and action. There are eighteen of these, drawn from ten government departments, and also involving experts from outside Westminster and Whitehall, together with some who have experience of poor neighbourhoods. Their work is based around five key themes – 'getting the people to work; getting the place to work; building a future for young people; access to services; and making the Government work better' (Social Exclusion Unit, 1998, p57, para.5.2).

In addition to horizontal integration across the compartmentalised divisions between government departments, policy action teams are also asked to integrate vertically with grassroots communities by '. . . consulting widely, particularly with people who live in poor neighbourhoods and drawing on lessons from good practice; give specific consideration to race and ethnic minority issues relevant to their topic; consider how to maximise the contribution of communities themselves, and what capacity building is needed to promote that; and to produce clear recommendations for follow up work' (p57, para. 5.3).

The timetable for work is brisk. There will be interim reports in April and July 1999 and the policy development work will be completed by December 1999. The work of the policy action teams will be cleared through the relevant Cabinet Committees, and the government has committed itself to pulling together the outcome of all the reports into a coherent national strategy, to which not only the government will commit itself, but also local authorities, other public organisations, businesses, the voluntary sector and others working in poor communities.

The Anglo-Catholic work ethic – a route out of poverty and the ghetto?

A crucial feature of the government's overall strategy, however, is a reliance on work rather than welfare as the main response to poverty and social exclusion. While New Labour shares with previous and other governments the substitution of workfare for welfare, its strategy goes further than this. Their Third Way, in Anthony Giddens terms, is to create a 'social investment state' based upon 'positive welfare' and inclusion (Giddens, 1998). In more concrete terms the declared aim is to offer education, training and employment as opportunities for escape out of poverty, out of the ghetto, out of dependence upon state welfare and as routes to inclusion in Middle England's mainstream. The difference in strategy from old Labour is encapsulated in the title of a recent Demos pamphlet – *Escaping Poverty: From Safety Nets to Networks of Opportunity* (Perri 6, 1997).

There are many attractions to this strategy, given that previous measures have tended to support people in continued poverty rather than to provide routes out of it. In this society, paid employment is one of the most important sources not only of income, but also of a sense of worth and status. Modern skills are a good route out of unemployment into decent paid jobs. Education, training and employment are therefore important components in any strategy for alleviating and preventing poverty and social exclusion.

However, a number of important caveats have to be registered. Work only works as a route out of poverty if jobs exist which are within the reach of the poor (both in geographical and skill and social terms). Networks only act as an escape route out of poverty if they provide a steady and secure progression through the many hazardous steps from unemployment into secure jobs. Those at the bottom of the ladder of demoralisation and dependence can climb out of poverty and back into employment and self-sufficiency if helped to regain confidence and skills by an integrated programme of social support, skill training and tailor-made job creation. However, for many people this is not a staircase moving steadily upwards, but a series of slippery slopes, with sudden steps up and slides down, like a game of snakes and ladders. Traditional welfare safety nets are still necessary, to underpin the networks of workfare opportunity, in any conception of a social investment state. For those who are old, sick, disabled or otherwise unable to work, the support systems and services of the traditional redistributive welfare state are still essential.

The strategy of creating networks out of poverty and the ghetto through education, training and employment also runs risks of further imbalancing the social composition of disadvantaged neighbourhoods. If the educable and the employable are helped to leave such neighbourhoods, to join the new middle class, such areas and estates are likely to be left with ever heavier and unviable concentrations of the poor, who are unable to climb out (Wilson, 1987). The strategy should rather be to create neighbourhood communities that are more mixed in terms of their forms of housing tenure, age composition, socio-economic background, ethnic diversity and so on.

The SEU has correctly criticised the succession of previous initiatives aimed at tackling the problems of poor neighbourhoods since the 1960s for failing to set in motion a virtuous circle of regeneration, with improvements in jobs, crime, education, health and housing all reinforcing each other. They have set themselves a bold challenge. The new strategy can only be effective if it combines networks of opportunity to climb out of poverty through education, training and employment, with the traditional support systems and services of the welfare state for those who are unable to work.

Conclusion

It is clear that New Labour policies towards the poor have a number of similarities with, but also crucial differences from, both old Labour and New Right policies. We have suggested that this is partly because of the Labour government's primary orientation towards the interests and insecurities of Middle England, rather than towards the traditional working class.

The government's pre-occupation with capturing the centre ground, creating a new long-term electoral coalition around the middle-income strata and supporting this hegemonic project with a new ideology of the middle way (between left and right and between state and market) is not only a very sophisticated political strategy. It reflects real changes in class structure, composition and identity in Britain, following de-industrialisation, the restructuring of the manufacturing sector, the decline of the manual trade unions, the rise of the service sector, the emergence of new white-collar employment groupings, and new skill and knowledge bases emerging around the new information and communication technologies.

We conclude that it may be necessary to give the people in this middle-income band greater security in their working lives, greater confidence in the future and a more reliable safety net if things go badly wrong for them before they can be expected to support more generous provisions for the poorest people and a serious attempt to create a more inclusive society. Realistic policies to end social exclusion may have to start with Middle England – the included but insecure.

We have analysed the government's social exclusion strategy as part of the creation of a middle way for the middle-income band, balancing fairness with enterprise, social justice with economic prudence. We discuss in particular the new emphasis on finding and creating routes out of poverty, social exclusion and the ghetto, and into inclusion in the middle-income strata, through education, training and employment. We see many of the attractions of this strategy, both for the government, the public purse, and for those who can find decent work as a result.

However, we conclude that this strategy cannot succeed, even in its own terms, if it is left to the processes of the labour market alone. It requires very detailed, planned and tailor-made micro-measures to support specific groups and individuals in developing the knowledge and skills that match both their interests and potential and the skill shortages and needs in the local economy.

Above all, such a strategy for those who want and are capable of paid employment must also be complemented by a strengthening, not a dismantling, of the support systems and services of the traditional welfare state, for those who are too old, sick or disabled to want or be able to take up paid work.

The social investment state proposed by the disciples of the Third Way needs to be undergirded by an economically redistributive welfare state.

Acknowledgment

The authors are grateful to Joseph Rowntree Foundation, LSE/STICERD Welfare State Programme and Sage Publications for permission to reproduce the illustrations in Figures 1, 2 and 3 respectively.

References

Community Development Project (1997a) *Gilding the Ghetto: The State and the Poverty Experiments,* London, Home Office Urban Deprivation Unit.

Community Development Project (1997b) *The Costs of Industrial Change,* London, Home Office Urban Deprivation Unit.

Craig, F. W. S. (1970) *British General Election Manifestos, 1918–1996,* Chichester, Political Reference Publications.
Dean, H. with Melrose, M. (1999) *Poverty, Riches and Social Citizenship,* Basingstoke, Macmillan.
Galbraith, J. K. (1992) *The Culture of Contentment,* Harmondsworth, Penguin.
Gershuny, J. (1993) 'Post-industrial career structures in Britain', in G. Esping-Andersen (ed.) *Changing Classes,* London, Sage.
Giddens, A. (1998) *The Third Way – The Renewal of Social Democracy,* Cambridge, Polity Press.
Hills, J. et al. (1993) *Investigating Welfare,* LSE Suntory Toyota International Centre for Economics and Related Disciplines Welfare State Programme, no. 92.
Hills, J. (ed.) (1996) *New Inequalities: The Changing Distribution of Income and Wealth in the United Kingdom.* Cambridge, Cambridge University Press.
Hobsbawm, E. (1994) *Age of Extremes,* London, Michael Joseph.
Joseph Rowntree Foundation (1995) *Inquiry into Income and Wealth,* York, Joseph Rowntree Foundation.
Jowell, R. et al. (eds) (1991) *British Social Attitudes: The 8th report,* Aldershot, Dartmouth.
Jowell, R. et al. (eds) (1996) *British Social Attitudes: The 13th report,* Aldershot, Dartmouth.
Marris, P. & Rein M. (1967) *Dilemmas of Social Reform: Poverty and Community Action in the United States,* Chicago, IL, University of Chicago Press.
Oppenheim, C. (ed.) (1998) *An Inclusive Society: Strategies for tackling poverty,* London, Institute for Public Policy Research.
Perri 6 (1997) *Escaping Poverty: From Safety Nets to Networks of Opportunity,* London, Demos.
Sassoon, D. (1996) *One Hundred Years of Socialism,* London, I. B. Tauris.
SEU (1997) Social Exclusion Unit: *Purpose, Work Priorities and Working Methods,* Briefing Document, December, London, Cabinet Office.
SEU (1998) *Bringing Britain Together: A National Strategy for Neighbourhood Renewal,* Cm 4045, London, The Stationery Office.
Wilcox, S. (ed.) (1996) *Housing Review, 1996/97,* York, Joseph Rowntree Foundation.
Wilson, W. J. (1987) *The Truly Disadvantaged,* Chicago, IL, University of Chicago Press.

4 Coming to terms with Culture

John Clarke

Ideas of culture have become increasingly significant within debates and conflicts about social welfare policies and practices. At the same time, forms of cultural analysis have been taken up within the study of social policy. On the one hand, culture – understood as a property or a characteristic of social groups – has been deployed to legitimate claims on social attention and social resources in relation to a range of forms of social differentiation, most obviously in relation to forms of ethnicity. On the other hand, cultural analysis has become more significant through the growing emphasis on treating social policy as a field which is 'socially constructed' or 'discursively constituted' (e.g. Hillyard and Watson, 1996; Leonard, 1997; Carter, 1998; O'Brien and Penna, 1998; Saraga, 1998). Alongside these two conceptions of culture lies a third in which culture acts as an axis of social explanation. Here, 'cultural explanations' of social problems are counterposed to 'structural explanations', e.g. in relation to conflicting perspectives on the 'underclass' (e.g. Morris, 1994; Katz, 1996). This chapter tries to separate out these different usages and their implications for social policy as well as arguing that there are important social conditions that underpin this conjunction of 'cultures' in the recent politics and analysis of social policy.

Culture as a field of difference

The most obvious impact of 'culture' in social policy has been its use as a marker of difference in conceptualising social orders composed of more than one homogeneous grouping. Culture registers the presence of difference – whether in terms of multiple 'racial' or ethnic cultures, diverse cultures of sexuality or geographical distinctions (e.g. in terms of different localities or the distinction between the city and the countryside). Culture has appeared in social policy primarily in relation to racialised social divisions. Azoulay (1997) has suggested that the construction of equivalences between culture, 'race' and ethnicity has been a central feature of the invention of multiculturalism. In social policy terms, this formulation can be seen in the emergence of 'multicultural education', and in the concerns to create 'anti-discriminatory' or 'anti-oppressive practice' in social work and related occupations. It is also visible in policy requirements, such as the 1989 Children Act's emphasis on the child's 'race, religion, language and culture' (section 22). This ambiguous equation of 'race' and culture was one outcome of the long struggles to dislocate the assumed correspondence of 'White' and 'British' identities in the conception of citizenship embedded in social welfare. Multiculturalism thus represents an uneasy accommo-dation between the previously hegemonic conceptions of the 'British way of life' and the struggles to articulate a position for minority ethnic groups that did not simply position them as 'immigrants'. Lewis has suggested that multiculturalism produced a new 'racialised subject' who 'is no longer the "immigrant" who must learn to do in Rome as the Romans do, but rather a category of person who, or group which, has distinct abilities and needs which must be met, but which are subordinate to those of the "majority"' (1998, p112).

Multiculturalism was formed as an accommodation or 'settlement' between conflicting conceptions of the relationships between 'race' and 'nation'. It both articulated differences and solidified them, treating them as embedded in plural cultures. It is probably more accurate to describe multiculturalism as a series of intersecting accommodations which varies between forms of welfare service, professional discourses and the political formations in specific geographical locations. So, educational multiculturalism was not precisely the same formation as social work's 'anti-oppressive practice', while the specific content of such practice varied between social services departments in local authorities despite the common professional commitment to such aims. Nevertheless, multiculturalism in this broad sense represented one sort of settlement between competing conceptions of the 'people', 'state' and 'welfare' implicated in the politics of social welfare (Hughes, 1998). Like all such political settlements, it is both a stabilising moment (becoming embedded or institutionalised in policy and practice) as well as remaining vulnerable to new challenges to its legitimacy.

This quasi-anthropological concept of culture as the 'way of life' – the accrued and continuing tradition – of a social group has been central to the development of 'multiculturalist' policies and practices in Britain and elsewhere (e.g. Baubock *et al.*, 1996). This view treats social groups as both 'owning' their own culture and being possessed or defined by it. In this view, a culture is a social unity: it is both internally unified and socially unifying. A culture is seen as a coherent or consistent field of 'values', accrued beliefs, traditions and orientations to the world. At the same time, it is shared by, and joins together, all of its 'members' as a social entity. Partly because of the emphasis on tradition, this conception of culture tends to view cultures as stable, unchanging or, at best, slowly adaptive. It is a view that prioritises the processes of classification or taxonomy – distinguishing between cultures (and the social groups that they constitute). It enables the differentiation and classification of different 'national cultures', different 'ethnic cultures', different 'religious cultures' and different 'local cultures'. This conception of culture as both constitutive of social difference and its primary social marker is accompanied by a number of problems. One is the issue of differentiated positions within a culture. Each cultural 'unity' will be inhabited differently by groups within its 'membership', whose places will be marked by the impact of other social divisions, e.g. gender or sexuality. A second problem is that such a concept of culture is ill-equipped to deal with culture-as-process. Cultures involve practices of creativity, transformation, realignment, deconstruction and reconstruction. For some commentators, this cultural dynamic is a matter of historical periodization. Giddens (1994, p5), for example, suggests that we have entered a 'post-traditional social order' in which values, positions and identities are no longer stabilised. I suspect that such distinctions overhomogenise the past (that which is pre-the-post) in a crude way and overemphasise the difference of the present. It may be that both the pace and the visibility of cultural transformations have increased in a world where cultural production, distribution and consumption are increasingly central to the technologies and processes of capital accumulation.

Nevertheless, the achievement of even a grudging and uneven conception of a diverse rather than a monocultural Britain has been subject to attempts to dislocate it in different ways. There has been a continuing tension about the relationships between 'minority ethnic cultures' and the 'dominant culture' of (white) Englishness/Britishness which is represented as both non-ethnic/non-culturally specific and the possessor of Culture in its aesthetic and value laden senses. This latter conception (of Culture as the/our 'way of life') has been given added weight by the significant place occupied by neo-conservative thinking in New Right politics (in both the UK and USA). Neo-conservatism aimed to preserve and revitalise 'tradition' in cultural terms that attempted to close the connections between 'race' and nation. These efforts were exemplified in the infamous Tebbit 'cricket test' directed at the identities and loyalties of 'Black British' people (relying on the assumed equivalence of White = English, or at least White = MCC). 'Culture' occupies a special place in neo-conservatism and I explore some aspects of this affinity in the following section.

However, it is worth noting that other processes have acted on the 'multiculturalist' settlement in Britain, destabilising it in different ways. One has been the drive towards individualising difference, particularly through the processes of economisation or marketisation in social welfare provision. In these processes difference has been recast as the variable wants of individual consumers. In such formulations, difference is both celebrated and 'de-socialised' (Clarke, 1998b). As Fiona Williams has argued, 'the whole notion of difference here is underexplained – it is seen as belonging to the individual and expressed through consumer choice. This imposes a market model upon the organisation of welfare in which consumer choices and preferences determine the nature and range of provision' (1994, p69). The rhetoric of consumerism, contracts and markets has been profoundly influential in the reconstruction of welfare systems, although whether this has actually 'empowered' consumers is another matter (see also Clarke, 1997, 1998c; Clarke and Newman, 1997, pp107–116). Finally, the formalism of multiculturalism (in which every group 'has' its culture) has been challenged by more dynamic conceptions and practices of cultural 'hybridisation' and transformation that refuse the settled, stable and essentialist views of culture as 'a way of life' or 'tradition' (e.g. Gilroy, 1993; Brah, 1996; Hall, 1996; Julien and Mercer, 1996; Lewis, 1998).

The final point that I want to draw out in this section concerns the political significance of 'culture'. I want to suggest that it has no distinctive or stable political identity; it is not signed up to any one political position or tendency. In the 1970s and 1980s it was certainly central to struggles to break hegemonic conceptions of the nation and the people in social policy as well as other domains of social life. Culture was one of the central means deployed to create a legitimate basis for claims on social attention and social resources. Culture was a crucial symbolic figure through which difference could be articulated; a means through which differences could be spoken of and spoken for (see e.g. Lowe, 1996). Culture was central to attempts to redefine the meanings, reach, membership and consequences of citizenship. Nevertheless, such a role in what might be termed 'progressive struggles' is not a guarantee of culture's political character. Indeed, one might argue that its successful use in such struggles has turned it into a valuable symbolic good. It becomes available as a potential political resource sought after and deployed by a range of political projects (see also Ross, 1998, ch. 9). Culture has been articulated to widely divergent political positions, playing an increasingly significant role in conflicts over rights to public institutions, public resources and public spaces. In these conflicts culture has been appropriated by dominant or majoritarian political projects. For example, it has been used as a rallying point in white 'preservationist' claims against multi-ethnic institutions and policies in the UK, USA and South Africa (seeking the control of access to and the content of schooling in the name of maintaining cultural traditions). Finally, this conception of culture was central to the recent mobilisation of the 'countryside' as a 'way of life' in the UK. The countryside was represented as a culture distinct from, and not understood or even abused by, 'urban folk'. This imagery of culture was put to work in defence of rural 'traditions' (fox hunting and the control of access to land). What is important in these diverse examples is that the possession of a culture provides a means of legitimating political claims on social resources (see also Cooper, 1998).

This is not an attempt to deny the political significance – or potency – of culture. On the contrary, it is clear that the term's currency – its social and political valorisation – has been increasing in the last two decades. As Ross has argued, 'respect for people's cultural identities – conventionally associated with gender, race, sexuality, nationality and ethnicity – has come to be seen as a major condition of equal access to income, health, education, free association, religious freedom, housing and employment.' (1998, p191). But this enhanced role makes it all the more important to draw analytical attention to the reifying consequences of the formulation in which culture = tradition =

way of life. These political and policy usages may be variants of 'necessary fictions' or 'strategic essentialism' in which the mobilisation of social forces requires them to be identified as a social, cultural or organisational unity (Weeks, 1996; Azoulay, 1997). In the process of social and political conflict, culture (like 'community') can provide a focus for collective action: the defence of black culture; the needs of the gay community; the interests of disabled people; and so on. At the same time, it is important to be attentive to the processes of conflict and negotiation that determine which interests, needs, values and orientations will be seen as part of that culture/community/group – and which will be excluded. Whether 'culture' is used self-consciously or not, we need to be attentive to the consequences for social policy and practice that may follow, in terms of the essentialising or homogenising effects for those subjected to and by such unifying conceptions of culture.

As a result, it is important to approach the study of cultures with an eye to their double-sidedness. They are unified and unifying entities, but are also the product of processes of construction that involve struggles over the dominant and subordinated elements that make up a culture. So, one aspect of examining specific cultures (or cultural formations) explores them as differentiating entities, constructing identities, attachments and a sense of collective belonging. In this respect, one might approach national cultures (examining the values, orientations, traditions and identities that differentiate French from German cultures). One might distinguish between different class cultures or different ethnic cultures. Alternatively, analysis could focus on different organisational cultures (distinguishing between those based in professionalism and others based in managerialism, for example). At each of these levels of analysis, it is possible to explore cultures as differentiated and differentiating entities. But it is equally important to treat each of those cultures as the product of struggles to determine what it means; to establish its dominant features and identities; to subordinate, marginalise or exclude others. These processes are at work at all levels of analysis. National cultures construct 'the people' and their 'way of life' selectively. Class or ethnic cultures construct their 'membership' and define the place of different groups within the culture. Organisational cultures represent the outcome of struggles to define the purpose, character and dominant modes of coordination within organisations. To put the point more generally, cultures are produced as temporary 'unities in difference'. Cultural analysis needs to address the specificity of this 'unity' and the 'differences' that have been accommodated or negotiated in producing this particular configuration. I will return to some of these issues in the final section of this chapter.

Culture as not-structure: explaining social problems

I now want to explore a different role that the term 'culture' has played in social policy, in which it serves as the organising principle for one approach to explaining social problems. At different times, poverty, disadvantage, delinquency, disorderliness, illegitimacy, ill health, unemployment and other 'social problems' have been the subject of explanations that give pre-eminence to the dimension of culture. As in the previous section, 'culture' here tends to be conceptualised as a 'way of life' – sets of traditions, values, beliefs and habits that characterise (or are believed to characterise) a distinctive social group. Poverty has long been surrounded by explanations that focus on the (supposed) cultural characteristics of poor people (Katz, 1989; Mann, 1994). Sometimes such explanation stress the existence of a distinct – and different – culture: a culture of poverty containing conceptions, values and beliefs that legitimate being in poverty and which are transmitted intergenerationally (most famously in Lewis, 1968). There are, of course, variants, e.g. around the culture or subculture debates around crime, delinquency and 'disaffected' youth (see Muncie, 1984). Such approaches to cultural explanations have been conducted predominantly within social reformist (or, in the US context, liberal) perspectives, as counterweights to individualist paradigms of theorising about disorderly conduct. More recently, cultural models of explanation have become realigned with their older heartland: the conservative concern with the production and maintenance of normative order. This tendency is most visible in the arguments about the 'underclass' and related disorders – incivility, delinquency, dismembered families, demoralised communities and so on (e.g. Murray, 1984, 1990; Davies, 1986; Dennis and Erdos, 1992; Dennis, 1993; Etzioni, 1994). The dominant model of cultural explanation is now normative. It explains 'social problems' as the result of either divergence from the norm (cultural or subcultural deviance: having the wrong culture) or as failure to follow the one true norm (a cultural deficit: having no culture or, at least, not enough).

There are many well-established challenges to such explanations of social problems. They typically rely on an overhomogenised view of poor people, treating them as a group separated from the rest of society. Such approaches have also

overemphasised the degree of cultural difference or distinc-
tiveness, where empirical studies of values and beliefs have
revealed little or no difference between the orientations of 'poor'
and 'non-poor' people (see e.g. Katz, 1989; Dean and Taylor-
Gooby, 1992). But I think that critiques of these approaches have
too readily rejected them on the grounds that they are cultural
explanations. As Morris notes: 'The "culture of poverty" view is
generally criticised for not placing the explanation of poverty
where it really lies, in the economic structure, but instead
encouraging a view of disadvantage as produced by a fatalistic
orientation and lack of motivation on the part of the individual, so
that poverty reproduces itself generation after generation' (1994,
p82). This certainly typifies the approach, but whether this
equates with a 'culturalist' perspective, which can be simply and
satisfactorily contrasted with 'structuralist' explanations, is more
problematic. The wish to refute or avoid the volitional emphasis
and the unimoral dimension of conservative cultural analysis has
resulted in a categorical distinction between culture and structure.
This has a number of problems, including foreclosing the
possibility of any more satisfactory cultural analysis being
developed. At the same time, the structuralist alternatives
developed in opposition to conservative culturalism have tended
to deny agency or the possibility of agency to those identified as
'victims of their structural position' – which is both an analytical
and a political problem.

Rather than rejecting such explanations because they are
cultural rather than structural, it may be worth dismantling these
conservative analyses a little more carefully. They might, for
example, be rejected because of their conception of human
nature (and its gendered character) and the relationship between
men, women and social order on which it is premised. They
might also be taken to task for their strange mix of moral
determinism and individual choice, such that individuals choose to
behave badly, but in a pre-given cultural or moral field where their
bad choices are perfectly rational (e.g. Murray, 1984). They
might be contested because of their narrow, impoverished and
static conception of culture (to say nothing of their imperfect
historical understanding of even the 'cultures of respectability' that
they celebrate). Finally, they might even be challenged for the
ways in which they equate culture and morality, at the same time
as conflating a human or social capacity for moral reflection with
the adoption of the one true morality (e.g. Dennis and Erdos,
1992, ch. 1). These slippages are endemic in Conservative and
neo-conservative theorising. They remain pressing analytical and
political issues, particularly as the peculiar cluster of neo-conser-

vative, communitarian, Christian socialist and merely rabidly illiberal threads continue to be woven into a very strange conception of social order at the heart of New Labour's commitment to 'modernisation' (Clarke and Newman, 1998).

Culture as the practice of producing meaning

After the first two sections, it may be tempting to think that culture is simply too unstable or even too regressive a concept to take further. Certainly, the emphasis on culture-as-tradition has powerful tendencies towards reifying or fixing particular configurations of social order. However, culture has also been the focal point for other modes of analysis which emphasise rather different sorts of social processes. Cultural analysis – particularly in the form of cultural studies – has placed a premium on the contingent and constructed character of social arrangements. In this form, culture does not stand for a fixed bundle of values, beliefs and habits, but a field or domain of social life in which meanings are produced and reproduced. In the process, some sets of meanings may achieve – or at least aim to achieve – the position of becoming 'taken for granted' or becoming the dominant 'way of life' of a social group. But this is the outcome of conflictual cultural processes in which alternative meanings are repressed, subordinated or incorporated. This approach to culture emphasises process and practice – it draws attention to the 'work' that goes into making, unmaking or fixing social meanings. As a result, it is the cultural realm – or level – that is the focus of attention, rather than 'a culture', or even 'some cultures'.

So why does it matter – what is at stake in cultural analysis for the practice of social policy? The term somewhat imprecisely defines a concern with meaning: it denotes the realm of ideas and images; the production, distribution and consumption of symbolic materials; the processes of discursive constitution or social construction; or the work and results of signifying practices. The 'cultural turn' in the social sciences centres on the claim that social life cannot be conceived of without meaning – the making and remakings of symbolic forms (Hall, 1997). It points to the spaces ignored by the classic dualisms of the social sciences: the gaps in the structuralist–individualist debates and the gaps in the structure–agency formulations. It does so by insisting that all social action is – *at the very least* – mediated by culture. This insistence on meaning or the irreducible role of the symbolic disrupts attempts to achieve simplifying closures in the social sciences. It resists a whole range of would-be determinisms by demanding attention be paid to how actions, institutions, alliances or policies are shaped, formed, formulated or imagined through the realm of culture. Even those deeply ingrained bits of social life that have always been thought of and represented as 'nature' are, as Gramsci (1971) insisted, the habits of 'second nature': the taken for granted and institutionalised cultural patterns and practices of a society.

The concern with culture in social analysis has foregrounded issues of practice, praxis and agency: the active production, circulation and consumption of symbolic resources (du Gay, 1997). Culture has provoked the rediscovery, rescue and reworking of issues that tended to be repressed by the dominant modes of social science thought. Culture cuts across established theoretical and disciplinary formations of the social sciences – refusing to 'settle' comfortably in any of them but providing a resource through which all of them can engage in the problems of meaning-making in social life (see e.g. Chaney, 1996; Cook *et al.*, forthcoming). Despite the importance of the word 'culture' in permitting or enabling these remakings of academic knowledge, it would be wrong to treat it as the only sign of the 'cultural turn'. It is possible to see a variety of forms and formulations through which this concern with meaning has been articulated. These include the central role of 'ideology' in Western Marxism in the 1970s; the renewed interest in phenomenology; the 'linguistic turn' drawing on Saussure, Wittgenstein and other tributaries; the emergence of 'labelling' and other varieties of symbolic interactionism; and the discoveries of discourse and social constructionism. None of these developments require the word 'culture', but they form part of what can be conveniently described as the cultural turn – because they create the intellectual concern with, and capacity for, analysing the symbolic practices involved in the processes of social construction/constitution. This is, of course, a slightly disingenuous observation in the way that it positions 'culture' as the dominant means of making sense of a variety of theoretical, epistemological and political shifts in the social sciences. Others have addressed these developments in other terms, e.g. as post-structuralism, social constructionism or postmodernism (Burr, 1995; Hillyard and Watson, 1996; Leonard, 1997; Carter, 1998; O'Brien and Penna, 1998; Taylor, 1998). This is not the place to debate the differences and their consequences, so I will merely note that the idea of the 'cultural turn' seems to me preferable because it is less theoretically and epistemologically specific. It captures a broad spectrum of changes without 'signing them up' to the more refined and exclusive positions implied in conceptions of post-structuralism or postmodernism (see also Clarke, 1998a). In this context, though, what matters is the general sense of what is made available for analysis though the intellectual changes that make up the 'cultural turn'.

In contrast to the uses of 'culture' discussed earlier, cultural analysis has tended to emphasise the fluidity or plasticity of social arrangements, particularly in contrast to the solidity that is conventionally attributed to 'natural' differences (Clarke, 1998b). Where culture-as-tradition foregrounds stability and reproduction (and risks reifying contingent sets of meanings), cultural analysis draws attention to the creative and conflictual production of culture. The socially constructed character of particular sets of norms, relations and differences has become a significant focus for the analysis of welfare policies and their institutional expressions (e.g. Taylor, 1997). In social policy, such arguments focused first on the reproduction of social divisions within welfare policies and practices (e.g. gender roles, racialised divisions, and distinctions between able-bodied and disabled). Subsequently, a more productive or constitutive emphasis has stressed how welfare policies and practices may actively construct, rather than merely reproduce or reflect, social differences, norms and power (e.g. Lewis, 1998; Saraga, 1998). Part of this process has involved exploring the social construction of specific 'social problems', 'client groups' and 'expert knowledges' in welfare policies and practices (e.g. Langan, 1998). It has also involved rethinking the politics of social welfare in analyses of how the meanings of 'the people', 'the nation' and 'the welfare state' have been constructed, contested and remade (e.g. Clarke and Newman, 1997; Hughes, 1998).

This emphasis on the contingent, constructed and fluid quality of the meanings and identities embodied in social welfare has been of considerable significance, not least for the way that it has broken up the universalising and eternalising effects of constructions of the 'normal' and 'natural' (Clarke, 1998b). While the stress on the constructed and the contingent is vital, I think it is necessary to try to grasp both 'fluidity' and 'solidification'. There are important analytical issues about how some meanings or constructions take on socially solidified forms, why some differences rather than others become socially valorised and why some norms become empowered as truths. There are some difficulties involved in trying to formulate the analytical tension between 'fragile' and 'solidified'. I have an attachment to Antonio Gramsci's geological metaphors. There is something significant about the imagery of searching out the 'deposits', 'sediments' and 'traces' of earlier philosophies that have settled into common sense (Gramsci, 1971). They testify to the experienced density and weight of social constructions and cultural formations. Although they are socially constructed and reconstructed, cultural formations appear as persistent, ingrained or immovable. The challenge is to keep both these aspects in view. There are also subsidiary questions about the relative densities of different cultural formations: some are more malleable, vulnerable to erosion or visibly contested than others. I would suggest that some of these questions concern the level of analysis at which the issues are being addressed. One might argue, for example, that the construction of 'the Nation' is changeable and contested. This is not difficult in the current context of shifting alignments of England, Britain and the UK, for example. One might also identify specific conflicts around attempts to 'fix' a particular set of meanings of 'the Nation'. For example, the 'Little Englander' wing of 1990s Conservatism attempted to construct a series of equivalences between White/English/British in the face of challenges that pluralised or destabilised the 'traditional' meanings of Britishness. But it is also important to register how some constructions of a Nation become sedimented in formal institutions and policies as well as in popular understandings (see e.g. Williams, 1985; Lewis, 1998). Although I have referred to the example of Nation here, the same methodological or analytical problems apply to the construction of specific social groups (the poor, the underclass, lone mothers etc.) or to constructions of need or desert in relation to social welfare (see e.g. Langan, 1998).

I want to draw out three other dimensions that are central to the analysis of such cultural formations. As well as being *'constructed'* – that is, produced by cultural practices – they are also changeable, contradictory and contested. By *changeable,* I mean to draw attention to the underlying conditions through which even the most apparently solidified and permanent formations/constructions have to be produced and reproduced. Their perceived 'naturalness' requires the work of continual cultural maintenance; not even the 'taken for granted' can be taken for granted. Even those who are attempting to reassert the 'natural order of things' (about masculine and feminine roles and identities, for example) know that they have to negotiate a society where the 'naturalness' of such differences can no longer be taken for granted as a shared assumption. Extra effort is now required to close off alternative constructions and to revitalise the 'normal and natural', precisely because those constructions have become destabilised by conflicting positions which insist (and have demonstrated) that gendered roles and identities are contingent and changeable. Indeed, it may be that the extra effort required to hold the 'tradition' in place accounts for the general bile and bad-temperedness of the neo-conservative 'revivalists'.

The stress on cultural formations being *contradictory* challenges those approaches to ideology, culture or discourse that treat them as essentially unified or coherently structured formations. As academics we may be prone to intellectual tidying and systematisation, but it is both theoretically and practically important to recognise that ideologies/discourses/cultural formations can be more than random collages of bits of knowledge or ideas without being forged into rigorously unified templates of thinking. This issue is developed in relation to 'common sense' about social problems in Clarke and Cochrane (1998). In a related vein, Dean's work (1998) on 'popular paradigms' has demonstrated the ways in which both political programmes and everyday thinking draw on complex and sometimes contradictory resources in making sense of social welfare. The analysis of the New Right in the USA and Britain has always posed the problem of how to deal with the intersection between neo-liberalism and neo-conservatism. The construction of a 'new' politics involved more than just adding bits from different currents of thought – and the tensions between the two currents were not resolved by allocating a different bit of social life to each (neo-liberalism gets the economy; neo-conservatism gets social order). The New Right posed analytical problems about how to understand the relations of dominance between the two strands and the constituencies that were mobilised through them, as well as the tactical 'ventriloquism' or vocalisation of different ideological themes or tropes for different contexts and audiences. There were also questions about the points of articulation between the different strands that allowed the construction of (temporary) alliances: the creation of an unstable 'unity in difference' (see Clarke, 1991, ch. 6). My aim here is not to go back over the New Right in detail, but to illustrate the need to think of political or cultural formations as complex and contradictory. The same set of problems could be posed just as easily in relation to New Labour (see Clarke and Newman, 1998). It is possible to discern different strands: communitarianism; neo-conservatism; Christian socialism; a limited social pluralism alongside more obvious continuities with the Thatcherite past around neo-liberal views of national and global economies; the commitments to 'flexible' labour markets and labour forces; as well as a commitment to the new managerialism in 'modernising' public services. Expecting coherence – or trying to impose it – detracts attention from more difficult, but possibly more important, questions about the internal and external contradictions embedded in such a formation. Without attention to those matters, it becomes impossible to examine how such contradictions are being negotiated, accommodated or managed within this formation. What sort of 'unstable equilibrium' does New Labour represent?

Finally, the idea of cultural formations/social constructions being *contested* is a claim that any specific social construction is likely to be engaged by different, and often conflicting, positions. Even the most hegemonic – the most 'taken for granted' – constructions or cultural formations have to negotiate their dominance against displaced or declining alternative conceptions of the world and against emergent alternative possibilities (Williams, 1989). The 'socialising' of social policy and the varied attempts to 'de-socialise' it provide a potent testimony to the contested status of social constructions. The political and intellectual struggles that have taken place around social welfare have recurrently revealed the 'social' basis of the distinctions and identities (e.g. around gender, age, 'race', disability and sexuality) articulated in welfare policy and practice. They have challenged the ways in which these distinctions have been represented as belonging to the realm of the natural/biological/medical (Clarke, 1998b, forthcoming; Saraga, 1998). However, the accomplishment of these 'socialised' understandings of social policy is itself a social construction. As such it is vulnerable to erosion, challenge and change. Indeed, it is possible to see a number of attempts to deny the 'social' character of differences, needs and problems in relation to social welfare to *de-socialise* them: to take the 'social' out of social policy (Clarke, forthcoming). Let me sketch three such de-socialising challenges, developed around morality, economics and management respectively.

The first – which we have already encountered in the guise of neo-conservative culturalism – is the attempt to redefine social problems as *'moral problems'* or *'moral disorders'*. 'Moral' is not a descriptive category but signals the aim of re-installing traditional morality and the forms of authority in which it is embedded. It links the neo-conservative critics of social welfare such as Charles Murray, the 'anti-liberal intelligentsia' politics articulated by Melanie Phillips among others and the strange strain of self-proclaimed 'ethical socialism' associated with Norman Dennis in particular. Here we see some of the tensions around the alliance of neo-liberalism and neo-conservatism mentioned above. This position is not individualist – it does not subscribe to the view that 'there is no such thing as society'. Rather, its proponents believe in society – but are extremely upset to discover that it is not what it used to be. More importantly, they are deeply committed to restoring past glories, eternal truths and a way of life in which everyone had their place and knew it.

Secondly, we have been subjected to consistent attempts to turn social policy into a subdivision of *economics,* posing welfare as being essentially a question about 'what we can afford'. This formulation has circulated globally, in national politics and within specific welfare providing organisations. It shifts the calculative framework within which issues of social needs, social rights or social justice might be posed. In the process, it attempts to subordinate the 'social' dimension to the apparently more fundamental realm of the 'economic'. This is a recurrent problem for the 'social': it appears as a secondary or residual category – what is left after the more basic or fundamental matters have been dealt with. So, the social also takes second place to the 'natural' (the various biological essences) and the 'medical' (in the determination of the forms and priorities of care (see Twigg, 1997)).

The third attempt to take the social out of social policy involves the impact of *managerialism* on the organisational regimes of the welfare state (Clarke and Newman, 1997). Here we can see continuing efforts to reduce social issues to matters of organisational business. Social policy has been reconstructed around the categories of efficiency, effectiveness and economy, definitions of core business and the ruthless capacity to make 'tough choices'. It has been sustained as a central strand of New Labour approaches to public services, visible in the drive to 'modernise' and in what we might describe as the 'dogmatic pragmatism' of the Blairite conviction that 'what counts is what works' (Newman, 1998). The cumulative effect of these diverse challenges to putting the social into social policy has been the creation of a complex and contradictory landscape for the current politics of social welfare. Organisational modernisers are challenged by both traditional paternalists and one-time radicals; efforts to expand civic rights encounter moral fundamentalists; and free marketeers find themselves at loggerheads with both social authoritarians and the socially excluded (or at least socially isolated) 'tax and spend' socialists. This is a contested, contradictory and changeable landscape indeed.

There are other analytical/methodological dimensions that I would want to place centrally in the development of a cultural analysis within social policy, though they are less vital to the argument being put forward here. Larry Grossberg has argued that cultural studies is 'radically contextualist':

An event or a practice (even a text) does not exist apart from the forces of the context that constitute it as what it is. Obviously, context is not merely background but the very conditions of possibility of something. It cannot be relegated to a series of footnotes or to an afterthought, to the first or last chapter. It is precisely what one is trying to analyse and it is the most difficult thing to construct. (Grossberg, 1997, p255)

Analysing contexts means treating them as both constitutive (of the event/practice being studied) and constituted (by previous practices, struggles etc.). Contexts are always historically specific moments, which means that studying culture is also a process of exploring 'conjunctures'. Conjunctural analysis means the task of understanding how multiple processes, trajectories and practices are condensed in the same place and time. We may abstract the bits that we want to focus on, but should not forget that it is their place in the conjuncture – the context – that gives them their current significance.

This view of culture as being constructed, changeable, contradictory and contested is clearly different in scope, level and character from the uses of culture discussed in the earlier sections. Rather than being a static category or form of causal explanation, it is better understood as a mode of analysis. It gives a particular – and important – inflection to what the 'social' in social policy means and offers ways of going about studying it. It also provides one route to sustaining connections between social policy and other fields of the social sciences, which have been experiencing their own variants of the 'cultural turn'. Both prospects seem to me to be good reasons for rescuing 'culture' from its limited incarnations as either 'tradition' or 'morality', and insisting on addressing cultural processes, practices and their consequences within social policy.

Acknowledgements

This chapter is part of a continuing effort to make sense of the relationship between cultural analysis and social policy. I am indebted to the Rethinking Social Policy group and the D218 course team at the Open University (particularly Sharon Gewirtz, Gordon Hughes, Gail Lewis and Esther Saraga) for helping me to think. Thanks are also due to Janet Newman and Larry Grossberg; to those who struggled with the paper at the SPA conference; and to the editors for supporting the endeavour.

References

Azoulay, K. G. (1997) 'Experience, empathy and strategic essentialism', *Cultural Studies*, vol. 11, no. 1, pp89–110.

Baubock, R., Heller, A. & Zolberg, A. R. (eds) (1996) *The Challenge of Diversity: Integration and Pluralism is Societies of Immigration*, Aldershot, Avebury.

Brah, A. (1996) *Cartographies of Diaspora: Contesting Identities*, London, Routledge.

Burr, V. (1995) *An Introduction to Social Constructionism*, London, Routledge.

Carter, J. (ed.) (1998) *Postmodernity and the Fragmentation of Social Welfare*, London, Routledge.

Chaney, D. (1996) *The Cultural Turn*, London, Routledge.

Clarke, J. *(1991) New Times and Old Enemies: Essays on Cultural Studies and America*, London, HarperCollins.

Clarke, J. (1997) 'Capturing the customer? Consumerism and social welfare', *Self, Agency and Society*, vol. 1, no. 1, pp55–73.

Clarke, J. (1998a) 'Thriving on chaos: managerialism and social welfare', in J. Carter (ed.) *Postmodernity and the Fragmentation of Social Welfare*, London, Routledge.

Clarke, J. (1998b) 'The trouble with normal: looking for the social in social policy', Inaugural Lecture, Faculty of Social Sciences, The Open University, March.

Clarke, J. (1998c) 'Consumerism,' in G. Hughes (ed.) *Imagining Welfare Futures*, London, Routledge.

Clarke, J. (forthcoming) 'Unfinished business? Struggles over the social in social policy', in P. Gilroy, L. Grossberg & A. MacRobbie (eds) *Without Guarantees: Stuart Hall and Cultural Studies*, Cambridge, Polity.

Clarke, J. & Cochrane, A. (1998) 'The social construction of social problems', in F. Saraga (ed.) *Embodying the Social: Constructions of Difference*, London, Routledge.

Clarke, J. & Newman, J. (1997) *The Managerial State: Power, Politics and Ideology in the Remaking of Social Welfare*, London, Sage.

Clarke, J. & Newman, J. (1998) 'A modern British people? New Labour and welfare reform', Occasional Paper no. 54, Department of Intercultural Communication and Management, Copenhagen Business School.

Cook, I., Crouch, D., Naylor, S. & Ryan, J. (eds) (forthcoming) *Cultural Turns/Geographical Turns: Perspectives on Cultural Geography*, London, Longman.

Cooper, D. (1998) *Governing out of Order. Space, Law and the Politics of Belonging*, London, Rivers Oram Press.

Davies, S. (1986) 'Towards the remoralization of society', in M. Loney with R. Bocock, J. Clarke, A. Cochrane, P. Graham & M. Wilson (eds) *The State or the Market: Politics and Welfare in Contemporary Britain*, London, Sage.

Dean, H. (1998) 'Popular paradigms and welfare values', *Critical Social Policy*, vol. 18, no. 2, pp131–156.

Dean, H. & Taylor-Gooby, P. (1992) *Dependency Culture: The Explosion of a Myth,* Hemel Hempstead, Harvester Wheatsheaf.
Dennis, N. (1993) *Rising Crime and the Dismembered Family,* London, IEA Health and Welfare Unit.
Dennis, N. & Erdos, G. (1992) *Families without Fatherhood,* London, IEA Health and Welfare Unit.
du Gay, P. (ed.) (1997) *Production of Culture/Cultures of Production,* London, Sage.
Etzioni, A. (1994) *The Spirit of Community: Rights, Responsibilities and the Communitarian Agenda,* New York, Crown.
Gilroy, P. (1993) *The Black Atlantic,* London, Verso.
Giddens, A. (1994) *Beyond Left and Right: The Future of Radical Politics,* Cambridge, Polity Press.
Gramsci, A. (1971) Selections from the Prison Notebooks, London, Lawrence & Wishart.
Grossberg, L. (1997) *Bringing It All Back Home: Essays on Cultural Studies,* Durham, NC, Duke University Press.
Hall, S. (1996) 'Gramsci's relevance for the study of ethnicities', in D. Morley & K.-H. Chen (eds) *Stuart Hall: Critical Dialogues in Cultural Studies,* London, Routledge.
Hall, S. (ed.) (1997) *Representation: Cultural Representation and Signifying Practices,* London, Sage.
Hillyard, P. & Watson, S. (1996) 'Postmodern social policy: a contradiction in terms? *Journal of Social Policy,* vol. 25, no. 3, pp321–346.
Hughes, G. (ed.) (1998) *Imagining Welfare Futures,* London, Routledge.
Julien, I. & Mercer, K. (1996) 'De margin and de centre', in D. Morley & K.-H. Chen (eds) *Stuart Hall: Critical Dialogues in Cultural Studies,* London, Routledge.
Katz, J. (1989) *The Undeserving Poor,* New York, Pantheon Books.
Katz, J. (ed.) (1996) *The Underclass Debate: Lessons from History,* London, Routledge.
Langan, M. (ed.) (1998) *Welfare: Needs, Rights and Risks,* London, Routledge.
Leonard, P. (1997) *Postmodern Welfare: Reconstructing an Emancipatory Project,* London, Sage.
Lewis, G. (1998) 'Welfare and the social construction of "race"', in E. Saraga (ed.) *Embodying the Social: Constructions of Difference,* London, Routledge.
Lewis, G. (ed.) (1998) *Forming Nation, Framing Welfare,* London, Routledge.
Lewis, O. (1968) 'The culture of poverty', in D. Moynihan (ed.) *Understanding Poverty,* New York, Basic Books.
Lowe, L. (1996) *Immigrant Acts: On Asian American Cultural Politics,* Durham, NC, Duke University Press.
Mann, K. (1994) 'Watching the defectives: observers of the underclass in the USA, Britain and Australia', *Critical Social Policy,* vol. 41, pp79–99.

Morris, L. (1994) *Dangerous Classes: the Underclass and Social Citzenship*, London, Routledge.

Muncie, J. (1984) *The Trouble with Kids Today: Youth and Crime in Post-war Britain*, London, Hutchinson.

Murray, C. (1984) *Losing Ground: American Social Policy 1950–1980*, New York, Basic Books.

Murray, C. (1990) *The Emerging British Underclass*, London, IEA Health and Welfare Unit.

Newman, J. (1998) 'What counts is what works? The evaluation of public services', paper presented to the Employment Research Unit Conference, University of Cardiff.

O'Brien, M. & Penna, S. (1998) *Theorising Welfare: Enlightment and Modern Society*, London, Sage.

Ross, A. (1998) *Real Love: In Pursuit of Cultural Justice*, London, Routledge.

Saraga, E. (ed.) (1998) *Embodying the Social: Constructions of Difference*, London, Routledge.

Taylor, D. (ed.) (1997) *Critical Social Policy*, London, Sage.

Taylor, D. (1998) 'Social identity and social policy: engagments with postmodern theory', *Journal of Social Policy*, vol. 27, no. 3, pp329–350.

Twigg, J. (1997) 'Deconstructing the 'social bath': help with bathing at home for older and disabled people', *Journal of Social Policy*, vol. 26, no. 2, pp211–232.

Weeks, J. (1996) 'The idea of a sexual community', *Soundings*, no. 2, pp71–84.

Williams, F. (1994) 'Social relations, welfare and the post-Fordism debate', in R. Burrows & B. Loader (eds) *Towards a Post-Fordist Welfare State?*, London, Routledge.

Williams, G. (1985) *When was Wales?*, Harmondsworth, Penguin.

Williams, R. (1989) *The Politics of Modernism: Against the New Conformists*, London, Verso

5 Sustainability: the twenty-first-century challenge for social policy

Michael Cahill

Introduction

In the 1980s the task for environmentalists was to persuade and convert, to sloganise and shock, but in the 1990s the agenda was widened to include engagement with the world of policy and government. In all this activity sustainability has been the key term. Although it has many definitions, it was popularised by the Brundtland Commission as 'meeting the needs of the present without compromising the ability of future generations to meet their own needs'. (Brundtland, 1987, p43) Sustainability gained global significance with its adoption at the Rio Earth Summit – the United Nations Conference on Environment and Development – in 1992. Since then in the UK Green pressure groups have come in from the cold and now form part of the environmental policy community. In local government the Local Agenda 21 initiative – created at Rio – has popularised sustainability usually in a way which entails a commitment to equity and social justice, and extends the remit to include social policy as well as the environment. Unfortunately under the Major government sustainability often meant little more than encouraging environmental awareness while maintaining its commitment to the free market economy. A New Labour government has meant that the Whitehall policy village is now engaged in a much more sophisticated debate on environmental options. In 1998 the government published a consultation paper on sustainable development with the full strategy document announced for 1999 (Department of Environment, Transport and the Regions (DETR), 1998a). Much of this work centres on areas which are social policy in a broad sense. In this chapter, after a discussion of the hold which consumerism has upon the national consciousness, I want to review the efforts which have been made to link environmental and social policy. This policy debate, however, cannot be abstracted from the context of UK society, which has an organising principle and ideology that is the very antithesis of sustainability.

Consumerism

Consumerism is now the dominant ideology in the UK. It is, to employ the stark and simple definition offered by Robert Bocock, 'the active ideology that the meaning of life is to be found in buying things and pre-packaged experiences' (Bocock, 1993, p.50) The material foundations of a consumerist society were being created fifty years ago, at the time that T. H. Marshall was outlining his theory of citizenship in his famous Cambridge lecture to explain the emergence of welfare state society in post-war Britain (Marshall, 1963). In the early 1950s numerous social democratic thinkers believed that the nationalisation measures of the 1945–51 Labour governments had produced a new variant of capitalism known as welfare capitalism. This was plausible enough until the 1970s, when mass unemployment and public expenditure cuts ended this phase. In the 1950s the consumer society was another manifestation of the changed nature of capitalism. The key development at that time was the rise of the mass working class market and the beginnings of a trend away from the public to the private in household expenditure and consumption. Contrary to the hopes of Richard Titmuss and others at that time, it is the values of consumer capitalism which have permeated the welfare state and not the other way round. So much so that in the late 1980s the Conservative government remodelled important parts of the welfare state using the metaphors of consumer and the market (Clarke, 1998). What is insufficiently recognised is the way in which consumerism was experienced on a personal level by the population. There is a now a close identification between many people and the products that they use, wear and drive. Market research is alive to this and firms deliberately aim goods at an aspirational market trading in people's desires. The self then becomes attached to consumer products and life without them seems intolerable because they have become part of ourselves – we have witnessed this process occurring with the car and it is now underway with the mobile phone. Clearly this makes the need to move to a more sustainable, less environmentally damaging way of life that much more difficult as many people do not just own consumer products but use them to define and express their identity (Dittmar, 1992).

The debate on the impact of consumerism on society began in the 1950s with the concerns about the influence of television advertising. The changed voting behaviour of the working class, as Labour lost three general elections in a row, seemed to betoken a shift in attitudes brought about by affluence. The long-term post-war crumbling of working class solidarity was the product not just of the changing occupational structure and the move from manufacturing to services in the British economy but also the appeal of the private and the domestic over the public. These trends, among them the rise of mass motoring and the gradual increase in the number of owner occupiers, changed the perceptions and aspirations of the UK population. Thatcherism's strength – and later New Labour's – was that it recognised and responded to this changed psychology of the electorate.

The status of consumer is the key to understanding the development of rights and obligations in the second half of the twentieth century. Consumerism, which had moved from the realm of the experience of the upper middle class in the Edwardian period to the middle classes as a whole in the inter-war years, was, after 1950, to be extended to the working class with the rise of mass motoring, mass tourism, the further extension of home ownership and the purchases of consumer durables for the home (see Bowden, 1994). This great increase in the purchasing power of the working class brought a realm of new opportunities, and coupled with an era of full employment, greatly increased the choices and freedom open to large numbers of people. Women gradually increased their participation in the workforce after the 1950s and their employment gave them a greater status in the wider society. Consumerism as an ideology is predicated upon the mass enjoyment of consumer goods and upon a continuously rising standard of living. Although since the mid-1970s there has been a significant pool of unemployment in the UK, this has not dented the consumer society, which continues to command wide support.

Consumerism has its own set of values and aspirations, centred on the self and the gratification of wants and desires. Consumerism is a culture which provides meaning and understanding for many in our society, be they white or black, men or women, young or old, straight or gay (Miles, 1998). It is able to appropriate and reinforce the symbols of those who seek to advance their identity. Diversity is a welcome concept for those involved in selling and marketing for it offers more opportunities to create niche markets for their goods. The cardinal virtue is choice, be that the choice of product, service or identity. Looking back, it now seems inevitable that the public services should be remodelled according to the image of the consumer for if we are consumers in every other part of our lives then why not in welfare? The problem for the poor is that they are simply not on the map in consumerism: they are invisible in the shopping malls and out-of-town hypermarkets, and if they use city centre shops then they purchase so little that they can be ignored by major retailers who know that discount stores and charity shops will supply their needs. What this induces is profound feelings of dissatisfaction with their lives. Admittedly not for all, as some people for a variety of reasons are able to withstand the ceaseless urging to spend and enjoy which is promoted by television advertising. Bauman believes that the poor who are excluded from the spending society look upon this as an individual failing and not something that can be remedied by collective action. 'It is this inadequacy, this inability to acquit oneself of the consumer's duties, that turns into bitterness at being left behind, disinherited or degraded, shut off or excluded from the social feast to which others gained entry' (Bauman, 1998, p38).

The ideology of personal freedom, in part responsible for the legislation on individual behaviour of the 1960s – divorce law reform, homosexual law reform – was assimilated by consumer society in a big way. There is an intense irony in the fact that the burgeoning consumer capitalism appropriated imagery and slogans from the counterculture of the 1960s which had been its implacable enemy. While some alternative businesses which owe their origins to this period, like Virgin, have flourished, the major change was in the style of mainstream firms, businesses and banks. Over the last twenty-five years banks have moved from being stuffy institutions who did their best to dissuade their customers from running up debts or acquiring overdrafts to making a major part of their business the selling of loans and the cultivation of debt – now renamed credit – among their customers.

Consumerism is a status which has to be earned. Paid work is essential for the great majority of people to become consumers; yet the shift from a manufacturing economy to a service economy has meant the end of employment in many communities. The closing of a major employer, the end of traditional apprenticeships, the movement of work from this country to the Third World has been accompanied by a seemingly national passion for the things that money can buy. If the 1960s are to be remembered for what some called the sexual revolution, then the 1980s witnessed the money revolution in which it became socially acceptable to trumpet one's wealth. Although the worst excesses of the get-rich-and-brag-about-it society are now at an end, what they have left behind is a commitment to a culture where money is the universal signifier and form of status. This is to argue not that there are no alternatives to this consumerist order but rather that they have been severely weakened. Those institutions which saw it as their role to socialise us into moral values no longer have the authority they once enjoyed – schools, churches, voluntary organisations like the Girl Guides, the Scouts. Membership has declined, which is unsurprising because the demands of paid work mean that there is less time for voluntary activity. Dual-earner families not only have both parents working but their children, once they reach their teens, will be keen to take up part-time work. One reading of what has happened in schools is that the pervasive stress on individual judgement and decision making – while clearly an advance on morality as authority handed down – has left school leavers more prey to the seductions of the consumer market place where choice is worshipped and the individual is sovereign. Despite the attention given to environmental issues in the curriculum, the most recent Mintel survey of young people's preferences reveals that teenagers aged 15–19 are the least concerned of any age group with environmental issues (Cowe, 1999). Moreover, in the USA those with the most education are the most susceptible to designer labels, status and prestige (Schor, 1998, p155).

The structural changes in the economy and society have meant that old ideologies have weakened and withered while new ones such as New Labour play to the desires and values fostered by the capitalist marketplace – but cannot transcend it. Has environmentalist ideology the capacity to generate sufficient support for a radical challenge to the prevailing orthodoxies? Certainly the last fifteen years have seen fundamentalist Green ideology lose out to the more pragmatic realist position which has been successful of late with the coming to power of the Socialist–Green coalition in Germany. The question which now needs to be confronted is whether Middle England wants to change its way of life in the ways which would be necessary for sustainability. The challenge for New Labour is to move on from environmental rhetoric and allay the suspicion that the government will not want environmental action to endanger its re-election for a second term. It may well be that it is in transport policy where the government faces the most significant test of its commitment to sustainability.

Transport policy

The urgent environmental problem of transport demonstrates the problems faced in changing travel behaviour so that it does less damage to the environment and public health. After many years of travel awareness activities by local authorities, the number of cars continues to rise while motorists are not using their vehicles less. This growth in the number of vehicles, the perceived need among some sections of the population for more roads and the impact on global warming of motor vehicle emissions meant that *A New Deal for Transport,* the government's White Paper on transport published in the summer of 1998, was bound to be a key environmental policy document (DETR, 1998b). There is much of substance in the document – the priority given to walking and cycling is welcome, as is the discussion of transport in the context of land use planning – and overall, it does outline an integrated transport policy. But it shirks the real challenge, which is to reduce the car dependence of the UK population, and accepts that traffic on our roads will continue to increase rather than outlining a national strategy to reduce it. To take a clear omission: one of the main causes of increased car-use mileage has been the movement of supermarkets to the edge of cities where car parking is provided free. An obvious way to restrict this is through taxation of the car parking spaces in out-of-town superstores, but reportedly this policy was removed from the draft of the White Paper because of the successful lobbying of Tesco and other major food retailers (Palast and Calvert, 1998). Road pricing is another instrument which will make the use of the car less attractive and lessen the car congestion which bedevils city centres and other urban areas but, disappointingly, there is no national policy and instead local authorities will be able to run pilot schemes (DETR, 1998c). The government has provided local authorities with new powers which will enable them, through the new Local Transport Plans, to widen travel choice, restrain the demand for more travel, integrate the various modes of travelling – walking, cycling, public transport and car use – and promote the linkage of transport with other policies. This involves the acceptance that transport policy can intensify social exclusion, especially for the one-third of households who do not have access to a car. The development of a car-dependent society has tended to exclude them: this is the case not only with out-of-town shopping centres but also with greenfield leisure centres, and hospital complexes built on the outskirts of towns and cities. Reducing car dependence is an obvious area where leadership is required to put into place a fiscal and policy package which makes the individual decision to leave the car at home and use public transport a rational choice rather than an act of altruism. Even then it is a moot point whether car dependence would be reduced sufficiently to meet the UK's international commitments on reducing carbon emissions, given that the car remains for many a compelling symbol of sexuality and status.

Clearly the adoption of environmentalist agendas by Conservative and New Labour governments demonstrates that they believe that environmental restructuring can occur within capitalist societies. The mechanisms of economic management can be utilised to achieve more environmentally benign economic behaviour. The economy can be restructured so that harmful industrial activity is discouraged through the fiscal system, energy sources are increasingly renewable and there is a major programme of recycling. 'Ecological modernisation' is obviously attractive to many in business and industry, as well as government, for it makes the case that environmental economic activity will be advantageous for a country, leading to job creation and new markets for the technology created (Weale, 1992).

Local Agenda 21

Local Agenda 21 (LA 21), organised by local authorities, aims to make sustainable development a reality in localities. It is an initiative which sprang from the Rio Summit of 1992. Its focus is the work of the local authority and the range of responsibilities that it has: for example, environmental health, transport, recycling and energy are core areas of LA 21 activity. In this way environmental issues are now being integrated with other policy areas with a stress on how people and their actions can improve or damage the environment. In the UK some local authorities have reviewed their activities in the light of the principles of sustainability; many have implemented environmental audits; while others have integrated the LA 21 process into their system of corporate management. Some councils have drawn up indicators which will measure progress towards local sustain-ability. These generally cover two areas: those that measure the quality of the environment and the way in which the local authority can respond to the stresses on it; and those which measure environmental efficiency in areas such as transport, industry and energy (Selman, 1996; Young, 1997, 1998). Local authorities have on the whole been sensitive to the ways in which these indicators can be constructed. There has been an awareness that it is easy to ignore the views of those who do not participate in environmental policy making but who are concerned about the environment. In this respect, it is sobering to note that recent research has revealed that most people have not even heard of the concept of sustainability even though one of its central planks is a stress on community empowerment (Macnaghten *et al.*, 1995). Probably the most important part of LA 21's work has been the construction in many cities of sustainability indicators which have been devised across a range of policy areas. It has had much less impact upon the social policy responsibilities of local government, such as social services or anti-poverty strategies, than on traditional environmental areas like waste management. This is hardly surprising, given the fact that it is only in the last decade that real links have begun to be made between environmental and social policy (Percy, 1998).

New Labour has given a new lease of life to LA 21, with the Prime Minister declaring at the New York Earth Summit in 1997 that he wanted all local authorities to have adopted LA 21 strategies by 2000. This was an important statement in the light of the recent report on perceptions of barriers to local sustainability which identified a lack of political will at the level of councillors and senior officers in local authorities (CAG Consultants 1998).

Local authorities espoused I A 21 because it extended their role in local governance, and this should be strengthened by the paragraphs in the White Paper *Modern Local Government* stating that local government should have a new duty to promote economic, social and environmental well-being (DETR, 1998d). Some new powers would need to be shared by local government with regional bodies in order to overcome problems of economic rivalry between different local authorities. A local authority, for example, will be reluctant to impose high parking charges to deter car-borne shoppers if neighbouring authorities have none and gain all the lost patronage.

The thrust of LA 21 enables issues of access and inequality to be encompassed in the search for sustainability. Lancashire County Council is one of the local authorities that has incorporated social objectives in its Green audit. One of the indicators that it has used in its review of the population of Lancashire is the percentage who live more than 1 km from five basic services – post office, primary school, food shop, general practitioner surgery and bus stop – thereby operationalising the concept of accessibility. It would be possible to build upon this in relation to walking and cycling. Areas could be assessed according to the degree to which they are friendly to pedestrians: to what extent are there useful places to walk to within 1 km? How many other people does one meet when walking?

Quality of life

All varieties of environmentalism, to a greater or lesser extent, are committed to a different set of values and aspirations than those of the consumer society. Consumer capitalism ignores the damage to the physical and natural environment which it produces and refuses to acknowledge limits to the production of more and more goods. Even in its own terms consumer capitalism, which sedulously cultivates desire in order to sell products and the promise of happiness, has failed. Research on individual life satisfaction and contentment reveals that the most economically advanced societies are no happier than poor societies; indeed, they are less so (Easterlin, 1980; Easterlin, 1995).

One of the key tasks facing advanced societies is to persuade large numbers of people that they will gain more satisfaction from life if they consume less. This is not an easy task as, for example, in the UK we have been through a period of celebration of consumption which has had its impact upon the values of all groups in society, although one might argue that the young have been most affected. A Demos market research survey revealed that 'consumer sceptics' were least numerous among eighteen- to thirty-four-year-olds (Wilkinson and Mulgan, 1995). In the United States Juliet Schor writes:

> Asked what constitutes 'the good life' people in 1991 focused far more on material goods and luxuries than they did in 1975. Items more likely to be part of the good life now than then include a vacation home, a swimming pool, a color TV, a second color TV, travel abroad, nice clothes, a car, a second car, a home of one's own, a job that pays much more than the average, and a lot of money. Less likely, or no more likely, to yield the good life, according to respondents were a happy marriage, one or more children, an interesting job, and a job that contributes to the welfare of society. (Schor, 1998, p15)

There is disturbing evidence that the concern with the accumulation of consumer goods and material success has not produced a happier society. Indeed, a 1986 study revealed that almost one-third of the population had reported psychological morbidity at some point in their lives (James, 1997, appendix 1).

Although imprecise, the concept of 'quality of life' does capture something important. As Seed and Lloyd describe it, there are five general components of the 'quality of life': physical and material well being; relations with other people; social, community and civic activities; personal development and fulfilment; and recreation (Seed and Lloyd, 1997, p19). In short, quality of life concerns the relationship between the individual, society and the environment. The fusion of environmental and social concerns revolves around the provision of social goods which can include freedom from crime, clean air, clean streets, parks, libraries and other civic amenities (Jacobs, 1997). These environmental and social goods lie outside of market regulation (see Jackson, 1996; Seed and Lloyd, 1997; Offer, 1996). 'Quality of life' can embrace the proximity of public libraries as well as bus stops, or even the existence of public libraries. 'Quality of life' is subjective; it will be interpreted differently from one individual to the next. For many people their quality of life is better measured by the number and range of consumer durables which they possess, and this is perhaps the dominant view in our society. When questioned, however, people agree that for them public amenities such as parks, libraries and public conveniences are also part of their quality of life. The extent to which the majority of the population can be mobilised in support of these social goods when they are threatened by, say, developers or road builders is unpredictable because the values of individual self advancement and private consumption are often stronger. There is, however, a widespread perception that there has been an erosion of the 'quality of life' in our society despite the increases in personal consumption. When people in Lancashire were asked to define what they meant by 'quality of life' they responded by choosing the following: having a more local job, not having to worry about money, better relationships with friends and family, more community spirit, and better amenities, especially for children (Lancashire County Council, 1997). This stress on improved social relationships – opportunities for more time with family and friends, more time to pursue interests – reveals that non-monetary considerations are important for many people and arguably have been squeezed in many people's lives in our work-and-spend society.

The Index of Sustainable Economic Welfare (ISEW) promoted by the New Economics Foundation attempts to measure the quality of life through time. Its authors accept that personal consumption is a contribution to individual welfare but include in their index many other activities such as unpaid domestic work and child care which contribute to individual well being but are ignored in conventional indices such as gross domestic product (GDP). They also include measures of economic inequality and environmental pollution. The ISEW subtracts 'defensive expenditures' such as the costs of road accidents or resource depletion. Since 1980 the ISEW has fallen by around 22 per cent (Friends of the Earth/New Economics Foundation, 1997; Jackson *et al.*, 1997). Clearly the way in which the components of such an index are weighted is crucial and open to debate.

In late 1998 the government produced a list of proposed 'headline' indicators designed to measure the UK's progress towards sustainable development: economic growth, public sector investment, employment, expected years of healthy life, qualifications at age 19, unfit homes, emission of greenhouse gases, days of air pollution, road traffic, rivers of good or fair quality, population of wild birds, new homes built on brownfield sites, and waste and waste disposal (DETR, 1998e). There are real questions as to the acceptability of GDP as an indicator of sustainability because it does not discriminate between sustainable and other forms of economic activity, including, for instance, the income generated by the use of natural capital and counting destructive forms of growth. The number of people who are below half average income is an indicator which would provide some measure of how the national wealth is distributed and could be added to the government's list.

Social economy

Because the operation of the global economy has meant that mass unemployment has dealt a blow to the notion of full employment, in those areas where jobs are scarce a dangerous culture of high unemployment, no hope and drug pushing has severely damaged the social fabric. Here the formal economy is only one way of earning a living alongside crime and drug trafficking. The challenge for government is to find some way of restoring hope to these areas, and it seems entirely sensible to envisage governments doing this by supporting and strengthening what is termed the 'social economy'. This takes various forms. Local Exchange Trading Schemes (LETS) have proliferated, particularly in the USA, Canada and the UK. They enable services and work to be performed for tokens or credits which can then be used to obtain other services. Members of the schemes themselves decide who they are going to exchange their token with and for which services. The coverage of these schemes is sporadic in the UK and, where they do exist, have not made major inroads into local economies, although one estimate is that 30,000 people are members of LETS schemes (Bowring, 1998). One study of five LETS in the UK found that about 40 per cent of the activities were domestic work and all could have been paid for in cash. (Seyfang, cited in O'Riordan, 1997, p18). LETS acknowledge, however, the amount of work which goes on outside the formal economy in cash-in-hand payments which remain outside the tax system (Williams, 1996). LETS schemes are an obvious alternative to money and would seem ideal for poor areas but so far they have, in the main, failed to attract the educationally deprived unemployed (Bowring, 1998, p93). This is an area where government backing for LETS in poor areas would foster not just more economic activity but equally the cultivation of local community leaders (Barnes *et al.*, 1996).

Credit unions are community organisations for saving and borrowing which operate on a non-profit-making basis. Members must live and work locally. Currently there are 585 credit unions in Great Britain with over 200,000 members (Mayo *et al.*, 1998). Many of them are based in rundown areas which have suffered greatly from the restructuring of the British economy over the past two decades; they are characterised by high unemployment, poor housing, underperforming schools and poor public transport. The policy of bank branch closures means that there are an increasing number of areas with no local source of finance for either personal customers or small businesses. As Mayo *et al.* comment: 'the neighbourhoods that have the most pressing need for capital are those that have the least access to it' (Mayo *et al.*, 1998, p3). Financial exclusion is linked to social exclusion: it is estimated that 26 per cent of people have no current account with a bank or a building society. 'The groups without bank accounts tend to be women, the young, the old, the unemployed, those both in low aid jobs and more likely to live in rented accommodation' (Conaty and Mayo, 1997).

The social economy, although relatively small, will undoubtedly have a growing role to play as jobs in the core economy become more short term and more scarce. There is a deeper worry for the next century. Consumer capitalism has encouraged a deskilling of the population: household economy skills – including knitting, sewing and cooking – have been downgraded and extinguished for many, which makes many people with low skills or no skills extremely dependent on the wage economy. The social economy is a resource, but there is a real possibility that many people will need the elementary protection afforded by the skills and resource sharing available in the household economy. The disintegration of stable family units is troubling because it means that opportunities for interdependence across generations is diminished.

Creating impetus for change

Just at the time when an ethic of cooperation and mutuality is required we have a dominant ideology of individualism and consumerism in which there are ceaseless admonitions to consume more and to view the good life in terms of greater material prosperity. There is much sense in the observation that the voluntary simplicity campaigns in USA and Western Europe, while admirable, will have little impact because they are addressed solely to individuals. The wish to consume is not just about consuming in order to display goods; it is also to be able to take part in a way of life, a culture of consumption. Consumption has become so much a part of selfhood that it is only a small minority who can be expected to opt out of it. It is fairly difficult to do so even if one wishes to. The car is a particularly good example of this. To give up driving a car is to withdraw from a range of activities which often then become much more difficult and time consuming. It is at the same time to cease to be able to fulfil certain responsibilities. Yet to argue – as Michael Jacobs has done recently – that 'environmentally sustainable consumption will not come about through individual choices, but through regulatory policies, collectively decided and imposed by the state' would seem to ignore the value of consumer boycotts and consumer campaigns, although clearly Jacobs is right when he says that these arguments must not remain at the individual consumer level to be effective (Jacobs, 1997).

In order to produce the necessary impetus at a political and social level to move towards a more sustainable level of consumption there are three useful concepts which are being developed: sustainability indicators, environmental space and ecological fooprints. The development of national and local sustainability indicators is an important step. The particular merit of the ISEW is that it measures the extent to which there has been an improvement or deterioration in the quality of life across a range of indicators: income inequality, unpaid domestic labour, environmental degradation, depletion of natural resources, long-term environmental damage, changes in capital stock and defensive expenditures (e.g. criminal justice). The implications of this analysis for the UK economy is to prioritise the 'social economy' – the informal economy and household and family labour. This sector is not inconsiderable: around 200,000 people are in credit unions and over 30,000 in LETS schemes, and 35,000 people receive an organic food box each week (Mayo *et al.*, 1997). All of this is important work, for much of it is restoring some sense of power to poor neighbourhoods. However, as Donnison remarks, LETS and the like are part of the 'complementary economy' – they are not in the mainstream economy (Donnison, 1998, pp101–102). The task then remains of how to reconceptualise the workings of the mainstream economy so that it is possible to think moving in a sustainable direction. Here the concept of 'environmental space' is promising.

'Environmental space', to quote Carley and Spapens, is

> the total amount of energy, non-renewable resources, land, water, wood and other resources which can be used globally or regionally: without environmental damage, without impinging on the rights of future generations, and within the context of equal rights to resource consumption and concern for the quality of life of all peoples of the world. (Carley and Spapens, 1998, p9)

The underlying principle is that environmental space is limited and the extents of these limits need to be worked out in order to enable developed countries to move towards a lower per capita resource use and developing countries to rise to a higher per capita level of resource use. A related concept is that of 'ecological footprint' to demonstrate the burdens which are being placed upon the earth by the rich world. It is estimated that the ecological footprint of London, i.e. the provision of food, materials and energy, would occupy a land mass 125 times its actual size (McLaren *et al*,, 1998, p126). Production should enhance quality of life – health, welfare, family and community – rather than material goods goals. Such a concept as Carley and Spapens concede is really more of a scheme in which to fit a range of policies and regulations, including ecological tax reform.

The 1999 Budget moved decisively in this direction with the announcement of the industrial energy tax which will be revenue neutral for the Treasury because of the associated reduction in employers' National Insurance contributions. Given the fact that all governments wish to encourage the level of employment, taxes on 'goods' such as jobs should be reduced while taxes on 'bads' such as pollution should increase. Poor people will need protection from future environmental tax changes. Pollution taxes could be socially regressive, i.e. they may fall most heavily on those who are least able to bear the cost. This can be illustrated by one of the most debated examples of an ecological tax proposal – a continuing and substantial increase in the tax on petrol. Such a tax would penalise those who live in rural and semi-rural areas where there is no alternative for many people to using a car if they wish to reach their work and other amenities. Proponents of ecological taxation admit the force of this argument and propose that payments should be made to these motorists to compensate them for the extra costs which they would have to bear. This is not the only tax that could be levied in support of an environmentally friendly transport policy. It is widely acknowledged that the existence of free parking at work has been one of the major reasons why the use of the car has greatly increased for commuter journeys over the last twenty years. Taxing employers for this parking space would, if it were passed onto the employee, tend to discourage them from using their car for these journeys. Those on low incomes are clearly hit the hardest when domestic fuel taxation is increased, and the state would need to protect them by rebates and by subsidising better standards of insulation in the home.

Conclusion

The discourse of sustainability has brought environmental and social policy much closer together. Under the Major government this had occurred only in some of the local authorities which had embraced the LA 21 process. Since May 1997 sustainability has become a credible concept in Whitehall and there has been a stream of policy documents from the Department of Environment, Transport and the Regions. Nonetheless, viewing the enormity of the environmental problems which confront us and the seeming addiction to consumption in our society, the move to a sustainable way of life remains the greatest challenge for the new century.

References

Barnes, H., North, P. & Walker, P. (1996) *LETS and Low Income,* London, New Economics Foundation.
Bauman, Z. (1998) *Work, Consumerism and the New Poor,* Buckingham, Open University Press.
Bocock, R. (1993) *Consumption,* London, Routledge.

Bowden, S. (1994) 'The New Consumerism', in Johnson, P. (ed.) *Twentieth-Century Britain: Economic, Social and Cultural Change*, London, Longman.

Bowring, F. (1998) 'LETS: an eco-socialist initiative?', *New Left Review*, vol. 232, November/December.

Brundtland Report (World Commission on Environment and Development) (1987) *Our Common Future*, Oxford, Oxford University Press.

CAG Consultants (1998) *Perceptions of National Barriers to Local Sustainability*, London, CAG Consultants.

Carley, M. & Spapens, P. (1998) *Sharing the World*, London, Earthscan.

Christie, I. & Nash, L. (eds) (1998) *The Good Life*, London, Demos.

Clarke, J. (1998) 'Consumerism', in G. Hughes (ed.) *Imagining Welfare Futures*, London, Routledge.

Conaty, P. & Mayo, E. (1997) *A Commitment to People and Place*, London, New Economics Foundation.

Cowe, R. (1999) 'Caring attitudes out of fashion', *Guardian*, 12 March.

Department of Environment, Transport and the Regions (1998a) *Opportunities for Change: Consultation Paper on a Revised UK Strategy for Sustainable Development*, London, The Stationery Office.

Department of Environment, Transport and the Regions (1998b) *A New Deal for Transport: Better for Everyone*, Cm 3950, London, Stationery Office.

Department of Environment, Transport and the Regions (1998c) *Breaking the Logjam: the Government's Consultation Paper on Fighting Traffic Congestion and Pollution through Road User and Workplace Charging*, London, The Stationery Office.

Department of Environment, Transport and the Regions (1998d) *Modern Local Government: in Touch with the People*, Cm 4014, London, The Stationery Office.

Department of the Environment, Transport and the Regions (1998e) *Sustainability Counts*, London, The Stationery Office.

Dittmar, H. (1992) *The Social Psychology of Material Possessions*, Hemel Hempstead, Harvester Wheatsheaf.

Donnison, D. (1998) *Policies for a Just Society*, Basingstoke, Macmillan.

Easterlin, R. A. (1980) *Birth and Fortune: the Impact of Numbers on Personal Welfare*, London: Grant McIntyre.

Easterlin, R. A. (1995) 'Will raising the incomes of all increase the happiness of all?', *Journal of Economic Behaviour and Organisation*, vol. 27, pp35–47.

Friends of the Earth/New Economics Foundation (1997) *More Isn't Always Better*, London, New Economics Foundation.

Jackson, T. (1996) *Material Concerns: Pollution, Profit and Quality of Life*, London, Routledge.

Jackson, T., Marks, N., Ralls, J. & Stymme, S. (1997) *Sustainable Economic Welfare in the UK 1950–1996*, London, New Economics Foundation.

Jacobs, M. (ed.) (1997) *Greening the Milennium: the New Politics of the Environment,* Oxford, Blackwell.

James, O. (1997) *Britain on the Couch,* London, Century Random House.

Lancashire County Council (1997) *Lancashire's Green Audit 2,* Preston, Lancashire County Council.

Macnaghten, P., Grove-White, R., Jacobs, M. & Wynne, B. (1995) *Public Perceptions and Sustainability in Lancashire: Indicators, institutions, participation,* Preston, Lancashire County Council.

Macnaghten, P. & Urry, J. (1998) *Contested Natures,* London, Sage.

Marshall, T. H. (1963) 'Citizenship and Social Class', in *Sociology at the Crossroads and Other Essays,* London, Heinemann.

Mayo, E., Thake, S. & Gibson, T. (1997) *Taking Power: an Agenda for Community Economic Renewal,* London, New Economics Foundation.

Mayo, E., Fisher, T., Conaty, P., Doling, J. & Mullineux, A. (1998) *Small is Bankable: Community Reinvestment in the UK,* York, Joseph Rowntree Foundation.

McLaren, D., Bullock, S. and Yosuf, N. (1998) *Tomorrow's World: Britain's share in a sustainable future,* London, Earthscan.

Miles, S. (1998) *Consumerism – as a Way of Life,* London, Sage.

Offer, A. (ed.) (1996) *In Pursuit of the Quality of Life,* Oxford, Clarendon Press.

O'Riordan, T. (ed.) (1997) *Ecotaxation,* London, Earthscan.

Palast, G. & Calvert, J. (1998) 'Lobbyists helped Tesco block car tax', *Observer,* 26 July.

Percy, S. (1998) 'Real progress or optimistic hype?', *Town and Country Planning,* January/February.

Schor, J. B. (1998) *The Overspent American,* New York, Basic Books.

Seed, P. & Lloyd, G. (1997) *Quality of Life,* London, Jessica Kingsley.

Selman, P. (1996) *Local Sustainability,* London, Paul Chapman.

Weale, A. (1992) *The New Politics of Pollution,* Manchester, Manchester University Press.

Wilkinson, H. & Mulgan, G. (1995) *Freedom's Children,* London, Demos.

Williams, C. (1996) 'Informal sector responses to unemployment: An evaluation of the potential of Local Economic Exchange Trading Schemes (LETS)', *Work, Employment and Society,* vol 10, no 2.

Young, S. (1997) 'Local Agenda 21; the renewal of democracy?', in M. Jacobs (ed.) *Greening the Milennium: the New Politics of the Environment,* Oxford, Blackwell.

Young, S. (1998) 'The United Kingdom: a mirage beyond the participation hurdle?', in W. M. Lafferty & K. Eckersley (eds) *From the Earth Summit to Local Agenda 21: Working towards sustainable development,* London, Earthscan.

6 Continuity or modernisation? The emergence of New Labour's welfare state

Tim Blackman and
Amanda Palmer

Introduction

This chapter discusses the emerging shape of New Labour's welfare state. It considers how the manifesto promises of Britain's first Labour government for eighteen years have unfolded since the May 1997 general election. Rhetoric and reality are compared, focusing in particular on health and social services and the welfare-to-work programme.

The chapter explores the new government's project of 'modernisation', assessing its relationship to earlier Conservative policies and the extent to which it represents a new agenda of pragmatic reformism, emphasising 'what works'. Much of the modernisation project represents a coherent reform agenda based on explicit objectives, but what kind of welfare state is emerging? Many of the new policies are modestly redistributive, but the existence of some unresolved contradictions threatens to perpetuate major problems. These include stigma caused by the targeting of specific groups that are seen to be too dependent upon the state, and uncertainty arising from a continuing dependency on markets in key areas such as employment and pension provision. The process of modernisation has also been a centralising one from the perspective of local government, which has so far seen little reversal of its loss of powers under the Conservatives.

From rhetoric to reality – the process of modernisation

Conservative Social Security Secretary Peter Lilley's Mais Lecture in 1993 has been identified as the start of the welfare state overhaul being continued by the Blair administration (Brindle and MacAskill, 1997). The speech forecast an unsustainable growth in benefits spending and painted a picture of 'an increasing proportion of the next generation being reared in dependency' (p15). Lilley advocated strengthening conditions attached to unemployment benefits, active help to enable people to return to work, and encouragement for making provision privately.

Targeting and selectivity in social policy were considerably strengthened by the Conservatives, shifting subsidies from collective provision to the individual and tightening eligibility criteria for benefits and services. For those who could afford to do so, exiting into the private sector was legitimate and even altruistic because it took pressure off public services. The new public management also revolutionised how public services were procured and run, expanding general management, curtailing professional autonomy, redefining users as customers and introducing a performance culture (Blackman, 1995). Whilst ideologically driven by politicians committed to market forces and competition, many aspects of these changes reflected real problems with managing public services, such as the difficulty for health authorities in planning strategically when they were also embroiled in the direct management of health care services. Further, the work of the Audit Commission – established in 1982 to keep the economy and efficiency of local government under review – revealed substantial local variations in costs and standards, often finding no correlation between levels of spending and the quality of services.

In the Labour Party's pre-election document, *New Labour: Because Britain Deserves Better* (1997a), Tony Blair promised to build 'a modern welfare state'. This implied a break with the past, but in fact continuity was also important:

> Some things the Conservatives got right. We will not change them .
> . . I want to renew faith in politics through a government that will
> govern in the interest of the many, the broad majority of people who
> work hard, play by the rules, pay their dues and feel let down by a
> political system that gives the breaks to the few, to an elite at the top
> increasingly out of touch with the rest of us. (Labour Party, 1997a,
> p1)

What those things were that the Conservatives got right is not
made clear, but the message is pragmatic and populist, appealing
to fairness and invoking the work ethic. Fairness, though, is not
the same as equality. New Labour is a party of equality of
opportunity and minimum standards. Its commitment to redistribution is conditional, favouring employment and children but not
with the degree of equality favoured by previous Labour administrations. Blair's address continued to say:

> I want a country in which people get on, do well, make a success of
> their lives . . . We need more successful entrepreneurs, not fewer of
> them But these life chances should be for all the people. And I want
> a society in which ambition and compassion are seen as partners not
> opposites – where we value public service as well as material wealth
> . . . but we must recognise also that the policies of 1997 cannot be
> those of 1947 or 1967. (Labour Party, 1997a, p2)

Underlying these messages is New Labour's 'Third Way' analysis:
working with the realities of globalisation and mobile capital, the
rise of individualism, and the dynamism of markets (cf. Chapter 2
above). The continuity with Conservative policy is not surprising
given how similar the analysis is to much Conservative thinking,
including a commitment to relatively low income and corporate
taxation. There is also an explicit rejection of old Labour, with
criticism of the 'outmoded' welfare structures of the post-war
Attlee governments and the large social spending increases of the
late 1960s. But there is an assertion of values of fairness and
public service which differs from broad Conservative ideology,
and the changes of the previous Conservative period prepared the
ground for New Labour welfare reforms rather than prefiguring
them.

Bonoli and Palier (1998) suggest that the main consequence
of the social policy changes that were made in both the UK and
France during the 1980s and early 1990s is that they opened up
new institutional opportunities for future reform rather than
brought about radical restructuring. Of particular significance,
they argue, is that the changes have affected patterns of political
support for aspects of the welfare state. The 1986 Social Security
Act, for example, reduced the value of the State Earnings Related

Pensions Scheme (SERPS) and promoted the transfer of some five million employees from state to private pension arrangements, weakening the extent of political stakeholding in state pension provision. SERPS was cut back again under the 1995 Social Security Act and the scene was set for New Labour's pension reforms which will further shift pension provision into the private sector (Department of Social Security, 1998a).

Thus, the Conservative era has made available to New Labour reform options that were previously unavailable and unacceptable politically. The new government considered reform of the welfare state to be unfinished business. Its manifesto for the 1997 general election boldly stated:

> We will be the party of *welfare reform*. In consultation and partnership with the people, we will design a modern welfare state based on rights and duties going together, fit for the modern world. (Labour Party, 1997a, p4)

This position sits uneasily with New Labour's cautious tax policies given evidence that the UK welfare state requires higher taxation just to maintain current standards of provision (Rowthorn, 1993). However, in his foreword to the welfare reform Green Paper, *New Ambitions for our Country,* Blair rejects the claim that his plans are 'cuts-driven' and argues that they are about spending money 'in the fairest and most effective way' (Department of Social Security, 1998b, piv). The Green Paper's agenda is dominated by issues of fairness and effectiveness in existing spending, and how these are to be improved within a strong financial discipline aimed at economic growth. 'Fair' is defined as supporting those in greatest need, whilst 'effective' is about helping people to help themselves. This is how New Labour envisages rights and responsibilities going together.

These principles of targeting assistance and promoting independence have a strong emphasis in all of New Labour's social policies, and especially in the welfare- to-work and benefits arena, where tougher eligibility rules are being combined with enhanced benefits for more severe needs and a strengthening of efforts to divert people from benefit dependency. Indeed, throughout the government's programme there is an emphasis on the desirability of employment and making work pay.

Overarching these principles is a commitment to performance management. New Labour's claim is one of being better managers than its Conservative predecessors, as well as reformers. The new government kept to the Conservatives' spending plans for two years while it undertook a comprehensive spending review across all departments. The review introduced a system of public service agreements between each department and the Treasury so that resources are allocated on the basis of objectives and targets (Chancellor of the Exchequer, 1998). Efficiency targets are designed to keep the pressure on services to reinvest in frontline services, and private–public partnerships are being extended into more areas. The sale of local and central government assets is being used to fund new investment in health, education, housing and transport.

Unlike its visionary use in the early post-war years, modernisation is used by New Labour in a pragmatic sense. It has enabled the government to reject aspects of the Conservative legacy, not because it has a new ideology but because it is claimed that they do not work, and to retain other aspects because it is argued that they do work.

Blair defined modernisation in a speech at the 1997 Trades Union Congress. It had four dimensions, the last two of which were concerned respectively with modernising government and creating a clear identity and role on the world stage. The first two dimensions addressed economic and welfare reform:

> The first is to create an economy fully attuned to a new global market; one that combines enterprise and flexibility with harnessing the creative potential of all our people. The second is to fashion a modern welfare state, where we maintain high levels of social inclusion based on values of community and social justice, but where the role of government changes so it is not necessary to provide all social provision, and fund all social provision, but to organise and regulate it most efficiently and fairly. (Blair, 1997a)

The approach is not free of ideology. Ideology is very important but is tempered by the use of evidence about priorities and effectiveness. Work provides the central focus of an anti-dependency ideology but is also embraced as the best way of lifting people out of poverty. In-work social security payments are being reorganised as tax allowances, and other benefits are being re-focused as a last resort for those who really cannot obtain employment. New Labour has appealed to evidence that most of the people they are targeting – especially young people, people over 50, disabled people and lone parents – want to work but face barriers such as lack of training, inadequate childcare and low wages. Maintaining people out of work has an opportunity cost: there are better purposes for public spending. Blair, for example, has made a point of stating that spending on disability and incapacity benefits exceeds the entire school budget in the UK (Blair, 1998). In aiming to achieve a shift from welfare to work, the government is building upon changes to social security policy made by the Conservatives by integrating social security with training and labour market policy.

Another focus of New Labour's agenda also appears to reveal continuity with the Conservatives – the emphasis on family values. The 1997 manifesto upholds family life as:

> . . . the most secure means of bringing up our children. Families are the core of our society. They are the first defence against anti-social behaviour. The breakdown of family life damages the fabric of our society. (Labour Party, 1997a, p25)

However, what the government has sought to do is to address the changes that have occurred in family life rather than criticise them. It is developing policy that recognises the extent of divorce, cohabitation and lone parenthood, but seeks to support the stability of all adult relationships for children and to target support on the early years of children's lives (Home Office, 1998). Great emphasis is placed upon enabling families to work, including single-parent families: 'Families without work are without independence. This is why we give so much emphasis to our welfare-to-work policies' (Labour Party, 1997a, p25). Thus, the modernisation of family policy is part of the anti-dependency drive and overall emphasis on work (cf. Chapter 7 below). For some, though, especially many lone parents, it appears to send a contradictory message that family life is an essential core for the healthy development of well-adjusted young people, yet going out to work should be regarded as the first responsibility of all citizens of working age.

Shifting ideologies: the case of health and social services

Labour's 1997 manifesto stated:

> . . . we will safeguard the basic principles of the NHS, which we founded, but will not return to the top-down management of the 1970s. So we will keep the planning and provision of healthcare separate, but put planning on a longer-term, decentralised and more co-operative basis. The key is to root out unnecessary administrative cost, and to spend money on the right things – frontline care. (Labour Party, 1997a, p4)

Labour promised to end waiting for cancer surgery, end the internal market within the National Health Service (NHS), remove 100,000 people from hospital waiting lists, end yearly purchaser-provider contracts in favour of three- to five-year agreements and raise spending in real terms on health care annually, targeting the money on patients not bureaucracy. A new patients' charter was promised, concentrating on quality and success of treatment. New money was to be found through the savings achieved by trimming expensive top-down management structures, estimated to cost some £1.5 billion a year. General practitioner (GP) fundholding was not necessarily to be abolished but there was an indication that some of the best of the newly forged relationships between GPs and hospitals would be retained, without allowing a two-tier system of health care to develop.

In confronting the problems of an NHS driven by the imperatives of the Conservatives' internal market, the new government formulated its modernisation agenda as one of 'integrated care, based on partnership and driven by performance' (Department of Health, 1997). Thus, annual contracts between health care commissioners and health care providers are being replaced with three-year service agreements, and the jungle of GP fundholders is being replaced by a jigsaw of primary care groups (PCGs).

The need for an integrated approach to health care has long been recognised but reforms under the Conservatives brought about growing separation between the administration of different public services. This approach was justified in terms of the clarity of purpose and executive decision-making power necessary to implement plans and act on feedback from performance measures, but a consequence has been that public service organisations, including the whole health care system and its interfaces with services such as social care, became fragmented.

Labour's response is set out in its White Paper *The New NHS: Modern, Dependable* (Department of Health, 1997). It includes a commitment to provide better information so that people are 'better able to care for themselves'; swift treatment with better coordination between health and social care staff; and prompt access to specialist hospital services, including 'seamless' links with primary health and social care (cf. Chapter 10 below). It proposes changes aimed at better value for money: a new drive for efficiency, quality and performance linked to reducing fragmentation and securing 'the cost advantages that collaboration can bring'; rigorous assessment of the clinical and cost-effectiveness of treatments; and better attuning of local services to local needs, with decisions about use of resources being taken by those who treat patients, although within a framework of national standards.

The White Paper describes the new PCGs as placing primary health care professionals 'in the driving seat in shaping health services in the future'. Again, the ground had been prepared by the Conservatives with their policy of a primary care led NHS. The new government sought to retain the advantages of GP fundholding while reducing inequalities in access to treatment by setting up PCGs to commission health services for local patients. It is also argued that they will be able to take better account of special health care needs and the wider public health agenda (Department of Health, 1997, para. 5.3).

PCGs will be able to adopt roles that entail a greater or lesser degree of responsibility, ranging from advising the local health authority about commissioning care to becoming freestanding primary care trusts, accountable to the health authority, which both commissions care and provides community health services for its population. Interestingly, this last option represents a return to a unified NHS with no purchaser–provider split. PCGs are also expected to cut transaction costs and bureaucracy, and to help primary health care practices develop information systems needed for integrated health care. They are being introduced into a new environment of flexibility in joint working and budgets across health and social services, including the transfer of functions. A further White Paper, *Partnership in Action,* sets out a legislative agenda in this area (Department of Health, 1998a).

Where this trajectory of change will take the NHS is unclear. If primary care trusts blossom and if the transfer to them of social care functions becomes widespread, the stage is set for an integration of community health services and social services. To some extent this scenario is akin to the pre-1974 NHS, but is more accurately prefigured in the Scandinavian system. The major difference, however, is that in Scandinavia both health care and social services are local government responsibilities whereas in Britain health care is a central government responsibility and social services are separately administered under local government.

The rationing debate has highlighted the democratic deficit in the NHS (Glendinning, 1998). Rationing, or 'priority setting' as it is described by the Department of Health, has always been a feature of the NHS but rationing by queuing is being supplemented by the use of evidence about clinical and cost effectiveness. New Labour's policy does not address the lack of democratic process in local priority setting with, for example, no intention of reinstating local councillors on health authorities following their removal by the Conservatives. Instead, local authority chief executives have been given a seat on health authorities and PCGs, which will make key rationing decisions at local level, have a solitary lay member who is actually appointed by the health authority in an astonishingly tokenistic role of representing the public. There have been moves, however, both to consult patients about the quality of care and to involve the public in priority setting exercises, but the new explicitness about rationing has not been matched by democratic reform.

At the time of writing, a number of manifesto promises in relation to health care have not yet come to fruition. The first year of the new government saw the total number of patients waiting to be admitted to hospital increase by 140,000. More money was allocated to reducing waiting lists in April 1998, together with targets for each NHS region to reduce their lists, and Labour reiterated its election pledge that lists will be cut by 100,000 by the time of the next general election. The new patients' charter has been converted into an initiative to create local charters to reflect local needs and conditions, rather than a uniform set of rights for patients and a uniform set of obligations upon the NHS.

One major area where the government's intentions remain unclear is the social and health care of older people. During the Conservative period a major retrenchment of state health care for older people took place, with the substitution of free long-term hospital care by means-tested social and nursing care. This was also a large-scale privatisation, as most residential care and an increasing amount of domiciliary care was provided by the private sector. Responsibility for paying for residential care for poorer older people was transferred from the national social security budget to local authority social services departments in 1993, and social services departments responded to growing numbers of older people with high care needs by tightening their eligibility criteria. Between 1993 and 1997 home care contact hours increased by nearly 50 per cent but the number of households receiving home care fell by 7 per cent as services were concentrated on providing more hours to fewer people (Department of Health, 1998b).

Whilst a more rational allocation of finite resources for social and health care might be emerging from the increased focus upon both needs assessment and the efficiency of care services, the trend is essentially one of more rigorous selectivity both by need and by income. However, the criteria for achieving this vary from local authority to local authority. Labour's manifesto promised a Royal Commission on Long Term Care to advise on future change, especially as costs were projected to rise substantially with the ageing of the population. The Royal Commission reported in March 1999 and was critical of means-testing personal care, recommending complete state funding which, it estimated, would add 0.3–0.4 per cent to taxation of earnings, pensions and investments (Sutherland, 1999).

Whether New Labour will reverse the privatisation of social and nursing care in response to the Royal Commission's recommendations is not known at the time of writing. The recommendations do not chime well with the Third Way approach, in contrast to those of the authors of the Note of Dissent (Joffe and Lipsey, 1999). The dissenters argue that universal state support for personal care would fail to target spending on the poorest older people and divert state funding from the need to improve services. They also point out that the Commission's recommendations contrast with the government's rejection of universal state-funded provision in the field of pensions.

It seems likely that we will not see a return to universalism but that we will see measures, already signalled in the *Modernising Social Services* White Paper, to tackle the growth of local inequalities in access to care and how much older people or their families have to pay for their care (Department of Health, 1998c). Social services departments ration their services according to their budget and use eligibility criteria and charging schemes that vary from local area to local area. The government is introducing national standards and frameworks which are designed to reduce these local variations, but the approach entails a number of unresolved issues. It is unclear how national standards can be realised in practice given the difficulty of defining substantive rights in health and social care. Local authorities are also concerned that the issue will result in a further erosion of local democracy by curtailing local budgetary discretion in favour of earmarking funds for specific services and the introduction of standardised national means-tests (Blackman, 1998).

Welfare-to-work and social exclusion: reshaping rights and responsibilities

The welfare-to-work New Deal has been emerging in New Labour policy throughout the time in which the party has held office. The original manifesto promises of March 1997 offered four choices to young people who had been out of work for over six months; remaining on benefit was not one of those options. The choices were to work with an employer offered £60 per week for six months to take on an unemployed young person with approved in-work training; to work with a voluntary organisation, also with training, and with a wage equal to benefit plus a fixed extra sum for at least six months; to work with the Environment Taskforce being paid a sum equal to benefit plus a fixed sum for six months, with day release for education and training; or to enter full-time education on an approved course for those without suitable qualifications, without loss of benefit.

The language of responsibility was heavily present in Labour's *New Deal for a New Britain* (Labour Party, 1997b). This stated that 'young people have a responsibility to seek work and to train. A life on permanent benefit should not be an option' (p2). These responsibilities were to be matched by the rights of young people to have job and training opportunities: 'We recognise that they have a responsibility to seek work and training, but that these obligations must be matched by the government's responsibility to promote real opportunities' (p3). Specifically, the commitment was to get 250,000 young people under twenty-five years old off benefit and into work or training, to offer subsidies to employers to take on young people and to penalise unemployed claimants who did not comply with the new system by reductions in benefits.

The New Deal for the long-term unemployed was a similar programme started in June 1998 which also included four new options: employers would be offered a £75 per week tax rebate to take on people unemployed for at least two years for a minimum six months' work and training; there would be more flexibility in how benefits and other payments could be spent in order to help the unemployed person back into work; the unemployed person could return to education for a work-related qualification or could consider 'business start', a form of assistance to start up a new self-employed venture.

The New Deal also targeted the half million lone parents claiming Income Support whose youngest child was beyond the first term of compulsory schooling. Here the main message was that many lone parents wanted to work but were prevented from doing so either by their childcare responsibilities or by loss of out-of-work benefits. There was, initially, no mention of the benefit penalties present in the schemes for the young and long-term unemployed. Instead, a strong 'sell' message went out to lone parents that they would be far better off in work. They were offered a chance to consult personal advisers about workplace re-entry and childcare, job training and job applications. The scheme was piloted with 40,000 lone parents in eight locations during 1997 and implemented nationally from October 1998.

The 'single gateway' principle in these initiatives involves a combination of testing eligibility for benefits and personal advice and assistance aimed at helping unemployed people into employment. Whilst eligibility criteria for benefit payments are being tightened, improvements in benefit levels are being made: the tax credits are more generous than the benefits they replace, and the Severe Disablement Allowance is to be reformed to provide much higher financial support without means-testing for people who become disabled under 20 years of age.

The targeting of the £7.7 million budget for Incapacity Benefit illustrates the principles of the government's approach. This benefit is paid to people of working age who are unable to work due to illness or disability. In 1995–96 just over two million people were in receipt of this benefit, more than double the number claiming equivalent benefits in 1981–82. This growth is partly due to an increase in the duration of claims rather than new claims, and the benefit has been funding early retirement for many claimants who could return to some kind of work. The benefit is to be more tightly focused as a last resort for those who, with advice and support, cannot find suitable part- or full-time employment and who have a recent National Insurance contribution record. Employment policy is being revised to offer both individual support through personal advisers and wider action on barriers to work, including addressing discrimination through the proposed new Disability Rights Commission.

In October 1998, a package of major changes in disability benefits was announced. From June 1999, the single gateway would simplify and integrate employment and benefits advice and services for disabled people, based on personal advisers, mirroring the New Deal initiatives for the young, the long-term unemployed and lone mothers. At the same time, earlier welfare-to-work measures were tightened; from 2001 all claimants for benefits, *including* lone parents, would be required to attend employment advice interviews or lose benefit.

By the end of November 1998, some 203,000 young people and 70,900 long-term unemployed had joined the New Deal (Department for Education and Employment, 1999). Of the 82,600 young people who had left the programme, 49 per cent had entered unsubsidised jobs. The equivalent figure for the long-term unemployed was 28 per cent.

In addition, other financial and practical help to families was designed to assist women with children into paid work. Some additional 50,000 trained childcare workers were promised within the lifetime of the parliament, further developed in the Green Budget of November 1997 by the announcement of £300 million from the Exchequer and National Lottery to increase the availability of childcare places. The Working Family Tax Credit would supplement low wages through the tax system, rather than the old style Family Credit which was operated through the benefit system, and low-waged families would be able to claim further tax credits towards childcare costs. Support for children in working families was further strengthened in the March 1999 Budget by replacing the married couple's allowance with a new family tax credit for low-to-moderate-income families from April 2001.

The March 1998 and 1999 Budgets refined many of these promises. The Working Family Tax Credit from October 1999 guarantees a minimum £200 per week to all families on low pay. The New Deal is being extended to people over 50 who have been unemployed for six months or more, guaranteeing a minimum income of £9,000 p.a. for the first year back in work. Child Benefit has been increased well above the rate of inflation, the April 1999 rise meaning that it has been boosted by 25 per cent since the general election. In contrast to the shift from universalism to selectivity in other areas of social policy, Child Benefit has been retained as a universal benefit payable, usually, to the mother, and left untaxed. However, the 1999 Budget signalled an intention to integrate the various types of support for children and it seems likely that future changes will reduce this support for higher earning families, as will be the case with the new family tax credit.

Throughout the first eighteen months of welfare-to-work reforms, it is evident that the emphasis of earlier Conservative governments on making benefits conditional upon the individual's responsibility to find paid work has been embraced and strengthened (Finn, 1998). The state's responsibility has also been clearly defined as providing employment services and a number of employment and training options, including benefits for those who are unable to work. But there is no state responsibility for directly creating employment, and local variations in unemployment remain marked in the UK (Penman and Hough, 1998). Paradoxically, however, there appears to be no relationship between the state of the local economy and the proportion of young people going into employment via the New Deal (House of Commons, 1998).

What kind of welfare state?

New Labour's welfare reforms are taking place against a backdrop of economic and demographic pressures caused by the national economy's openness and vulnerability to the global economy, and an ageing population. Further, most of the electorate appear to support a tax policy that takes no more than 40 per cent of their incomes, rather than the 60 per cent which is typical of the Scandinavian welfare states. Budgetary discipline, the rationalisation of bureaucracy and containment of costs therefore dominate the agenda. New money is conditional on modernisation and performance, from regional hospital waiting list targets to finding employment.

However, the reforms are more than straightforward responses to these pressures. They represent a political choice from among alternative strategies. The Commission on Social Justice (1994) summarised these alternatives as a 'Levellers' Britain', a 'Deregulators' Britain' and an 'Investors' Britain'. The option of a Levellers' Britain is based exclusively on greater equality through redistribution via the tax and benefit systems. The Deregulators' Britain is at the opposite extreme, based on economic entrepreneurialism, acceptance of inequality, and reductions in public services and public spending. The Commission's preferred option was an Investors' Britain. This recognises the dynamism of markets but seeks to harness it by investing in education and other measures to maximise employment opportunities, together with a set of social principles based on the centrality of work, adequate social security for those who cannot work and strong families. Clearly, the New Labour welfare state is closest to an Investors' Britain.

But investment in the welfare state is as yet comparatively modest and limited by a desire to keep corporate and wealth taxation relatively low, and only marginally to strengthen the progressive nature of income tax. A year after the election, a Labour Party brochure trumpeted that corporation tax had been cut to the lowest in Europe and that there had been no increase in income tax, and this was further celebrated in March 1999 Budget Statement (Labour Party, 1998a; Chancellor of the Exchequer, 1999). Even so, the new government's windfall tax on the excess profits of the utility companies privatised under the Conservatives generated £5.2 billion for investment in job subsidies, training, work placements and school infrastructure. In addition, the March 1998 Budget was deceptively redistributive. Whilst income tax was not changed, one estimate is that £10 billion was raised in other tax and national insurance changes which would largely benefit low-income households through job creation incentives, tax credits and child benefits (*The Observer*, 22 March 1998). The March 1999 Budget cut income tax but was also redistributive, especially for families.

The government has managed the *presentation* of its strategy in terms designed to appeal to public opinion rather than lead it. When the March 1998 Budget was described as 'an exercise in moving money from wealthier to poorer families', the Chancellor corrected the interpretation: 'The redistribution is in favour of work, and it is helping people – lower income, middle income, upper income – who work' (*The Guardian*, 19 March 1998). At the same time, Tony Blair wrote to Labour Party members with the message that:

The budget was new Labour from start to finish. New Labour because it was both radical and modernising, a budget for fairness and a budget for enterprise. *The poorest 20 per cent of families will gain four times as much as the wealthiest 20 per cent from the announcements made in the budget'* (original emphasis; Labour Party, 1998b).

The tax and benefit transfers following the March 1998 Budget were not dramatic however. The poorest 20 per cent of households benefited to the tune of about £3 a week, compared with losses of around £1.50 a week for the top half of the income distribution. Redistribution was sharper for families with children, with lone parents seeing their incomes rise on average by £3.32 a week. The significance of the Budget, though, was in its status as the first progressively redistributive package for two decades and in the direction it set for future change in this direction. Thus, whilst the March 1999 Budget was a tax-cutting budget, introducing a new 10 per cent tax band benefiting low earners and cutting the basic rate of income tax by 1 per cent, it was also redistributive. For example, by 2001–02 a single-wage household with two children under eleven years old earning £200 per week should see their net income increase by 15.2 per cent, compared with 5.1 per cent if they earn £400 and 2 per cent if they earn £600 per week (Treasury, 1999). The figures are less impressive, for deliberate policy reasons, for earners without children. The equivalent percentage increases in net incomes are 4.4, 3.1 and 0.5 per cent.

The break with old Labour is that redistribution includes a retreat from universalism. For example, the government has signalled its intention to restrict support for children received by higher rate taxpayers; the state pension is being merged into a means-tested minimum income guarantee; and incapacity benefit – a national insurance benefit – is to be means-tested against income from private medical insurance or private or occupational pensions. State support is also increasingly conditional, especially with regard to the responsibility of all those of working age to find employment. Thus, whilst the March 1999 Budget was redistributive towards working families, it was far less generous towards families with no wage earner.

New Labour is seeking to balance targeted social policies with an economic policy of working with global capitalism, which means ensuring that labour is flexible and companies are competitive. There is little will to intervene actively with employment generation measures and it is extremely unlikely that anything resembling full employment will be achieved. Social inclusion informs its approach, with the selective targeting of particular groups. This figures prominently in its philosophy, which has sought to re-establish the one-nation ideology of post-war social democracy:

> . . . the people of Britain found it morally unacceptable that so many should have no stake. They saw it as an offence against decency that work should be allowed to disappear from so many areas of the country, work, to be replaced by an economy built on benefits, crime, petty thieving and drugs. For a country famous for its sense of fair play it was a source of national shame that visitors should see beggars on the streets and that Britain should have shot up the international league tables for inequality. (Blair, 1997b)

However, New Labour's drive to tackle social exclusion, led by the Social Exclusion Unit, bears little resemblance to the one-nation policies of earlier post-war Labour governments, especially their level of regional development funding. Some aspects of the strategy are major policy programmes, such as welfare-to-work, the national childcare strategy, the reform of pensions and the minimum wage. There is also a wide-ranging commitment through the Ministerial Social Exclusion Network, whose ministers draw together social exclusion issues in their own departments. But the main focus is selective, targeting lone parents, young people and deprived neighbourhoods. Area-based policies have also seen a renaissance, with the announcement of a series of new Employment, Education and Health Action Zones.

The selective approach is being justified because of its potential to address interconnected problems where agencies need to work together to focus on an issue. The first phase of work of the Social Exclusion Unit has focused on truancy and school exclusions, rough sleeping and rundown neighbourhoods. The Unit's reports are very reminiscent of similar reports produced during the 1970s, with their emphasis on local employment, education, access to services and interagency working (Social Exclusion Unit, 1998). However, the Conservative legacy is evident in overtones of the underclass thesis – the argument that a section of society has become disconnected from employment and mainstream values, creating a financial burden for taxpayers and a threat to social order. This approach owes much to Peter Mandelson who, when Minister without Portfolio, spoke at the Fabian Society in the following terms:

> . . . a permanently excluded underclass actually hinders flexibility rather than enhancing it. If we are to promote flexibility we must find ways of getting people off dependency and into the labour market . . . . Let us be crystal clear on this point. The people we are concerned

about, those in danger of dropping off the end of the ladder of opportunity and becoming disengaged from society, will not have their long-term problems addressed by an extra pound a week on their benefits. (Mandelson, 1997)

There is a thin line between targeting and labelling, and New Labour's 'rights and responsibilities' discourse on welfare has been challenged for emphasising the responsibility of unemployed people to seek work while having little to say about the responsibilities of the state or companies to provide employment. Without a greater emphasis on this responsibility there is, as Alcock (1998) comments, a danger of pathologisation which creates the idea that because some people are the victims of social exclusion, they must also be responsible for causing their situation.

In terms of public spending, those areas of social policy where there is still considerable stakeholding across all sections of the electorate are being prioritised, namely education and health. The Comprehensive Spending Review resulted in more new money for these two departments than all other government departments combined, with education spending set to increase at 5.1 per cent and health at 4.7 per cent per year above inflation over the three years from 1998–99. However, spending is vulnerable where there is weaker stakeholding among the public. Thus, the welfare reform Green Paper states:

With people living longer, it is inevitable that provision for retirement will increase. We expect that much of this increase will be delivered by private and mutual providers and that the proportion of the welfare budget funded by the tax payer will not increase. We would expect Government spending to give greater emphasis to measures which prevent poverty, such as education and health, as more people move into independence and off benefit. (Department of Social Security, 1998a, p82)

This strategy is reflected in pension proposals, where public opinion polls have shown majority support for requiring people who can afford to do so to make their own provision (Atkinson and Mortimore, 1998). The pensions Green Paper sets out the government's intention to promote private pension contributions with the aim that public spending on pensions should decline as a share of gross domestic product from 5.4 per cent today to 4.5 per cent in 2050 (Department of Social Security, 1998a). At the same time, the poorest pensioners will benefit from higher public spending to boost income support and encourage its take-up. In general, the government is 'moving out of areas where it need not be, and – in those areas where public service matters – setting clear targets for modern, efficient and effective services' (Chancellor of the Exchequer, 1998).

Conclusion

Whilst the Conservatives' approach to social policy was ideological in the sense of uncritically equating the profit motive with efficiency and quality, New Labour's approach claims to be rational, focusing on performance against explicit standards and targets. The emphasis on partnership can also be seen as a rational response to the fact that social welfare is co-produced: education is co-produced through school–parent links; employment is co-produced by workers' willingness to train and work productively, and employers willingness to create jobs; health and social care by recognising the roles of self-care and family carers; and urban renewal by linking public and private sector resources. Acknowledging that welfare outcomes are co-produced is an important antidote to the worst features of statism and professionalism, but it is a strategy that relies upon the availability and adequacy of employment, family care and public infrastructure. There is a danger that public policy will not be sufficiently strong to create the conditions and resources for this.

There can be no doubt that the new government has systematically, and with some speed, acted upon its promises of welfare reform contained in the 1997 election manifesto. There is nothing in the manifesto which has not received some considerable attention within twenty months of taking office. The shift, as promised, has been from welfare to work, and employees are to be afforded the protection of a minimum wage and enhanced rights. Work holds the key, alongside judicious saving and insurance for the future.

It is too early to say what kind of welfare state is going to emerge or what impact it will have on the large issues such as social inequality and quality of life in old age. What is clear is that the British welfare state is still on a trajectory of change, and that the conditions for this change were created by welfare state reforms made in the 1980s. Given the early signs, the main concern has to be whether the rhetoric of a one nation Britain will extend in practice to a welfare state in which all feel they have a stake when it remains modestly funded. The prospects for a welfare state which is an active agent of social and democratic progress will not be good if increasing numbers of the more affluent pay their own way privately, universal provision continues to be eroded, democracy fails to be reinvigorated at local level, and the poor become targeted and stigmatised by the state.

References

Alcock, P. (1998) 'Labour in power: four Labour social policy initiatives one year on', *Community Care,* 26 November–2 December, pp17–24.

Atkinson, S. and Mortimore, R. (1998) 'Blair – one year on', paper prepared for PSA Conference, University of Keele, April, London, MORI, Internet: http://www.mori.com/pubinfo/blairone.htm.

Blackman, T. (1995) *Urban Policy in Practice,* London: Routledge.

Blackman, T. (1998) 'Facing up to underfunding: equity and retrenchment in community care', *Social Policy & Administration,* vol. 32, no. 2, pp182–195.

Blair, A. (1997a) 'The modernisation of Britain', *Speech to the 1997 Trades Union Congress, Brighton, 9 September,* Internet: http://britain-info.org/bis/fordom/other/970909pm.htm.

Blair, A. (1997b) *Speech by the Prime Minister, 2 June, at the Aylesbury Estate, Southwark,* Internet: http://www.cabinet-office.gov.uk/seu/index/more.html#speech by the prime minister.

Blair, A. (1998) 'Unveiling Labour's welfare revolution', *Progress,* vol. 7, p23.

Bonoli, G. & Palier, B. (1998) 'Changing the politics of social programmes: innovative change in British and French welfare reforms', *Journal of European Social Policy,* vol. 8, no. 4, pp317–330.

Brindle, D. & MacAskill, E. (1997) 'All change, please: no room on board', *The Guardian,* 16 December, p15.

Chancellor of the Exchequer (1998) *Statement by the Chancellor of the Exchequer on the Comprehensive Spending Review,* 14 July, Internet: http://www.hm-treasury.gov.uk/pub/html/csr/statement.html.

Chancellor of the Exchequer (1999) *Budget Statement, 9 March,* Internet: http://www.hm-treasury.gov.uk/budget99/speech.html.

Commission on Social Justice (1994) *Social Justice: Strategies for National Renewal,* London, Vintage.

Department for Education and Employment (1999) *Statistical First Release, 28 January,* Internet: http://www.open.gov.uk.

Department of Health (1997) *The New NHS: Modern, Dependable,* London, The Stationery Office.

Department of Health (1998a) *Partnership in Action,* London, The Stationery Office.

Department of Health (1998b) *Health and Personal Social Services for England 1998,* London, The Stationery Office.

Department of Health (1998c) *Modernising Social Services,* London, The Stationery Office.

Department of Social Security (1998a) *A New Contract for Welfare: Partnership in Pensions,* London, The Stationery Office.

Department of Social Security (1998b) *New Ambitions for Our Country: a New Contract for Welfare,* London, The Stationery Office.

Finn, D. (1998) 'Labour's 'New Deal' for the unemployed and the stricter benefit regime', in E. Brunsden, H. Dean & R. Woods (eds) *Social Policy Review 10,* London, Social Policy Association.

Glendinning, C. (1998) 'From general practice to primary care: developments in primary health services 1990–1998', in E. Brunsden, H. Dean & R. Woods (eds), *Social Policy Review 10,* London, Social Policy Association.

Home Office (1998) *Supporting Families: A Consultation Document,* London, The Stationery Office.

House of Commons (1998) *Hansard Debates for 10 December 1998 (pt 26) New Deal,* Internet: www.parliament.uk.

Joffe, J. & Lipsey, D. (1999) 'Note of dissent', in S. Sutherland (Chairman) *With Respect to Old Age: Long Term Care – Rights and Responsibilities,* A Report by the Royal Commission on Long Term Care, London, The Stationery Office.

Labour Party (1997a) *New Labour: Because Britain Deserves Better,* London: The Labour Party.

Labour Party (1997b) *New Deal for a New Britain,* London: The Labour Party

Labour Party (1998a) *Together We're Making Britain Better,* London: The Labour Party.

Labour Party (1998b) Letter from the Prime Minister to Labour Party members, 20 April.

Mandelson, P. (1997) *Extract from a speech by the Minister without Portfolio, on 14 August, at the Fabian Society,* Internet: http://www.cabinet-office.gov.uk/seu/index/more.html#extract from a speech by the minister.

Penman, A. and Hough, J. (1998) *Unemployment by Constituency, November 1998,* Research Paper 98/119, London, House of Commons Library.

Rowthorn, B. (1993) 'Saving the welfare state', *New Economy,* Sample Issue, Autumn, pp36–40.

Social Exclusion Unit (1998) *Bringing Britain Together: A national strategy for neighbourhood renewal,* London, The Stationery Office.

Sutherland, S. (Chairman) (1999) *With Respect to Old Age: Long Term Care – Rights and Responsibilities,* A Report by the Royal Commission on Long Term Care, London, The Stationery Office.

Treasury (1999) *Budget Illustrative Tables,* Internet: http://www.inlandrevenue.gov.uk/legal_docs/pr99.htm.

7 New Labour, new families?

Hilary Land

'I can save the family' was the headline in the *Daily Mail* on 29 September 1998, above the lead article describing how Tony Blair was going to launch 'a crusade to safeguard traditional family life'. A month later, the Green Paper *Supporting Families* was published, setting out plans to improve family prosperity, strengthen marriage, make it easier to balance work and home, tackle serious problems 'such as domestic violence, truancy and school age pregnancy' and ensure all families 'have access to the advice and support they need'. The Home Secretary wrote the foreword to this paper, pointing out that this was 'the first time any government had published a consultation paper on the family' (Home Office 1998, p3). Meanwhile, during 1998 the government had already announced a number of policy initiatives, such as the introduction of the Working Families Tax Credit (WFTC), a national childcare strategy (Department of Health, 1998), a welfare-to-work programme for lone parents as well as for young people and disabled people, pension splitting on divorce and measures aimed at making employment more 'family friendly'. In addition, a number of policy reviews were under way, in particular reviews of state and private pension provision, the funding of care in old age and the Child Support Agency. How far these policy changes will influence how men and women or young and old actually behave towards each other – at least in the short term – will depend on the extent to which these changes are consistent with people's beliefs about family responsibilities. History provides many examples of how government intentions to make people support their relatives more or differently are resisted if policies are out of line with their everyday lives and views about family obligations. In this respect the 1991 Child Support Act is but one example in a long line of legislation. When in July 1998 the Green Paper *Children First* was published by the Department of Social Security (DSS, 1998a), announcing that the Child Support Agency was to be reformed, seven out of ten lone mothers claiming Income Support had sought to avoid claiming maintenance from the father of their children, and one-third of fathers assessed for maintenance were paying nothing.

Concern among politicians and policy makers that 'the family' is somehow threatened or in crisis is not new either. Such anxieties found expression in the 1834 Report of the Poor Law Commission as well as in debates on the family in Edwardian England. However, the extent to which family policies have become explicit is new. It is no longer the case, as Roy Parker and I argued twenty years ago (Land and Parker, 1978) that the UK has only a set of implicit family policies.

This chapter first examines the reasons for, and objectives of, these policy changes. Secondly, it looks at whether is the model of the family underpinning the proposed policies is very different from the traditional male breadwinner model. Indeed, is there a single model or, reflecting the diversity of family life, several? Why are changes necessary and what are their objectives? Is there coherence or contradiction at the heart of government policy? Gordon Brown, in his 1998 Budget proposed reforming and integrating the tax and benefit systems 'in order to improve work incentives, reduce poverty and welfare dependency and strengthen community and family life' (Treasury, 1998, p37). These objectives are not necessarily compatible as Pamela Meadows, then director of the Policy Studies Institute, told the House of Commons Social Security Committee. 'The debate tends to be muddled because it is not clear whether the objective is to reward work or to improve the well-being of families. The two objectives, while not incompatible, produce different policy recommendations, depending on the relative importance of each' (Social Security Committee, 1998a, para. 24). Gordon Brown also said in his Budget speech that as far as state welfare is concerned 'support should be provided on the basis of identifiable needs of children, not on whether there happen to be one parent or two'. In other words, 'additional support should be provided not on the basis of family structure but on the basis of family need' (*Financial Times*, 8 March 1998). But is this consistent with the Prime Minister's objective of strengthening marriage and safeguarding '*traditional* family life'? (emphasis added).

The demise of the male breadwinner and the rise of the lone mother

Since the beginning of the welfare state in the UK, the model of the family underpinning the tax and benefit systems has been that of the male breadwinner supporting a dependent wife and children. This male breadwinner model assumes most men can and do earn 'a family wage'. Although accepted over 100 years ago by the Trade Union Movement as an ideal, it was a model to which the majority of working class families never conformed. The labour market in a market economy cannot deliver high enough wages to all fathers. In any case wages have other functions. In the past twenty years, with the return to pre-Second-World-War deregulated, 'flexible' labour markets, accompanied by levels of male unemployment which would have been politically unacceptable in the earlier post-war decades, the numbers of men for whom a wage, let alone a family wage, is out of reach has grown. The number of children living in households in which there is no one in employment has doubled since 1979. In 1997 there were more than two and a quarter million children under sixteen years old in families receiving Income Support (IS) - the benefit which replaced Supplementary Benefit in 1988 - as Table 1 shows.

Table 1: Number of children dependent on Supplementary Benefit/Income Support (thousands)

Year	Age of child Under 11	11–16	16–18	Total
1979	724	284	29	1,037
1989	1,558	451	90	2,099
1993	2,251	688	161	3,100
1997	1,655	624	124	2,399

Source: DSS Social Security Statistics, 1979, 1989, 1993, 1997

Altogether two-thirds of lone-parent families and one in twelve two-parent families were dependent on IS in 1997. One-third of these families were headed by a man. It is harder to support a family on one wage as the increase in the uptake and cost of Family Credit (FC) (and family Income Supplement (FIS), the benefit which had preceded it) illustrates. By the end of 1997 nearly three-quarters of a million families with one and a half million children, accounting for one in six lone-parent families and 7 per cent of two-parent families, were receiving FC. Overall FC (FIS) claimants have increased threefold in ten years and sevenfold in twenty years. In nearly half (322,000) of these families the main earner was a man (DSS, 1998b, p19). The disproportionate number of children of lone mothers among recipients of means-tested benefits reflects the extent to which lack of qualifications and skills place women, as well as men, at a disadvantage in the labour market of the 1990s. As Table 2 shows, gender, marital status and motherhood make little difference to the employment prospects of women if they are highly educated. Among the unqualified, however, the disadvantage of lack of education is compounded by these characteristics so that overall only a small proportion of lone mothers are in paid work.

Table 2: Employment by levels of highest education attainment (per cent)

	Degree	'A' Levels	GCSEs	No qualifications	Average
Men and women	86	75	74	52	73
Women in general	83	71	70	47	67
Women with children	79	68	64	40	62
Lone mothers	79	56	48	21	42

Source: NOMIS database; Education and Employment Committee (1998, para. 17).

Table 3: Distribution of children in households where income is below half the national average by age and family type in Great Britain, 1997 (thousands)

	Before housing costs		After housing costs	
Age of child	1-parent family	2-parent family	1-parent family	2-parent family
0 – 4	190	500	460	720
5 – 10	370	720	640	900
11 – 16	290	620	460	740
17 or more	30	70	40	90
All children	870	1,920	1,590	2,430

Source: House of Commons, *Written Answer*, 5 May 1998, col. 378.

These figures expose the problem of combining the care and maintenance of children if there is only one parent on modest wages and that parent is the mother. During the 1980s the majority of lone mothers became dependent on means-tested benefits. By the mid-1990s, three-fifths of children on IS were in lone-parent families. Not surprisingly the proportion of children living in households in which the income is below half the national household average grew from one in ten in 1979 to one in three by the early 1990s. Table 3 shows the distribution of poor children by age and family composition.

Any strategy which aims to reduce poverty – particularly child poverty – must include lone parents and their children. However, this raises moral and social questions, as well as economic ones. Before the establishment of the post-1945 welfare state, lone parents, with the exception of widows, were treated as second-class citizens both in principle and in practice. To do otherwise, it was argued would encourage immorality and undermine marriage. Unmarried mothers and their children were particularly harshly treated. Their claims on the post-war welfare state were considerably strengthened, although in practice they faced discrimination from local health, welfare and housing authorities (see Kiernan *et al.*, 1998). Their rights to support from the social security system, albeit means-tested benefits, were less restricted than in many European states; for example, they were not required to register for employment until their youngest child was of school leaving age, in contrast to the age of *starting* school as was the case in some countries. Until the 1980s the majority avoided dependence on means-tested benefits (only one in five were claimants in the early 1960s) and in the first of the Conservative government's social security reviews in the mid-1980s, lone parents were not perceived to be a problem and received little negative attention. Indeed, in the new IS scheme introduced in 1988, on top of the family premium they were given the additional premium that was to become so controversial in 1997. By the end of the 1980s this had changed. Their numbers had grown and the proportion dependent on state benefits had increased. The dominant stereotype of the lone mother became the welfare mother playing the system and worse, encouraging irresponsibility among young men by making them redundant as fathers. The growth in their numbers in the first half of the 1980s was due in large part to divorce. However, after 1986 it was the increasing number of births to never-married mothers which accounted disproportionately for the growth. At the end of the 1970s only one in ten live births occurred outside marriage. By the end of the 1980s this proportion had nearly trebled. In 1997 it had reached 37 per cent. This trend was fuelled not, as is popularly believed, by a growth in the proportion of pregnant women having a baby on their own – this proportion has remained remarkably constant over several decades (see Kiernan *et al.*, 1998) – but by the growth in cohabitation. The majority of births to never-married women are registered by both parents and most of them are living at the same address, although cohabiting relationships, like marriages, can break down. Indeed, they are generally more fragile than marriages, and it is this that is the dominant cause of lone parenthood among never-married mothers.

These rapid and unanticipated changes raised questions not only about the cost to the taxpayer (benefits for lone parents increased from three billion pounds to five and a half billion pounds (1992–23 prices between 1985 and 1991 (DSS, 1993)) but also about the responsibilities of fathers, whether married or not. The policy response was to make the biological father responsible for the maintenance of his children and their mother as long as she was caring for them. DNA testing to establish paternity made this feasible with a degree of certainty impossible to achieve in the past. The 1991 Child Support Act for the first time in English law made the marital and household status of the lone mother irrelevant in determining her claims for maintenance either on the father or on the state. In other words, the dependency of women and children and the paternity of those children were no longer to be established and sustained primarily by the marriage contract as the male breadwinner model implies. There were penalties if mothers refused to name the father of their child(ren) without 'good cause'. Although there was, and is, widespread support for the principle that fathers should support their children, this proved to be very controversial when the Child Support Agency attempted to put this principle into practice, not least because its effect was not limited to the poor. The spectacular failure of the Child Support Agency to get more fathers to pay maintenance is another story (see Barnes *et al.*, 1998; Kiernan *et al.*, 1998). However, this failure led the Conservative government to develop a number of policies, the debates about which frame the family policies which the Labour government in turn are currently developing.

Key debates

Marriage

Cohabitation continued to increase and marriage to decline. In 1995 there were half the number of first marriages and double the number of divorces compared with 1970. The total number of marriages was the lowest figure recorded since 1926 (ONS, 1998a, 50). If divorce rates persist at their 1993 and 1994 levels it is estimated that two in five marriages are likely to end in divorce. Nevertheless on average, recent marriages are expected to last twenty-six years and nearly half of all couples will celebrate their silver wedding (*ibid.*, p51). The proportion of children living in two-parent families has fallen from nine out of ten in the early 1970s to four out of five in the mid-1990s. A million children live in stepfamilies with both natural and stepchildren. Questions were raised about why the state was not supporting marriage as the preferred state in which to bring up children. With the introduction of independent taxation in 1990 and the decline in the value of the married couples allowance (MCA), the subsidy to marriage enjoyed mainly by husbands was 'withering on the vine', as Nigel Lawson, who introduced independent taxation, intended that it should (Lawson, 1992). This subsidy was costing five billion pounds in foregone revenue when independent taxation was introduced in 1990. The decline in its value coincided with the increase in and indexation of child benefit, which John Major introduced in 1992. Gordon Brown explicitly linked the decline in the MCA with increased benefits for children. He said in his 1998 Budget: 'measures to increase support for children will be partly funded by reducing the rate of relief on the married couple allowance' (Treasury, 1998, p67). Concern that neither the tax nor the benefit system were actively being used to encourage marriage over cohabitation or lone parenthood grew in the mid-1990s. The lone parent's premium and one parent benefit, to which all lone parents including those in employment were entitled, were used as examples of how the benefit system appeared to penalise marriage. It was forgotten that these benefits were introduced because lone parents had additional needs. In November 1996 Peter Lilley announced the abolition of these benefits. As a member of the Shadow Cabinet, Harriet Harman opposed the cut because it 'will not cut the divorce rate or keep one family together but it will make hundreds of thousands of the poorer children worse off'. However, once in power, constrained by a promise not to increase income tax and to contain the social security bill, the new Labour government implemented the cut in 1998.

Childcare

The question of childcare moved up the policy agenda. Until the late 1970s combining childcare with paid employment was not a problem for many lone parents. Many could rely on their own mothers, with whom they lived or lived near; lone parents had priority in the allocation of what local authority day care places there were; and the benefit rules, both for FIS (the predecessor of FC) and Supplementary Benefit (the predecessor of IS), took full account of the costs of day care. All this changed in the 1980s. The 1977 Housing (Homeless Persons) Act for the first time had given local authorities housing departments the duty to rehouse homeless families irrespective of their marital status. This gave lone mothers a route into local authority housing. However, as a consequence of the housing policies of the 1980s and 1990s, this meant neither they nor the housing departments could give priority to their need to be near family or friends. This reduced or removed their access to 'free' daycare. This dislocation of lone parents from supportive family and friends as well as from possible employment has remained significant. A study in 1995 found that 30 per cent of lone parents reported experiencing homelessness in the previous ten years and 22 per cent had been accepted as homeless by the council. This compares with 6 and 4 per cent respectively of all households. Over the same period the housing benefit system penalised families who shared their accommodation with other adults. At the same time ill-considered changes in the treatment of working expenses in the benefit system meant that mothers who had to pay for childcare were discouraged either from maintaining contact with the labour market while on IS or from moving off IS more fully into employment and claiming FC. When the government began to develop policies to encourage lone mothers back into paid employment it was impossible to ignore the question of childcare. It was made easier to combine part-time employment with claiming benefit when, in 1994, the number of hours of employment defining eligibility for FC was dropped to sixteen from twenty-four hours per week. However, the loss of school meals and reduction in assistance with housing costs incurred when making this shift dampened the impact of this change for many families. In 1994 a childcare disregard was introduced in the FC but its impact was 'rather less than anticipated' (DSS, 1996, p31) – only 10 per cent of the number expected took advantage of it. Modest increases were made in funds for after-school places but even when the DSS began to pilot their welfare-to-work programme in 1997 it was still unclear how the necessary affordable childcare places would be forthcoming.

Labour markets

Changes in the labour market and family structure have not been confined solely to poor families. As Table 4 shows, there has been a significant fall in the number of full-time jobs, disproportionately affecting men as the traditional male manufacturing sectors declined. The male breadwinner model became less common among higher income groups too. Overall, between the early 1970s and 1996 the proportion of families dependent entirely on a male breadwinner fell from around two-fifths to one-quarter (ONS, 1998a, p81). Conversely over the same period, the proportion of married couple families with dependent children in which both parents were in paid employment increased from about half to over three-fifths (idem).

Much of this increase was accounted for by the second earner's part-time employment for, as Table 4 shows, the growth in employment over the past 30 years is mainly accounted for by part-time jobs occupied by women. However, mothers in professional and managerial occupations are increasingly likely to be in full-time employment, even when the children are very young. Not only did the economic activity rates of married mothers in the 1980s overtake those of lone mothers, but by the mid-1990s they were more likely than lone mothers to be employed full-time. Just as lone parents find it difficult to combine breadwinning with the care of young children, so too do couples when both have full-

Table 4: Historical trends in the number of part-time and full-time employees in employment in Great Britain (thousands)

Year	FT Total	Female	PT Total	Female
1951	19,239	6,041	832	779
1961	19,794	5,698	1,999	1,851
1971	18,308	5,413	3,341	2,757
1981	16,407	5,481	4,442	3,789
1991	16,877	5,802	4,615	4,114
1995	15,348	5,728	5,890	4,780

Sources: Kiernan et al. (1998, p253); Labour Market Trends, March 1997.

time jobs. This is particularly the case in the UK where not only is there very little state provision of day care compared with the rest of the EU but also where working full-time means working long hours. Both men and women employed full-time in the UK have the longest average working hours in the European Union (EU): nearly forty-six hours compared with an EU average of forty-one hours for men and forty hours compared with an average of thirty-nine hours for women (ONS, 1998a, p83). This is an increase for both men and women over the past ten years. Moreover, more than one in five of all men in employment in the UK work over fifty hours a week (one in five women work over forty hours) and this is likely to coincide with the time when fathers have young children. In this context the EU Working Time directive which sets a maximum working week of forty-eight hours could be of considerable significance to parents and children in the UK. Informal childcare from partners, parents and relatives has remained important. However, the number of employed parents of pre-school and primary school children who depend on formal childcare as well has grown. In the absence of any increase in state provision of day care, the numbers of child minders and private nurseries have grown dramatically (threefold and sevenfold respectively) in the past decade, and the question of how day care should be paid for has become a policy issue. The need for after-school care has also become evident as children have become dependent on adults to escort them to and from school and their parents' journeys to work have lengthened.

The demise of the male breadwinner not only raises questions about responsibilities for the maintenance of children and how this should be shared between parents and between parents and the state, but also about responsibilities for caring for children. When such care is embedded in the marriage contract implied in the male breadwinner model and therefore provided within the family or exchanged between friends, like so much of women's unpaid work, it is only noticed by the policy makers when it is no longer forthcoming. Then demands for the provision of replacement services or the money to purchase them in the marketplace begin to be made. The Working Families Tax Credit with the additional childcare credit, the welfare-to-work programme and the national childcare strategy are three of the Labour government's key routes into a reappraisal of the state's responsibility to share with parents both the financial support and the care of children. In other words, the issues involved go beyond concerns about child poverty.

New Labour strategy: a critical account

As Tony Blair wrote in the foreword to the Green Paper, *A New Contract for Welfare*, published in the spring of 1998, 'the welfare state isn't just about a few benefits paid to the most needy' (DSS, 1998c). Describing the system of benefits, taxes and charges as 'a contract between us as citizens', he emphasised that 'this contract should be one that is fair not just for the existing generation, bur fair between the generations' (pv). Central to the concept of citizenship is work – *paid* work. 'We want to rebuild the system around work and security. Work for those who can; security for those who cannot' (*ibid.*, piii). Despite Frank Field's departure from office, the centrality of 'work' to the government's reform of the tax and benefit system as well as to family policies has remained.

Summing up Gordon Brown's Spring Budget in 1998, *The Mirror's* headline declared 'Your country needs YOU back at work' (18 March 1998). The format of this front page, with a picture of Gordon Brown pointing at the reader, was reminiscent of First World War recruiting posters. The Budget outlined the government's proposals to develop welfare-to-work programmes to include young people, lone parents, the long-term unemployed and people with long-standing illness or disability. The most generously supported New Deal package is for the young unemployed, and it was the first to go nationwide in April 1998. It offers participants, all of whom must have been receiving the Jobseekers Allowance (JSA) for six months, advice followed either by work with an employer, a voluntary sector organisation or with the Environment Taskforce, or full-time education or training. Employers taking on a young person receive up to £60 a week subsidy plus £750 towards training costs. It is estimated that the scheme will cost £2.6 billion between 1997 and 2002 (Treasury, 1998, p43). Childless partners of the young unemployed must also participate in the scheme. Subsequently young lone parents have also been included if they have been receiving IS for six months. The New Deal for lone parents introduced in July 1997 built on the eight pilot projects initiated earlier by Peter Lilley. This was extended first to all new and repeat claimants in April 1998 and to all IS claimants in October 1998. In contrast to the New Deal for young people, employers may only receive a subsidy of £750 for training. There is very limited support (£30 million) for those wanting or needing education and training before taking up employment apart from government training schemes, on which they receive £10 on top of their benefit. This New Deal scheme is expected to cost a modest £190 million over the five years from 1997. Lone parents are not expected to participate until their youngest child has reached school age, and Harriet Harman assured them that attendance for a preliminary interview would *not* be compulsory. Her successor, Alistair Darling, has different views. He announced in October 1998 that *all* benefit claimants of working age including lone parents and disabled people will be required to attend an interview at a job centre with a personal job adviser. He said that this was 'good news for those out of work who will be given better advice and opportunities to work. But bad news for those who abuse the system, and bad news for those who try to claim benefits they are not entitled to be on' (quoted in 'Reform to Curb Welfare Abuse', *The Independent,* 29 October 1998). It is clear that the government is giving priority to short-term intensive job search assistance rather than raising skill levels as far as lone mothers are concerned.

The House of Commons Education and Employment committee were critical:

> we heard powerful and convincing evidence that lone mothers and women returners saw education and training opportunities as a way of boosting confidence and upgrading their chance of finding rewarding and fulfilling jobs. Moreover with better qualifications lone mothers can find higher paid jobs and can more easily afford childcare. . . . To help lone parents into unrewarding, low paid employment with little or no skills development is not enough. (Education and Employment Committee, 1998, para. 1).

They had received evidence that currently 40 per cent of lone mothers between the ages of 20 and 40 years had no qualifications at all. The National Council for One Parent Families had told the Committee that 69 per cent of lone parents were concentrated in traditionally low paying jobs, many of them in the ten lowest paid occupations in the UK. The Committee drew this to the attention of Harriet Harman, then Secretary of State for Social Security. In reply she stressed the importance of 'making sure that children are not brought up in workless households, it is part of our programme for tackling social exclusion' (*ibid.*, Minutes of Evidence, Q. 198). She also made it clear that an initial aim was to increase lone parents economic activity rates to those of mothers with partners (*idem,* Q. 211), for these were higher even among the unqualified (see Table 2). The message to lone mothers seems to be that any job is better than providing full-time care for their own children at home.

The New Deal programme does not address the question of the availability and cost of childcare, except that it is anticipated that 50,000 young people in the programme will train as childcare workers and that some lone mothers might become childcare workers too. Under the national childcare strategy £260 million will be spent between 1999 and 2003 through the Out-of-School-Care Initiative and New Opportunities Fund. This is in addition to the £54 million spent on childcare provision during 1998–99 (Department for Education and Employment, press release, 1 June 1998). In 1998 there were 850,000 childcare places for the 5.1 million children aged under eight years in England (*idem*). As mothers with pre-school children are not required to participate in the programme, the question of the most expensive form of day care could be avoided. However, had the training and education of lone parents been a priority then some of the shortcomings of the national childcare strategy would have had to have been addressed.

The Further Education Student Support Advisory Group, also reporting in the summer of 1998, regretted that the Childcare Tax Credit (CTC) will not be available for a parent in full-time education needing childcare even if their partner is in employment and receiving the WFTC. 'We are concerned that the current and new government initiatives available will not provide the financial help needed to meet the costs incurred by people who need childcare but cannot afford to pay for it. Even the extra provision in FE will not necessarily be available for students free of charge' (Further Education Student Support Advisory Group, 1998, p23). Doubling access funds to £12 million plus an additional £1.5 million for the half of all further education colleges who have childcare facilities are welcome but very modest developments. Higher education is no better. The Dearing Committee reporting in 1997, although committed to lifelong learning, did not even have 'children' or 'childcare' in the index of their main report (National Committee of Inquiry into Higher Education, 1997). This was despite the evidence they received that the availability and cost of childcare was a major concern among mature students. Overall a commitment to raising the skills of lone mothers and investing in their human capital is not evident either in the New Deal for lone parents or in the national childcare strategy. It is considerably less than in the New Deal for young people. Is this because the latter includes a majority of actual or potential male breadwinners? Unemployment rates among young men are significantly higher than among young women (ONS, 1998a, pp87 and 89).

Once in employment, lone parents along with two-parent families will be eligible for the WFTC, which will replace FC in October 1999. All parents will gain from the increased child credit for children under eleven years old (increased to take account of the £2.50 increase made to child benefit in the 1998 Budget), the increase in the threshold from £79 to £90 a week before the credit starts to be withdrawn and the reduction in the taper from 70 to 55 per cent. If they use registered day care all, including the lowest earners who currently get nothing from the FC childcare disregard because they already get maximum FC, will gain from the CTC. The credit will be over 70 per cent of childcare costs of a maximum of £70 for one child and £150 for two. In his 1998 Pre-Budget Report, Gordon Brown announced that this credit will be extended to children up to age fourteen and, in the case of children with a disability, to sixteen.

The government estimates that by 2001 the WFTC will be reaching some 1.5 million families and costing £5 billion. This, together with the increase in child benefit, represents a significant redistribution of resources from childless couples who are losing their MCA to families with children, especially poorer families. Unlike FC, the WFTC will be administered by employers in the wage packet unless, in the case only of two parent families, they choose that the credit is paid like FC, directly to the caring parent. This is to meet the criticism that past and current research evidence show that money for children is most effectively used if given directly to the parent responsible for feeding and clothing them, i.e. in most cases the mother (Goode *et al.*, 1998). However, if most two-parent families continue to collect help with the cost of children via the benefit book and the purse, the objective of the WFTC, which is 'to make work pay' by making it clearer that low earners are better off in work than out of work, will be defeated. This is unlikely to happen, at least for long. First, the majority (95 per cent) of two-parent families on FC are currently dependent solely on a male breadwinner, so the bargaining position of the mother is weak relative to the father. Second, mothers who give up paid employment while the children are young (as the unskilled are likely to do) will have to convince their partners that it is worthwhile for them to return to work even if there is less money in his wage packet as a result. The Institute of Fiscal Studies (IFS) predicts that there will be 'significant incentives for second earners, mainly women, in couples to leave employment altogether. These effects are consistent with the government's statement that "the highest priority must be to get one member of workless households into work"' (Social Security Committee, 1998, appendix 6). The male breadwinner model is being reinstated among low wage earners. Their employers will have to pay a minimum wage but are not expected to pay a family wage. The poorly qualified, unskilled men, who have been disadvantaged by the structural changes in the labour market over recent decades, can after all contemplate settling down, having a 'traditional' family and becoming responsible citizens.

The implications for women are rather different. Mothers face a reduced choice of caring for their children full-time themselves once their children are school age unless they have a partner. Lone mothers must become breadwinners and, like men, rely on other poorly paid women to care for their children. Lone mothers claiming the WFTC will not be penalised if they refuse to name the father of their children, which is an advantage to those who fear the consequences of doing so but a disadvantage to those who may have to pay if they want the help of the CSA in getting maintenance from those fathers. Care provided within the family and home is no longer counted as work and a valuable contribution to society as it was in Beveridge's version of the male breadwinner model. In the revised model mothers are not even second-class citizens. Beveridge argued that wives and widows had claims on their husbands' state pensions because of their services as wives and mothers. This year the pension which widows can inherit from their husband's SERPS is halved as a result of the 1988 Social Security Act, and in the proposed stakeholder's pension men and women must save for their own pension. The carer's pension only includes mothers as carers until their youngest child is 5 years old. Under the 1975 Pension Act mothers were counted as carers until their child was 16 unless they earned enough to pay national insurance contributions. Under the pension-splitting reforms, however, divorced women will have greater claims on their husband's private or occupational pensions – if they have one. Altogether the stakeholder's and carer's pension scheme is estimated to cost £5 billion by 2030. However, by 2030 the government will be saving £3.5 billion a year because of raising women's pension age from 60 to 65 years (DSS, 1998c, ch. 6).

Another illustration of the devaluing of women as carers is that the CTC can only be used for formal childcare – which excludes family and friends, even if they are paid (as many are). They may register as childminders but care provided in the child's own home is also excluded. (If all informal carers registered the IFS estimate that the cost of the CTC would be £4 billion. The government are not expecting this and estimate that the CTC will cost £200 million in 2000–01 (Social Security Committee, 1998b, Q. 346 and Q. 351).) Yet familiarity with the carer and continuity of care are highly valued by mothers who share the care of their children with others. Registration is no guarantee of the quality of care provided, nor does it come with additional resources to ensure that childcare workers will be better trained and rewarded as the Social Security Committee noted (*ibid.*, Q. 340). Turnover is high in this rapidly expanding sector (estimated to include 400,000 workers in 1997) at the bottom end of the labour market. Other countries such as Australia and France have combined increasing support for parents with improved pay and conditions for childcare workers. In the UK, as the Assistant Director of the

Revenue and Personal Tax Division, responsible for the WFTC, told the Social Security Committee in October 1998, 'the childcare tax credit element is essentially looking at the demand side. It is providing demand for affordable childcare' (*ibid.*, Q. 338). The private market and voluntary sector are expected to supply the necessary places, with local authorities left to coordinate and regulate the provision.

The Green Paper *Supporting Families* makes much of encouraging family-friendly employment practices, but the proposed policies are modest. The implementation of the Part-time Work Directive in April 2000 will considerably reduce discrimination against part-time workers, 80 per cent of whom are women and many of whom have caring responsibilities. Aligning maternity leave and maternity pay to eighteen weeks still leaves a far less generous scheme than in the rest of the EU. The right to three months' unpaid parental leave is a timid step of little use to those who cannot afford to take it. Scandinavian experience shows that more pro-active policies are necessary if fathers are to become more involved with their young children. Similarly the right to take leave to look after a sick child or relative will be of less value to those who cannot afford to lose pay. Other EU countries introduced paid leave for this purpose twenty years ago. Recent research estimated that 30 per cent of lone mothers were prevented from working either because of their own or their child's ill health. If the children of lone mothers are less healthy for whatever reason, it is important that their mothers are given the resources to care for them.

The new Labour government has given more priority to families with children than previous Conservative governments and there has been a significant redistribution of resources from childless couples to poorer families. However, policies are based on a clear distinction between families with working parents and those entirely dependent on state benefits. Indeed, the stigma associated with the latter group is growing. The ambivalence towards mothers with young children taking paid employment, in particular full-time employment, which underpinned many social policies in the post-1945 welfare state has almost disappeared. The tax and social security systems have been reformed to assist mothers to behave more like fathers, i.e. as workers. However, in practice the WFTC may re-establish the male breadwinner model among poorer two-parent families and it is now clear that lone mothers should be in the labour market. There is very little support for fathers to become more involved in the care of the children, despite the rhetoric.

Overall genuinely family-friendly employment policies will only flourish in a culture which values the time, effort and skills spent on caring for the family as much as it values the activities associated with paid work. Sadly the current government's emphasis on work – *paid* work – as the only badge of citizenship which gives men and women claims on resources, is undermining moves towards family-friendly practices. It is not surprising that more young women are delaying having children or deciding to remain childless. Only 12 per cent of women born in the 1940s remained childless. This proportion is projected double for women born in 1972 (ONS, 1998b, p14). Tony Blair and his Cabinet colleagues recognise that the welfare state represents a contract between the generations. However, if the government is serious about establishing a contract which is fair to all citizens – young and old, men and women – the model of the family and the concept of work embedded in current social and economic policies will have to change and broaden.

References

Barnes, H., Day, P. & Cronin, N. (1998) *Trial and Error – a Review of UK Child Support Policy,* London, FPSC.

Department of Health (1998) *Meeting the Childcare Challenge,* Cm 3959, London, The Stationery Office.

DSS (1993) *The Growth in Social Security,* London, HMSO.

DSS (1996) *Social Security Department's Report, The Government's Expenditure Plans 1996/97 to 1998/99,* Cm 3213, London, HMSO.

DSS (1998a) *Children First. A New Approach to Child Support,* Cm 3992, London, The Stationery Office.

DSS (1998b) *Social Security Statistics 1997,* London, The Stationery Office.

DSS (1998c) *New Ambitions for Our Country: A New Contract for Welfare,* Cm 3805, London, The Stationery Office.

Education and Employment Committee (1998) *Pathways into Work for Lone Parents,* Seventh Report, HC 646, London, The Stationery Office.

Further Education Student Support Advisory Group (1998) *New Arrangements for Effective Student Support in Further Education,* London, Department for Education and Employment.

Goode, J., Callender, C. & Lister, R. (1998) *Purse or Wallet? Gender Inequalities and Income Distribution Within Families on Benefit,* London, PSI.

Home Office (1998) *Supporting Families,* Cm 3991, London, The Stationery Office.

Kiernan, K., Land, H. & Lewis, J. (1998) *Lone Mothers in Twentieth Century Britain,* Oxford, Oxford University Press.

Land, H. & Parker, R. (1978) 'The hidden dimensions of family policy', in S. Kammerman and A. Kahn (eds) *Family Policy in Fourteen Countries,* New York, Columbia University Press.

Lawson, N. (1992) *The View from Number Eleven,* London, Bantam Press.

National Committee of Inquiry into Higher Education (1997) *Higher Education in a Learning Society,* London, HMSO.

ONS (1998a) *Social Trends 28,* London, The Stationery Office.

ONS (1998b) *Population Trends,* Winter.

Social Security Committee (1998a) *Tax and Benefits: an Interim Report,* First Report, HC 283, London, The Stationery Office.

Social Security Committee (1998b) *Minutes of Evidence,* First Report, HC 29, London, The Stationery Office.

Treasury (1998) *Financial Statement and Budget Report,* HC 620, London, The Stationery Office.

8 Education Action Zones: emblems of the Third Way?

Sharon Gewirtz

The Education Action Zone (EAZ) policy was one of a range of initiatives introduced by New Labour in its first year of office to tackle the twin problems of 'underperforming schools' and 'social exclusion'. In September 1998, the first twelve EAZs began work, with thirteen commencing in January 1999 and a further tranche planned for 2000. Their brief is to raise standards, cut truancy, improve discipline and boost staying on rates in 'areas of social and economic disadvantage with poor educational achievement and expectations' (Labour Party, 1995). There is an expectation that EAZs 'will explicitly encourage innovation using the additional flexibility' they are being offered (Department for Education and Employment (DfEE), 1997a), which includes the opportunity for participating schools to opt out of the national agreement on teachers' pay and conditions. Each zone, made up of up to twenty schools, is to operate for three years, with the possibility of an extension to five. Zones are meant to be run by Education Action Fora (EAF) made up of 'local partners' - school governors, parents, businesses and community organisations. Funding is also based on the principle of 'partnership', with each zone receiving up to £1 million per year from a combination of state and private-sector sources.[1]

The amount of money being invested in EAZs is small in relation to the DfEE's overall budget for schools. Indeed, £1 million is substantially less than the annual budget for an average-sized secondary school, suggesting that the significance of the policy may well be more symbolic than substantive. Certainly, its proponents have suggested that EAZs symbolise something important. More specifically, they have been heralded as piloting new modes of educational association and governance - a 'Third Way' between the 'stifling statism' of old labour and the 'ruthless free-for-all' of the market (*Times Education Supplement,* 1998). Secretary of State for Education, David Blunkett, said, on announcing the successful bids for the first twenty-five EAZs, that 'This is the beginning of an entirely new way of delivering the education service. It is about partnership based on success rather than outdated dogma on either side' (Carvel, 1998a, p4). Stephen Byers - School Standards Minister at the time - was quoted as saying that 'The purpose of [EAZs] is that the Government believes that there is a third way in public services' (Hackett, 1998) and he described EAZs as forerunners for the future delivery of the public services in the next century. In a similar vein, Margaret Hodge, as Chair of the Commons Education and Employment Select Committee, argued that 'The development of the Third Way is perhaps best seen in the development of education action zones' (Hodge, 1998, p15). Meanwhile, DfEE officials described the initiative at its launch in 1998 as 'the centrepiece of Labour's modernisation agenda' (Carvel, 1998b).

In this paper, I take seriously some of these grand claims, arguing that the EAZ policy does indeed appear to be emblematic of New Labour's hitherto elusive 'Third Way' and that it therefore provides a valuable focal point for interrogating aspects of Third Way theory. The paper is in three parts. In the first part, I concep-tualise the EAZ initiative as an 'umbrella policy' encompassing a complex amalgam of strategies which, in a number of senses, can be seen to represent New Labour's approach to education and social policy as a whole. Next, I draw upon research into the impact of Conservative policy on schooling to speculate about possible tensions within the EAZ initiative. Finally, I use these speculations to raise questions about the desirability and viability of a Third Way for education.

Conceptualising EAZs as emblems of the Third Way

Whilst the Third Way (TTW) is a concept that has considerable interpretational elasticity - with rather different versions produced by Blair (1998), Giddens (1998), Le Grand (1998) and Kellner (1998a,b), amongst others (see also Chapters 1, 2 and 3 above) - what does seem to be agreed by its proponents is that it signifies a 'robust pragmatism', an openness to innovation and a commitment to 'what works' (Blair, 1998; Le Grand, 1998) rather than the 'outdated dogma' (Blunkett, cited in Carvel, 1998a) of the Old Left and the New Right. There is also an acceptance of what Giddens (1998, pp18-19) refers to as 'the central socialist value of social justice', although, according to Le Grand (1998, p27), 'it is not egalitarian . . . but it is the kind of social justice that relies on ensuring minimum standards and equality of opportunity rather than on redistribution and equality of outcome'. A popular cynical reading of TTW is that it represents an attempt on the part of New Labour politicians and fellow-traveller social theorists to somehow develop a coherent post-hoc theoretical justification for a rag-bag set of policies shaped more by electoral expedience than principle. It also might be suggested that TTW rests on stereotyped versions of the 'Old Left' and the 'New Right'. However, whether or not we instinctively believe TTW to be coherent, viable or desirable, or that the first and second ways ever really existed, the fact is that New Labour is in the process of developing and implementing a set of education and social policies which self consciously draw on a mixture of strategies associated with the very different traditions of Social Democracy and the New Right. The arguments presented in this paper are therefore based on the presumptions that: (a) TTW provides a convenient shorthand for characterising the eclectic and pragmatic mix of strategies which has come to represent New Labourism; and (b) however inchoate, TTW has become an influential normative theory of welfare reform which needs to be subjected to critical, 'grounded' examination.

Analysis of key documents (DfEE 1997a, 1998, 1999) and various declarations made by the architects of EAZs suggests that implicit within the policy are nine discrete strategies for tackling underperformance. Some of these represent consolidations, extensions or intensifications of policy trends set in train by Conservative administrations in the 1980s and 1990s which were inspired by New Right thinking, whilst others have more in common with ideas of Social Democracy. It is this apparently pragmatic fusion of strategies which characterises the policy as a possible exemplar of TTW.

I now want to identify the strategies and some of their key features, before going on to discuss possible tensions between them.

Marketisation

The EAZ policy does not explicitly contain within it provisions to extend the marketisation of education. The emphasis is on collaboration and partnership, not competition; consensus, not conflict; and on community not consumer accountability. However, closer scrutiny of New Labour policy suggests that there is, in fact, a consolidation of marketisation strategies. This is evidenced in the proposed extension of the Conservative-initiated scheme for the establishment of selective specialist schools which will, in effect, increase the market diversity available to (some) consumers - and, crucially, there is an expectation of a specialist school in every zone. Marketisation is also manifested in the primacy accorded to parental choice by New Labour's education policy architects, reflected in the ruling that primary schools cannot limit choice in their efforts to bring class sizes down to below thirty (Thornton, 1998). Moreover, the government has as yet left the Conservative's per capita funding formula intact, which means that school income will continue to be determined largely on the basis of market success. In addition, league tables of examination results have been retained, if in a revised 'performance-trends' format, with the consequence that parents are still being encouraged to choose schools on the basis of examination performance.

All of this means that the EAZ policy is operating in the context of a marketised education system in which schools continue to benefit according to how many and what type of students they attract, even though EAZ schools may gain some additional income via their participation in the scheme. Therefore, whilst marketisation is not a high-profile strategy, the market and the covert academic selection which goes with it (Gewirtz *et al.*, 1995; West *et al.*, 1997) are potentially influential forces in EAZs, and may sit uneasily alongside the policy's emphasis on cooperation, collaboration and redistribution.

Managerialisation

As a consequence of a range of Conservative education policies, the managerialist technologies of target-setting, performance monitoring, auditing and a whole repertoire of devices advocated by the school improvement and effectiveness lobby were enthusiastically taken on board by many head teachers. Whilst Clarke and Newman (1997, px) are right to point out that the impact of managerialisation is uneven, contested and messy, it is nevertheless the case that managerial technologies change what goes on in schools, producing 'a new grid of visibilities for the conduct of organisations and those who inhabit them' (Rose 1996, p55). To put it somewhat crudely, those activities that can be measured and which contribute to hegemonic constructions of success are valorised, whilst activities and students which do not contribute to league table or other public indicators of success are devalorised. However, until the 1997 Education Act,[2] passed just before the general election was called, such managerial devices were not an explicit part of the formal policy framework, but they had become part of the everyday lives of schools because of the pressures generated by exam league tables and Ofsted inspections. Other managerial strategies which prevailed under the Conservatives included a growth in the casualisation of teachers' work and the use of 'flexible' staffing strategies, to which special needs teachers were especially vulnerable (Gewirtz *et al.*, 1995), and the utilisation of the contract model for resource allocation, where schools who wished to gain extra funds could tender for technology college status.

New Labour's intention to consolidate and extend the formalisation of such strategies is marked by a range of developments but is particularly evident in the EAZ policy, which contains a number of managerialising elements. First, there is the use of the contract model, whereby local 'partnerships' have to tender for zone status. This represents a mechanism by which the government can ensure that funds are allocated to schools which appear to conform to centrally-approved ideas about what works best in education. Thus the documentation sent to bidders contains very explicit messages about what is expected. For example, zones are expected to 'build on national initiatives such as the literacy and numeracy hours', by, for instance, adapting the national curriculum to enable 'an extra focus on literacy and numeracy' (DfEE, 1997a, p8). Second, there is the further deregulation of teachers' labour, manifested in the call for zones to put forward proposals for innovative staffing contracts and a flexibilisation of teachers' work. Third, the EAZ policy actively promotes performance monitoring, target-setting and action plans which, like the contract model, make it possible for the government to try and ensure that participating schools implement government-set goals for education - for example 'improvement in National Curriculum statutory assessments . . . improved attendance, higher rates of recruitment and retention of teachers and headteachers, reduced exclusions or better progression from school to work' (DfEE, 1997a, p3).

Finally, there is the emphasis on 'value for money' which the 'Guidance notes' stated would be one of the criteria used in assessing the quality of applications (DfEE, 1998, p4). This is part of what Rose (1996, p55) has referred to as 'budgetization', a technology of government which 'transforms the activity of the budget holder . . . providing new ways of ensuring the responsibility and fidelity of agents who remain formal[ly] autonomous'.

Privatisation

I am not referring here to the wholesale privatisation of education. Rather, I am using the term to signify processes by which the private sector is enabled to take on a more extensive role in the funding and running of schools. The EAZ policy is a privatisation strategy insofar as it has been designed to extend what are referred to as partnerships between the public and private sectors. More specifically, there is an expectation that the private sector will sponsor and have 'a central role' in the running of zones. Public-private partnerships are not new in education. A number of Conservative initiatives developed these in a variety of ways. For example: the expectation that schools would co-opt individuals with business interests onto their governing bodies; the 'outsourcing' of various services ranging from school cleaning and catering to teacher supply; the steady growth in the number of Private Finance Initiatives in education; and the City Technology Colleges (CTCs) initiative within which businesses contributed to the start-up costs of schools and in return were given a significant role in running them. However, what is different about the public-private partnership envisaged within the EAZ policy is the opportunity it gives for private companies to run groups of schools 'outside the normal framework of municipal control' (Carvel, 1998c, p2) and possibly make a profit from doing so. As it turns out, it looks as if, of the first twenty-five zones, the day-to-day running of only one, Lambeth, will be managed by a private company. However, the use of a private firm to manage only one zone in the first tranche may make the privatisation of local school provision more widely acceptable and thus play an important legitimating role.

Traditionalism

EAZs are being established against a background of government support for more traditional pedagogical practices. For example, New Labour believes that 'setting [i.e. grouping of students by ability] should be the norm in secondary schools' and that 'it is worth considering in primary schools' (DfEE, 1997b, p38). Again this strategy is not peculiar to New Labour. Conservative policies of national testing, league tables, the reduction of continuous assessment at GCSE level and the establishment of a new inspection regime combined to encourage conservative pedagogies in schools, but the Conservative government apparently did not see a need to intervene directly to shape schools' pedagogic strategies. New Labour has taken that step, by introducing the highly prescriptive literacy and numeracy hours in primary schools and slimming down the primary curriculum so there is more time to focus on 'the basics'. Schools in EAZs are allowed to adapt the national curriculum to provide an extra focus on literacy and numeracy. These policies are based on an acceptance of what some academics (e.g. Atkin and Black, 1997) have suggested are spurious international surveys carried out by school effectiveness and improvement researchers.

Experimentation

Somewhat paradoxically, alongside its claimed preference for traditional teaching methods, New Labour, via its EAZ policy, has expressed a formal commitment to experimentation in education. Like the Conservative government's CTCs, EAZs are ostensibly designed to develop innovative approaches to the problem of educational underperformance in disadvantaged areas. In practice, given the DfEE's expectation that primary schools will prioritise basic skills and that secondaries will develop work-related curricula (DfEE, 1997a), it is questionable how much genuine experimentation there is likely to be in EAZs. However, as I discuss below, innovation as a discourse can be viewed as an additional managerialist strategy which may have a powerful disciplinary effect on schools.

Redistribution

Under the Conservatives, redistribution was not a prominent discourse. However, significant redistributions did occur - mainly via the market and grant-maintained schools mechanisms - which tended to favour the most advantaged students and discriminate against working-class and minority-ethnic families (Gewirtz *et al.*, 1995). When the Conservatives did channel extra resources into disadvantaged areas through the CTC and technology college status initiatives, the additional funds went to individual schools rather than groups of schools, and these schools were able to use selection by 'aptitude' to produce relatively advantaged intakes (Whitty *et al.*, 1993). In contrast, EAZs are designed to channel extra resources into whole 'areas of relative disadvantage' (DfEE, 1998, p2).

However, the EAZ initiative does not appear to be a straight-forwardly redistributive policy of the old (ideal typical) Beveridgean kind, that is, a redistribution based purely on need. Rather, it looks like EAZs will produce what might be termed a 'managerialised redistribution' in that money is being allocated not solely on the basis of any objective criterion of disadvantage, like that used by the Inner London Education Authority to allocate resources to Education Priority Areas in the 1960s (Plewis, 1998), but using a range of criteria (DfEE, 1998, p3-4), including 'how the proposals are likely to contribute to improved teaching and learning . . .; how they address barriers such as truancy, exclusions and poor expectations . . .'; and 'the strength of the partnership proposed'. In particular, there needs to be 'a central role for business' both in running the zone and in helping students move from education into training and work.

It is also possible that the perpetuation of markets and the managerial emphasis on outputs and outcomes will provide an incentive for EAZ schools to become selective - either overtly, by attaining specialist school status, or by more covert means - and as a result take the more advantaged children from the local area.

Integration of traditionally distinct welfare domains

Although David Blunkett and his advisers have in various pronouncements tended to dismiss those who argue that the best way to improve schools is to tackle poverty (e.g. Barber, 1996), the EAZ initiative appears to be based upon a belief that education underperformance needs to be dealt with in conjunction with the amelioration of other forms of disadvantage. Hence the DfEE encouraged those proposing to set up EAZs to draw in agencies and charities involved in health, social care and crime prevention, and develop links to other strategies - e.g. Health Action Zones, Employment Zones and projects funded through the Single Regeneration Budget. This emphasis on cross-welfare links, or to use New Labour parlance, 'joined-up government' (Social Exclusion Unit, 1998), suggests an implicit recognition that disadvantage has multiple causes and that 'tackling it requires strategies that bring together agencies that more usually work in isolation' (Whitty, 1998, p5). This implicit focus on the structural causes of educational underachievement marks a significant departure from Conservative policy, which was based on the belief that there was in fact 'no such thing as society' and stressed instead individual and institutional responsibility for school improvement. However, there are doubts about how effective strategies of welfare integration can be when they are not supported by substantial material investment, for recognising that educational achievement can be raised by tackling unemployment and improving health and housing provision involves significant financial investment in employment creation, health and housing, in addition to better coordination between service providers (Cochrane, forthcoming).

Responsibilisation

I am referring here to strategies designed to inculcate a culture of self-discipline or self-surveillance amongst welfare subjects. Responsibilisation is a process by which individuals (or collectivities) are 'offered' 'active involvement in action to resolve the kind of issues hitherto held to be the responsibility of authorized governmental agencies' (Rose, 1996, p29). Like marketisation and managerialisation, responsibilisation is not new, but it appears to be a strategy that is being pursued more vigorously by New Labour than their Conservative predecessors. Under the Conservatives, discourses of individual responsibilisation were particularly evident in the *Parents' Charter* (Department of Education and Science (DES), 1991; Department for Education (DfE), 1994a), in the government's approach to 'Pupils with Problems' (DfE, 1994b; Evans and Vincent, 1997) and in the increased use of home-school contracts. However, New Labour plans to extend responsibilisation in education by making home-school contracts compulsory, centrally dictating and placing on the statute books the amount of time students are expected to spend on homework and setting up 'family learning schemes'. New Labour's 1997 White Paper on education states that 'family learning'

> is a powerful tool for reaching some of the most disadvantaged in our society. It has the potential to reinforce the role of the family and change attitudes to education, helping build strong local communities and widening participation in learning. (DfEE, 1997b, p53)

These sentiments are echoed in the DfEE's (1997a, 1999) literature on EAZs. Whilst some parents might feel supported by such strategies, and whilst 'family learning' initiatives may help raise literacy levels in schools, the emphasis on parental responsibility also has the potential to be used as a mechanism for pathologising parents, particularly working-class parents - because it is only in relation to 'the disadvantaged' that the need for 'family learning' is discussed within New Labour discourse. In this sense, discourses of responsibilisation have much in common with the thesis of cultural deprivation - popularised by the publication in 1962 in America of Riesman's *The Culturally Deprived Child* and accepted by the Plowden Report (Central Advisory Council for Education, 1967) - which held that low attainment of working-class children was the result of cognitive, linguistic and/or motivational defects rooted in culturally deficient socialisation in the home. The thesis of cultural deprivation was criticised for effectively laying the blame for inequalities in educational outcomes on the losers in the system and ignoring the ways in which the structure and culture of provision produce differential educational outcomes. Parallel concerns could be attached to strategies of responsibilisation - although the redistributional and welfare-integrational aspects of the EAZ policy, discussed above, do appear to indicate that its architects do not hold those schools and individuals deemed to be poor educational performers *entirely* responsible for their own 'failures'.

Associationalisation

I use this somewhat awkward term to refer to attempts to facilitate new forms of civic association and collective responsibility, influenced by some of the communitarian ideas of writers like Putnam (1993) and Etzioni (1996). In these writings, communitarianism and associated narratives, like social capital formation and mutuality, are presented as antidotes to the socially destructive nature of rampant neo-liberalism, on the one hand, and 'the dependency culture' produced by excessive collectivism on the other. Within these variants of communitarian thinking, associationalisation goes hand-in-hand with responsibilisation and redistribution. If we want to build a society that is rich in 'social capital', so the argument goes, then we all need to live 'responsibly', ensure that our children do not grow up in poverty and develop relations of mutuality within 'a thriving civil society - from networks of neighbourhoods to extended families, community groups to religious organisations, local businesses to local public services, youth clubs to parent-teacher associations, playgroups to police on the beat' (Commission on Social Justice, 1994, pp308-309). Within this context, the establishment of EAF involving a range of groups, including parents, educators, other welfare providers and businesses, can be viewed as an attempt to create new forms of active citizenship and thus help build social capital.

This associationalising strategy represents a marked shift from Conservative policy, which eschewed a collective approach to the running of schools, preferring to emphasise consumerism, competition and devolved management. However, there are notable exclusions from the list of groups which the DfEE would like to see represented on EAF, namely teacher associations and unions. Presumably this is a deliberate omission, for such groups are seen by New Labour's policy architects, like the former Education Minister, Stephen Byers, to epitomise the very 'vested interests [which] for too long held back our school system' (Carvel, 1998a).

Tensions and contradictions

This brief account of the various strategies incorporated within the EAZ policy has highlighted the apparently eclectic and pragmatic nature of educational New Labourism. The education market introduced by the Conservatives is being perpetuated and is likely to remain a potent force, continuing to shape the activities of schools; New Labour is experimenting with new forms of privatisation; and strategies of managerialisation, responsibilisation and pedagogic traditionalism are being employed perhaps more stridently, or at least more explicitly, than was the case under the Conservatives. But alongside these neo-liberal and neo-conservative devices, we are also seeing the adoption of strategies, like redistribution and welfare integration, which have a more Social Democratic or possibly, in the case of associationalisation, Christian Democratic feel to them. From my description of these strategies, some tensions and contradictions within the EAZ policy, and educational New Labourism more generally, will already be apparent. In this section I want to draw attention to and examine some of these, focusing on three sets of tensions.

Experimentation vs. marketisation, managerialisation and traditionalism

First, there is a set of tensions between the expectation that EAZs will be test beds of innovation and the continued, and intensified, use of strategies of marketisation and managerialisation operating within a discursive context which constructs pedagogic traditionalism as desirable. A number of studies of the Conservative education reforms of the 1980s and 1990s indicated that, in general, markets and managerialism discourage pedagogic and curriculum innovation (Gewirtz *et al.*, 1995; Halpin *et al.*, 1997; Woods *et al.*, 1998). Although we cannot predict precisely what effects the triad of markets, managerialism and discourses of traditionalism will have in EAZs, since much will depend on local contingencies and the particular responses of individual actors, we can speculate on the basis of what we already know about what these technologies do to schools.

I want to deal with the possible effects of the market first. Schools in EAZs are likely to still want to be successful in market terms and, therefore, to maximise their league table perfor-mances. In areas where there is a socio-economic mix, and some of the zones will be located in such areas, the most cost-effective way for schools to do this is to attract middle-class students who are likely to attain higher marks with minimal investment. Because head teachers tend to believe that most middle-class parents are pedagogically conservative (Gewirtz *et al.*, 1995), schools in mixed-class areas may be reluctant to innovate. Conversely, schools positioned low down in the league tables and serving exclusively working-class constituencies deemed unlikely ever to produce high test scores may feel they have nothing to lose by attempting to improve attendance and attainment through more experimental approaches to the curriculum and its mode of delivery. However, if such schools want to innovate in collabo-rative ways with other schools, they will have to overcome the divisions and conflicts which markets can produce at a local level

(Macbeth *et al.*, 1995; Bridges and Husbands, 1996; Gewirtz, 1997a).

It is not just the market which can inhibit genuine pedagogic experimentation. The various managerialising strategies currently in play are designed to ensure that school processes are geared to performance indicators set by central government. Whilst, in theory, genuinely innovative pedagogical practices have the potential to raise test scores and thus contribute to schools reaching their targets, in practice the culture of 'performativity' (Lyotard 1984) is more likely to inhibit authentic innovation.

First, performance monitoring tends to narrow the scope of valued activity in schools, producing an emphasis on the instrumental and academic aspects of schooling at the expense of the expressive and the social (Gewirtz *et al.*, 1995). Yet if EAZ schools are to be test beds of innovation, one would expect them to attend to the expressive and social as well as the academic and cognitive. In addition, target-setting provides no encouragement for teachers to focus on those students who are far from achieving the level which the targets relate to (Gewirtz *et al.*, 1995; Plewis, 1998; Gillborn and Youdell, forthcoming). If the EAZ policy is to produce authentically innovative solutions to educational underperformance, one would expect schools to focus on the lowest-attaining students. Given the short time scale of the EAZ experiment, we may see an exacerbation of these effects: genuine innovation involves taking risks and schools may not feel that three years is enough time to take risks. Traditional methods may be viewed as a safer bet, even though they may be less effective at motivating the lowest-attaining students.

Second, managerial practices can discourage innovation because they tend to limit the scope for participative decision making and autonomous teacher activity. Because teachers have to conform to narrow goals set by the state, their work comes to be governed by a technical or instrumental rather than a substantive rationality (Robertson, 1996; Smyth and Shacklock, 1998).

Third, excessive performance monitoring can produce competition within schools which discourages forms of interdisciplinary collaboration conducive to innovation (Gewirtz, 1997b). Moreover, all of these things can combine to sap teachers' morale and generate stress which is unconducive to the development of genuinely innovative practices. About half of the first twenty-five zones were reported to be planning to employ Advanced Skills Teachers.[3] It will be interesting to see to what extent this will relieve teacher stress and raise morale, and the extent to which the new grade will breed conflict and resentment, creating more stress and an accompanying decline in morale.

Finally, there are already indications that the contract model of resource allocation has acted to inhibit innovation (Rafferty, 1998), possibly because the DfEE's literature for potential bidders placed a great emphasis on literacy, numeracy and the fact that zones would get priority access to funds tied to existing DfEE initiatives. Contenders for zone status may therefore have felt reluctant to deviate from what appeared to be expected of them by a government which has been strident in its advocacy of traditional approaches to teaching. There are, nevertheless, indications of plans for innovative practices in some of the successful bids. However, the extent to which these will be successfully translated into practice, given the barriers of markets and managerialism, will need to be subjected to empirical scrutiny. Furthermore, it will be necessary to monitor the extent to which some of the so-called innovations may actually turn out to represent a return to older vocationalised ways of doing things (Socialist Teachers Alliance, 1998).

However, it is possible that whilst EAZs may not result in much authentic innovation, the *discourse of innovation* - within which experimentation is compulsory, expected to be perpetual and intended to meet tightly specified objectives - may produce a different kind of effect in EAZ schools. The expectation of permanent innovation is likely to constitute an additional pressure on school personnel which, like budgetisation, has the powerful disciplinary potential 'to act upon the personal capacities of subjects, channelling the conduct of individuals into certain patterns' (du Gay, 1996, p138). Innovation may thus turn out to be one of a number of discourses through which new managerial subjects in schools are coming to be constituted and imagined. It is through such managerial discourses that '"administrators", "public servants" and "practitioners" come to see themselves as "business managers", "purchasers", "contractors", "strategists", "leaders"' (Clarke and Newman, 1997, p92) - and innovators.

Associationalisation vs. privatisation, responsibilisation, marketisation and managerialisation

The second set of tensions I want to address lie between the privatising, responsibilising, marketising and managerialising elements of the policy, on the one hand, and the association-alising ones on the other.

First, the emphasis on public-private partnerships sits somewhat uneasily alongside claims that EAF could prefigure a revivified civil society within which parents and other community members are 'empowered' to take more control of local services (Halpin, 1999). It is questionable, where private companies are involved, how far they are likely to want to cede control to parents and other community groups in any meaningful way where this might conflict with their own commercial interests. The cosy rhetoric of social capital theory may therefore gloss over deep-seated and irresolvable conflicts amongst the so-called partners who are meant to be associating together.

Moreover, practices designed to promote social capital have the potential to exclude as well as include (Campbell, 1995; Hughes and Mooney, 1998). In the case of EAZs, exclusions may be manufactured in a number of ways. I have already alluded to the exclusion of teacher unions from the DfEE's list of recommended members for EAF. Presumably, this is, at least in part, because they would oppose the abolition of national pay and conditions for teachers.[4] But, if private companies are not only included but given a central role in the running of zones, there will be additional voices and interests who are excluded or at least marginalised: for example, teachers opposed to a further intensi-fication of their work and the loss of autonomy associated with managerialisation; parents opposed to sponsoring companies directing advertising at their children who are effectively a captive audience when at school; those opposed to the ethical practices of some of the companies involved (for example, the lead sponsor in Lambeth is Shell); and those opposed to any involvement of private companies in the provision of education.

Yet, if zones are to be effective in combating social exclusion, they will need to draw in groups who are traditionally margin-alised by the school system. Whilst strategies of responsibilisation, like family literacy or intergenerational learning schemes, may have the potential to facilitate perceptions of inclusivity amongst members of traditionally marginalised groups whilst boosting their literacy skills, these strategies also have the potential to make people feel they are being constructed as a problem, hence exacerbating their perceptions of marginality. Much depends on how such policies are enacted on the ground. Thus there is a need to attend to the nature and patterns of the inclusions and exclusions - in terms of class, ethnicity and gender - which may be constitutive of and constructed by the associationalising and responsibilising processes involved in the development of EAZs.

It would also seem that markets and managerialisation are unconducive to associationalisation. Authentic associativeness rests on members of the association having a relatively high degree of decision-making autonomy. Yet managerialisation limits the capacity of those involved in the running of schools to make decisions about what Susan Robertson has referred to as:

the big ticket items such as: What is it that we want children to know? How do we provide opportunities for students to genuinely participate in the learning process? What does it mean to educate a critical citizenry? (Robertson, 1996, pp43-44)

Moreover, in a market context, parents are constructed as consumers. This does not seem to be easily compatible with the partnership role for parents which would be an essential component of authentic associationalisation. A meaningful partnership between parents and other EAF members will depend on parents being able to trust these other members. Yet the market creates an incentive for schools and their business sponsors to manipulate information, rather than genuinely inform parents and children (Gewirtz et al., 1995, p136). This means that, however open head teachers and business representatives are, in a market situation parents can never be entirely confident that they are not being deceived by service providers keen to retain their custom.

Redistribution vs. marketisation and managerialisation

There are a number of reasons why we may have to be sceptical about how extensively redistributive the EAZ policy will be. First, there is the question of the amount of money being awarded, which Plewis (1998) has described as 'minuscule', with the funds for each zone amounting to 'just 0.06 per cent of total current expenditure' on education:

> Bearing in mind recent estimates which suggest that a third of all children live in poverty, then even if all the pupils living in EAZs were living in poverty (which they won't be), only a small proportion of poor children will benefit from any extra resources. On this basis, it is difficult to see how the introduction of a small number of less than generously funded EAZs can have much effect either on standards or on educational inequalities.

But aside from the relatively limited quantity of funds being allocated, there are other aspects of the policy which may compromise its redistributive potential.

Markets in mixed-class and multi-ethnic areas, within which students are allocated to schools by methods other than random selection, have the potential to exacerbate inequalities of access and heighten polarisation on the basis of class, gender and ethnicity. Polarisation is produced by a combination of how parents choose schools and schools' selective and exclusionary practices. More specifically, many parents make choices on the basis of what they believe to be the class and ethnic composition of schools (Gewirtz et al., 1995; Bagley, 1996; Noden et al., 1997), and, in a market situation, oversubscribed schools tend to displace responsibility for those children deemed to be low attainers or badly behaved to schools with few resources to cater for them effectively. In addition, the compound effects of various forms of racism mean that some groups of minority-ethnic children are more likely to be represented in under-resourced and/or non-selective schools.

Given the continued existence of markets, it is difficult to see how EAZs will be able to interrupt these processes of polarisation. Most EAZ schools are likely to be initially undersubscribed, predominantly working class, with disproportionate numbers of children from ethnic minorities, and unpopular with middle-class families. In addition, the acquisition of zone status may have a stigmatising effect on schools, further inhibiting applications from middle-class families. Such schools are typically caught up in a vicious circle - they find it difficult to improve their raw examination scores without first attracting more middle-class children but are unable to attract more middle-class children without first improving their examination results.

However, it may be that some EAZ schools are able to break this circle, perhaps by becoming specialist schools. Using their newly acquired designation as specialist EAZ schools, and the additional resources attached to specialisation and participation in an action zone, such schools might, through hard work and skill, succeed in improving their image amongst local middle-class families. In this way they might attract more middle-class children, thereby increasing their per-capita-based funding and embarking on a spiral of 'improvement'. But this kind of development could not be read as a simple redistribution in favour of the least advantaged schools. Those higher-attaining, middle-class students newly selected for such schools would have to come from other local schools, possibly outside the zones, and these schools may as a result embark upon their own spiral of decline and have to accept the 'less desirable' excluded students from the now-popular EAZ schools. It is also quite possible that the extra resourcing for EAZ schools and any extra money being offered to teachers working in them will exacerbate teacher, as well as student, recruitment difficulties in neighbouring, non-zone schools, thereby lowering morale and the quality of provision in these schools.

Thus, whilst the EAZ policy might result in a redistribution of resources which may favour some EAZ schools, overall, what we might see if we look at local education systems as a whole is a perpetuation of polarisation, with middle-class, mainly white students benefiting from the redistribution at the expense of their working-class and minority-ethnic counterparts.

It will also be important to monitor processes of differentiation and polarisation by class, gender and ethnicity within EAZ schools. As I have already argued, managerial practices like target-setting tend to lead teachers to focus on those students just below the required level. In addition, traditional pedagogical practices like setting and whole-class teaching, which are central features of the literacy and numeracy hours being promoted by the DfEE, also have the potential to disadvantage students deemed to be 'less able' and, in the case of setting, students from minority-ethnic families (Gillborn and Youdell, forthcoming).

Conclusions

One of the most crucial weaknesses of Third Way theory is that the strategies of reform which TTW is seen to comprise are commonly discussed in fairly decontextualised and compartmentalised ways. Thus, for instance, Le Grand (1998) argues that TTW, as manifested in New Labour policy, is characterised by four values - community, opportunity, responsibility and accountability. Although he acknowledges potential tensions between these values - particularly 'between encouraging freedom of action by communities and the centralisation that may result from vigorously holding them to account' (1998, p27) - Le Grand appears to dismiss these as relatively inconsequential, and instead prefers to emphasise consistencies. In a similar vein, Giddens claims that TTW accepts the central socialist value of social justice but rejects the widespread direct payment of benefits. He avoids the thorny question of how, in practice, the two positions can be pursued simultaneously, by simply stating that 'Of course reforming the welfare state in the real world is a messy and difficult business'. 'How to cope with rising inequality' is conveniently included in a long list of 'fundamental issues' that Giddens has not had space to discuss, but upon which, he assures us, 'there can be a clear route separating the new politics from the two alternative positions' (Giddens, 1998, p21).

What the inherent tensions discussed in this paper point to is that, rather than the abstract, compartmentalised theorisation that is typical of the TTW genre, there is a need for a grounded consideration of the lived consequences of the combined effects of the range of reform strategies which characterise the eclecticism and pragmatism of contemporary social policy. To use Giddens' phraseology, there is a need for an examination of the 'messy' complexity of welfare state reforms in 'the real world'.

What I have tried to do here, by focusing on the EAZ policy, is to indicate how the tensions between the various strands identified as constituting TTW might be played out at 'street level'.

The most positive dimensions of the EAZ policy mix are its redistributional and 'welfare-integrational' aspects. These appear to indicate a recognition that educational underperformance has structural causes. This represents a significant shift from the denial of any association between poverty and poor educational attainment which underpinned the Conservative educational reforms of the 1980s and 1990s. And it is also a welcome development within educational New Labourism, whose advocates in the past have tended to deride, as perpetrators of an 'excuse culture', those who argue that the best way to raise educational performance is to tackle poverty. However, as I have argued in the paper, the extent of actual redistribution looks limited, and the history of British urban policy (Higgins *et al.*, 1983; Cochrane, forthcoming) tells us that, without substantial material investment, better coordination between welfare sectors is unlikely to lead to any significant improvement in opportunities for the most disadvantaged sections of society.

A more fundamental problem with the EAZ policy mix is that social justice, redistribution, pedagogic innovation and a revivified civil society are, in practice, most probably incompatible with a perpetuation of markets, managerialism and privatisation. Markets, managerialism and privatisation may inhibit authentic innovation, will almost inevitably foster redistributions in favour of the most advantaged, and are likely to produce exclusions and circumscribe institutional and individual autonomy over many of the things that matter. Thus, whilst the pragmatism and eclecticism of TTW may sound attractive in theory, in practice particular strands of Third Way-ism are likely to dominate and prevent the realisation of others. I would suggest, therefore, that as long as markets, managerialism and privatisation remain significant forces in education, the likelihood of an inclusive education system and any authentic redistribution, associationalisation or pedagogic innovation emerging will be extremely remote if not impossible. In effect, it may be very difficult to see much difference between the New Right way and the so-called Third Way.

Acknowledgements

I am grateful to John Clarke, Hartley Dean and Roberta Woods for their detailed and very helpful comments on an earlier draft of this paper.

Notes

1 For the first round of zones, DfEE (1998) stipulated that half of the funding should come from the private sector. For the second round, DfEE (1999) guaranteed £500,000 per zone per annum, with an additional £250,000 available to match private sector funding, pound for pound. Private sector funding can include 'benefits in kind'.

2 Under the 1997 Act each governing body is required to set performance targets for its pupils in all public examinations and key stage assessments and make them public.

3 A new grade designed to provide a financial incentive for talented teachers to stay in the classroom rather than take up management posts.

4 Of the first twenty-five zones, eleven were reported to be considering disapplying the Teachers' Pay and Conditions Order.

References

Atkin, J. M. & Black, P. (1997) 'Policy perils of international comparisons; the TIMMS case', *Phi Delta Kappan*, vol. 79, no. 1, pp22-28.

Bagley, C. (1996) 'Black and white unite or fight', *British Educational Research Journal*, vol. 22, no. 5, pp569-80.

Barber, M. (1996) *The Learning Game: Arguments for an Education Revolution*, London, Victor Gollanz.

Blair, T. (1998) *The Third Way: New Politics for the New Century*, London, The Fabian Society.

Bridges, D. & Husbands, C. (eds) (1996) *Consorting and Collaborating in the Education Market Place*, London, Falmer Press.

Campbell, B. (1995) 'Old fogeys and angry young men: a critique of communitarianism', *Soundings*, issue 1, Autumn.

Carvel, J. (1998a) 'Schools to be given radical overhaul', *Guardian*, 24 June.

Carvel, J. (1998b) 'Labour revolt on private schools plan', *Guardian*, 7 January.

Carvel, J. (1998c) 'First signposts to the third way', *Guardian*, 5 May.

Central Advisory Council for Education (England) (1967) *Children and their Primary Schools*, The Plowden Report, London, HMSO.

Clarke, J. & Newman, J. (1997) *The Managerial State*, London, SAGE.

Cochrane, A. (forthcoming) 'Just another failed urban experiment? The legacy of urban development corporations', in R. Imrie & H. Thomas (eds) *British Urban Policy and Urban Development Corporations*, 2nd edn, London, Paul Chapman.

Commission on Social Justice (1994) *Social Justice: Strategies for National Renewal*, London, Vintage.

DES (1991) *The Parent's Charter: You and Your Child's Education*, London, HMSO.

DfE (1994a) *Our Children's Education: The Up-dated Parent's Charter,* London, HMSO.

DfE (1994b) *Pupils with Problems,* London, HMSO.

DfEE (1997a) *Education Action Zones: An Introduction,* London, DfEE.

DfEE (1997b) *Excellence in Schools,* London, The Stationery Office.

DfEE (1998) *Guidance on Completing the Form,* London, DfEE.

DfEE (1999) *Meet the Challenge: Education Action Zones,* London, DfEE.

du Gay (1996) *Consumption and Identity at Work,* London, SAGE.

Etzioni, A. (1996) 'The responsive community: a communitarian perspective', *American Sociological Review,* vol. 61, February, pp1-11.

Evans, J. & Vincent, C. (1997) 'Parental choice and special education', in R. Glatter, P. Woods & C. Bagley (eds) *Choice and Diversity in Schooling: Perspectives and Prospects,* London, Routledge.

Gewirtz, S. (1997a) 'The education market, labour relations in schools and teacher unionism in the UK', in R. Glatter, P. Woods & C. Bagley (eds) *Choice and Diversity in Schooling: Perspectives and Prospects,* London, Routledge.

Gewirtz, S. (1997b) 'Post-welfarism and the reconstruction of teachers' work in the UK', *Journal of Education Policy,* vol. 12, no. 4, pp217-231.

Gewirtz, S., Ball, S. J. & Bowe, R. (1995) *Markets, Choice and Equity in Education,* Buckingham, Open University Press.

Giddens, A. (1998) 'After the left's paralysis', *New Statesman,* 1 May.

Gillborn, D. & Youdell, D. (forthcoming) *Rationing Education* (working title), Buckingham, Open University Press.

Hackett (1998) 'Historic ideology seeks a third way', *Times Educational Supplement,* 24 April.

Halpin, D. (1999) 'Investing in social capital: EAZs and the renewal of civil society', lecture given at the Education Action Zones Invitational Seminar, National Union of Teachers, Hamilton House, London, 28 January.

Halpin, D., Power, S. & Fitz, J. (1997) 'Opting into the past? Grant-maintained schools and the reinvention of tradition', in R. Glatter, P. Woods & C. Bagley (eds) *Choice and Diversity in Schooling: Perspectives and Prospects,* London, Routledge.

Higgins, J., Deakin, N., Edwards, J. & Wicks, M. (1983) *Government and Urban Policy. Inside the Policy-making Process,* Oxford, Blackwell.

Hodge, M. (1998) 'A pragmatic ideology', *Times Educational Supplement,* 12 June.

Hughes, G. & Mooney, G. (1998) 'Community', in G. Hughes (ed.) *Imagining Welfare Futures,* London, Routledge.

Kellner, P. (1998a) 'A new "ism" for our times', *New Stateman,* 22 May.

Kellner, P. (1998b) 'Our mutual friends', *Times Educational Supplement,* 19 June.

Labour Party (1995) *Excellence for Everyone: Labour's Crusade to Raise Standards,* London, Labour Party.

Le Grand, J. (1998) 'The Third Way begins with Cora', *New Statesman*, 6 March.

Lyotard, J-F (1984) *The Postmodern Condition*, trans. G. Bennington & G. Massumi, Minneapolis, MN, University of Minnesota Press.

Macbeth, A., McReath, D. & Aitchison, J. (eds) (1995) *Collaborate or Compete? Educational Partnerships in a Market Economy*, London, Falmer Press.

Noden, P., West, A. & David, M. (1997) 'You can't always get what you want - choices and destinations at the transfer to secondary schools in London', paper presented to the Parental Choice and Market Forces Seminar, King's College London, 10 February.

Plewis, I. (1998) 'Inequalities, targets and Education Action Zones', *New Economy*, vol. 5.

Putnam, R. (1993) 'The prosperous community: social capital and public life', *The American Prospect*, vol. 13, Spring.

Rafferty, F. (1998) 'Action zone bids "not sexy enough"', *Times Educational Supplement*, 5 June.

Robertson, S. (1996) 'Teachers' work, restructuring and postfordism: constructing the new "professionalism"', in I. Goodson & A. Hargreaves (eds) *Teachers' Professional Lives*, London, Falmer Press.

Rose, N. (1996) 'Governing "advanced" liberal democracies', in A. Barry, T. Osborne & N. Rose (eds) *Foucault and Political Reason: Liberalism, Neo-liberalism and Rationalities of Government*, London, UCL Press.

Smyth, J. & Shacklock, G. (1998) *Re-Making Teaching*, London, Routledge.

Social Exclusion Unit (1998) *Truancy and School Exclusion*, London, The Stationery Office.

Socialist Teachers Alliance (1998) *Trojan Horses: Education Action Zones: The Case against the Privatisation of Education*, London, Socialist Teachers Alliance.

Times Educational Supplement (1998) 'The third way emerges', *Times Educational Supplement*, 20 March.

Thornton, K. (1998) 'Class size cannot limit choice, ministers warn', *Times Educational Supplement*, 12 June.

West, A., Pennell, H. & Noden, P. (1997) *Admissions to Secondary School: Changing Policy and Practice*, London, Centre for Educational Research, London School of Economics and Political Science.

Whitty, G. (1998) 'New Labour, education and disadvantage', lecture given at Department of Applied Social Studies and Social Research, University of Oxford, 24 February.

Whitty, G., Edwards, T. & Gewirtz, S. (1993) *Specialisation and Choice in Urban Education: the City Technology College Experiment*, London, Routledge.

Woods, P., Bagley, C. & Glatter, R. (1998) *School Choice and Competition: Markets in the Public Interest?* Buckingham, Open University Press.

9 Making the market work? New Labour and the housing question

Peter A. Kemp

Introduction

In order to understand New Labour's housing policy it is important to consider the legacy left behind after 18 years of radical Conservative government. The Thatcher and Major administrations introduced major changes in housing policy during their years in power. By 1997, housing policy and provision were significantly different from what they had been in 1979. Of course, even after Mrs Thatcher became Prime Minister, there was an important degree of policy continuity with the past (Malpass, 1990). Nevertheless, the 1979 election marked a major departure in terms of key aspects of policy and of intention compared with previous post-war governments, whether Conservative or Labour. While many of the developments in housing provision during this period were the product of exogenous social, economic and demographic forces and trends, the actions of government (not just in housing, but also in other policy arenas) were also significant factors behind many of the changes that took place.

However, it was not merely in respect of housing policy and provision that the Conservative governments of Margaret Thatcher and John Major were able to make significant changes.

The Conservatives also helped to alter housing policy discourse. The ways in which the 'housing question' was debated, the nature and perception of the housing problems that seemed to require policy attention, and the solutions that those debates and perceptions seemed to imply were fundamentally reconstituted under the Conservatives. When the Labour Party returned to office in 1997, therefore, the landscape of debate about the housing question was very different from what it had been when they published their housing policy review twenty years earlier (Department of the Environment (DoE), 1977).

The aim of this paper is to examine how New Labour has responded to this altered terrain. How has New Labour interpreted and presented the housing question? What problems has it identified and how has it proposed to tackle them? In some ways, it can be said that New Labour is searching for a post-Thatcherite settlement in housing, as in other areas of social policy. But at this stage, the full details of that approach have not yet been fully developed and many details have still to be worked out. Nevertheless, it is possible to discern at least in outline some of the key features of New Labour's approach to the housing question. The paper begins by briefly reviewing the post-war settlement in housing policy which the Conservatives sought to undermine. It then recalls some of the key developments under the Conservatives, before moving on to outline housing policy under New Labour. The final section seeks to draw some conclusions about how New Labour has defined and addressed the housing question.

The post-war housing question

According to Malpass (1986), the housing problem as it was understood by governments from the First World War until the late 1960s was 'essentially about quantity, quality and price'. Consequently, housing policy was very largely designed to address these three elements of the problem, though the balance of attention between them varied over time and between Conservative and Labour governments.

The provision of rented housing by local authorities was an important part of the post-war welfare state settlement in Britain. Following the Second World War, policy focused on tackling the severe housing shortage that had developed during the hostilities. In this 'era of reconstruction' (Harloe, 1995), house building by local authorities played the most important role, though construction for the owner-occupied market became increasingly important from the 1950s onwards. Throughout this period of housing shortage, housing was a politically important issue and both Labour and Conservative governments felt compelled to maintain a high level of housing output (Merrett, 1979; Malpass, 1998). The politically sensitive housing shortage also helps to explain why private sector rent control was kept in place after the war. The failure of the unsubsidised private market to supply new homes to let was a major factor behind the importance attached to council house building.

From the mid-1950s, once the housing shortage had begun to abate, more attention was devoted to tackling the poor quality of the nineteenth-century housing stock, much of which was deemed unfit for human habitation. The problem of private sector slum housing was tackled by demolishing and replacing it by new local authority housing, either in the cleared, inner city sites or on the urban periphery. Here again, local authority and new town housing was seen as the solution to the failings of the private housing market (Merrett, 1979).

The high cost of housing relative to incomes was largely tackled on the supply side, by reducing rents to below the market price. This was done by means of 'bricks-and-mortar' subsidies to council housing and rent controls in the private sector. Less attention was given to demand-side subsidies such as housing allowances to enable households pay the market price of their accommodation (Cullingworth, 1979). An important exception here was mortgage interest tax relief, which acted to boost the purchasing power of home buyers (to the extent that it did not simply increase house prices). In these ways, governments sought to reduce the share of household incomes devoted to housing to a level they could be expected to afford.

By the late 1960s and early 1970s, considerable progress had been made towards tackling what were perceived to be the most severe housing problems. From the late 1960s, housing policy focused less on slum clearance and rebuilding by local authorities and more on rehabilitation of the existing stock by private landlords and owner-occupiers and, after 1974, when generous capital subsidies were introduced, by housing associations. In the mid-1970s, Labour's Housing Policy Review (DoE, 1977) concluded that there was no longer a national housing problem, but rather a series of localised problems, which were essentially residual in nature and confined to the poor and those with 'special needs', such as elderly and disabled people. The Green Paper presented council housing as an important and unquestioned form of provision (albeit second best to owner-occupation) for those who had, or wished, to rent their accommodation.

The housing question under the Conservatives, 1979–97

The Conservatives came to power in 1979 determined to introduce major changes in policy and overturn the post-war settlement in housing. As in other policy areas, they sought to roll back the state, reduce public expenditure and extend the role of private enterprise in housing as in other areas of public policy. In essence, the Conservatives employed what Fraser (1989) has called a 'reprivatisation' discourse to redefine the housing question and to justify the radical changes which they sought to achieve. To some extent, this shift in the discourse surrounding the housing question reflected the new-found influence of neo-liberal ideas and especially what Piven (1986) has referred to as the 'revivalist romance' with markets in the advanced industrial democracies.

The Conservatives' principal housing policy objective was to expand owner-occupation. This aim was to be achieved in a number of ways, the most important of which was by giving council tenants the right to buy their home at a substantial discount from the market value. The Conservatives presented home ownership not only as the preferred and, indeed, the ideal tenure, but also one that had almost mystical qualities. According to Michael Heseltine, then Secretary of State for the Environment, there was in Britain 'a deeply ingrained desire for home ownership', a spirit that the government wished to foster. Owner-occupation, he claimed, stimulates 'the attitudes of independence and self-reliance that are the bedrock of a free society'.

As well as seeking to expand owner-occupation, the Conservatives aimed to reduce public expenditure on housing, minimise the role of local authority housing and revive the privately rented sector (see Malpass and Murie, 1994). Council house sales helped to achieve the first three of these four objectives simultaneously. Initially, the Conservatives accepted the need for continued council house building, but hoped to confine it to a residual role, addressing 'special needs' groups such as elderly and disabled people, rather than general housing needs (Forrest and Murie, 1988).

From 1987, the Conservatives switched the focus of their attention towards the demunicipalisation of rented housing (Kemp, 1989; Hills, 1998), though extending owner-occupation remained the most important objective. The Conservatives now argued that councils should cease to see themselves as providers of rented housing and instead act as enablers, facilitating provision by other agencies (DoE, 1987). In this way, the role of councils as housing landlords came to be seriously questioned for the first time since the Second World War. Councils were presented as inflexible and bureaucratic monoliths, overlarge, unresponsive to tenants' wishes and out of touch with modern society. In their place, the government wished to foster the creation of a more market-oriented, pluralist system of rented housing provision. Demunicipalisation was to be achieved by reviving the privately rented sector, transferring as much as possible of the existing housing stock over to alternative landlords, and switching the focus of new building away from local authorities and towards housing associations.

By the time that the Conservatives left office in 1997, major changes had taken place in housing provision. Indeed, housing was one of the few areas of the welfare state where the Conservative governments of 1979–97 were able to effect significant retrenchment and restructuring. Unlike most other aspects of social policy, net public expenditure on housing was significantly reduced, especially if mortgage interest relief is taken into account (Table 1). The composition of government spending on housing was also changed (Hills, 1998). Assistance with housing costs in social housing was shifted from 'indiscriminate' bricks-and-mortar subsidies to means-tested support and in

Table 1: Real net public expenditure on housing in the UK, 1979–80 to 1996–97 (£bn at 1995–96 prices)

	1979/80	1996/97
Net current	6.0	–0.1
Net capital	8.5	3.0
Housing benefits	2.6	12.4
Total public spending	17.1	15.3
Mortgage interest relief	4.2	2.6
Spending as % of GDP	3.3	2.1
Spending as % of GGE	7.4	5.1

Notes: in net current expenditure, housing revenue account surpluses contributing to the cost of housing benefit are treated as negative spending. Housing benefits includes rents of supplementary benefit recipients before 1983 and income support mortgage interest payments. GDP is gross domestic product; GGE is general government expenditure.

Source: Hills (1998, table 5.1).

particular housing benefit. The cost of mortgage interest relief rapidly escalated during the 1980s, but in the 1990s it was dramatically reduced as the rate of relief was cut back by the Major government. In addition, charges were increased in the sense that social housing rents rose over the period at a much faster rate that retail prices or average earnings (Wilcox, 1997; Hills, 1998).

The ownership of the housing stock was also transformed, with a shift from public to private, during the Conservatives' period in office. Owner-occupation increased from 56 per cent of the housing stock in Britain in 1981 to 67 per cent in 1996. Private renting ceased to decline after rent deregulation in 1988 and in fact expanded marginally for the first time in seventy years. The housing association sector doubled in size, from 2 to 4 per cent of the stock, over the same period. Meanwhile, council housing declined from 30 per cent of the stock in 1981 to only 19 per cent by 1996 (Wilcox, 1997). As well as sales to sitting tenants under the right to buy, over fifty local councils sold their entire stock of rented homes, mainly to newly set up housing associations (Mullins *et al.*, 1995; Wilcox, 1997). In Scotland, one Scottish authority sold its entire stock and a number of others transferred small amounts of run-down housing, mainly to community-based housing associations. In addition, Scottish Homes – a quasi-government agency responsible for registration, monitoring and funding of housing associations – transferred over half of the 75,000 dwellings it inherited from the Scottish Special Housing Association in 1989 to new social landlords (Taylor, 1998).

New social housing production was switched away from local councils and increasingly towards housing associations. Public sector completions declined from 86,027 new dwellings in 1980 to only 863 in 1996. By the time that the Conservatives left office, therefore, local authorities had all but ceased to be a major supplier of new rented homes. Although housing associations were able to increase their output of new dwellings by half over this period, this failed to compensate fully for the decline in public sector completions.

Finally, social rented housing, as in other areas of social policy, was also subjected to the disciplines of the 'new public management' (Pollit, 1990) imposed by the Conservatives. For example, local authorities and housing associations were required to produce annual performance indicators for housing management. Compulsory competitive tendering was also introduced for local authority housing management services, though most contracts were ultimately won by in-house teams.

In summary, there is no doubt that the landscape of housing provision was significantly different in 1997 from what it had been when Labour left office in 1979 (Malpass, 1998). While some of these changes were the product of exogenous social and economic trends, many were either the result of, or accelerated by, government policy. The outcome of all these changes was that social rented housing had become fragmented and destabilised by the time the Conservatives lost office. Local authority housing appeared old fashioned and its very existence was being seriously questioned for the first time in the post-war period. Council housing had ceased to be the solution and was increasingly seen as part of the problem (Kemp, 1989).

Housing policy under New Labour

Throughout the Conservatives' eighteen years in government, the Labour opposition was largely on the defensive, defending the old and accommodating itself to the new, rather than generating a radical, new alternative vision of its own. In government, New Labour appears to have accepted much of the analysis and many of the policy prescriptions of the Conservatives – in many ways, that is what is new about New Labour housing policy (Kemp, 1999). They have adopted a 'modified reprivatisation' discourse, one stripped of the ideological fundamentalism with which it was imbued by the previous government. In place of the Conservatives' obsession with home ownership and its mission to demunicipalise rented housing at all costs, New Labour has dismissed ideology and self-consciously adopted the mantra, 'what matters is what works'. Nevertheless, what works in most cases is apparently the market; or, at least, what does not appear to be working is the municipal provision of rented housing.

Before the 1997 election, New Labour made few housing policy commitments, though it did promise to allow the phased 'release' of capital receipts from the sale of council houses, to abolish the compulsion on local authorities to put housing management out to competitive tender and to repeal the restrictions introduced by the Housing Act 1996 on the rights of homeless people to be rehoused in council accommodation (Malpass, 1998). These commitments apart, during Labour's first year in office, housing policy continued more or less as it was before the general election. Major decisions on housing policy were deferred until after the departmental 'Comprehensive Spending Reviews' (CSRs) – set up by the government shortly after it came to office – were completed in the summer of 1998. Even then, it was still not fully clear what was New Labour's housing strategy and some commentators suggested that this was because the government did not have one (Whitehead, 1998). Certainly, by early 1999, major silences remained over a number of key issues. However, in Scotland a Green Paper on housing policy (Scottish Office, 1999) was published in February 1999, shortly before this article was completed. The following discussion of New Labour's housing policy is based on the CSR statement on housing policy (Prescott, 1998), a number of publications, speeches and articles by Ministers (e.g. Armstrong, 1998), and the Scottish Green Paper.

The housing CSR

The CSR statement on housing policy in England shed important light on New Labour's housing intentions, but nevertheless failed to outline a clear vision or strategy for housing. In fact, it read very much like a spending plan rather than a prospectus for housing policy under New Labour. As one critic put it, 'Far from being a comprehensive statement of housing policy, this really is a three year budget for housing. The big policy questions have yet to be answered' (Blake, 1998, p21). It was also notable that many of these big issues were also ones that would require difficult decisions ('hard choices') to be made. Major unresolved issues (affecting England, Wales and Scotland) included the long-term level of social housing rents, the structure of social housing rents, and the balance between bricks-and-mortar subsidies and housing benefit incentives. The CSR also failed to address the structural deficiencies of housing benefit, including the impact of the scheme on work incentives and on housing decisions (Kemp, 1998). Although New Labour initially promised radical reform and possibly even cuts, it subsequently backed away from major changes (to the relief of many vested interests). The government instead promised to 'streamline' the structure of the scheme and to improve administration.

Somewhat unexpectedly, housing (along with urban regeneration) was one of the 'winners' from the CSR in terms of increased public expenditure, though not on the scale of the extra resources devoted to the headline services of health and education. Under the CSR settlement, spending on housing and urban regeneration was planned to increase by around £5 billion over the three years from 1999–2000 to 2001–02. Most of the additional spending was to be targeted on the improvement of local authority housing and on urban regeneration programmes such as the New Deal for communities and the Single Regeneration Budget. The additional spending did not reflect a new commitment to housing policy as such, but rather the fact that good housing was essential to the success of the government's strategy for tackling social exclusion. As Hilary Armstrong explained, 'investment in housing is part of our wider agenda for tackling social exclusion' (quoted in Whitehead, 1998, p11).

The extra spending represented an increase over the historically low housing planning totals for 1997–98 and 1998–99 that were inherited from the Conservatives and retained by New Labour as one of its pre-election pledges. Shelter's magazine *Roof* calculated that New Labour planned to spend less on housing during its expected five-year term of office than the Conservatives had spent during their last five years in government. In other words, from *Roof's* point of view, the extra spending resulting from the CSR only looked good because the previous two years were so bad. Be that as it may, it was never likely that New Labour would be able to raise spending up to anything like its former levels. Housing net capital spending had been more than halved in real terms under the Conservatives and, given New Labour's commitment not to increase income tax, its determination to keep the PSBR under very tight control and its other pressing priorities, restoring the cuts was never a realistic option.

While the CSR statement shed only partial light on New Labour's housing plans, a major speech by the Minister for Housing and Local Government in England and Wales, Hilary Armstrong, provided further insights. According to the Minister, there were 'four cornerstones' of New Labour's housing policy. The government's aim, she said, was 'to offer everyone the opportunity of a decent home and so promote social cohesion, well-being and self-dependence' (Armstrong, 1998, p2). In order to achieve that goal, she argued, the government had a duty to:

● make the housing market work for all the people, to protect the vulnerable and reduce the scope for exploitation;
● maximise the effectiveness, efficiency and accessibility of public services;
● empower people as stakeholders in the homes and communities where they live;
● strengthen communities, their stability and sustainability.

Making the market work?

The Housing Minister's speech made clear New Labour's commitment to, and preference for, the market model of housing provision. While she accepted that market failure could make intervention necessary, this should be limited in scope:

> Our over-riding aim is to make the housing market work for all the people. If the housing market worked perfectly there would be no need or rationale for government intervention but the free market can not accommodate the needs and aspirations of all. Government must intervene – but that intervention must be limited and strategic, empowering and enabling, not centralising and controlling. (Armstrong, 1998, p3)

The proposals outlined by the government in relation to the private housing market were all relatively minor, albeit important in their own right. The fact that, other than the new initiative on rough sleeping, none of them had significant implications for public expenditure is probably significant. In so far as each of the measures had cost implications, the burden would largely fall on the market rather than the taxpayer.

Armstrong argued that one of the most serious examples of market failure was rough sleeping on the streets by homeless people. The incidence of rough sleeping increased considerably in the late 1980s, but subsequently declined, in part because of the Rough Sleepers Initiative (RSI) introduced by the Conservatives in the early 1990s. The RSI remained in place, but with enhanced resources and a remit extended to Scotland and a larger number of provincial cities in England. Rough sleeping was one of the first topics to be tackled by the Prime Minster's new Social Exclusion Unit (SEU, 1998a). Following the publication of the SEU's report, the government announced that it aimed to reduce rough sleeping to as near to zero as possible. This was to be achieved by better coordination of housing, health, training and employment programmes aimed at rough sleepers; a new coordinating body in London led by a so-called 'tsar'; increased resources; and action to prevent vulnerable people leaving institutions (such as care homes, prisons and the armed forces) from becoming homeless.

In the privately rented housing market, three actions were either taken or proposed. First, new limits were introduced on the rate at which 'fair rents' could be increased on the remaining stock of (pre-1989) regulated private and housing association tenancies. Over the previous decade, registered fair rents increased at a much faster rate than either the retail price index or average earnings; and some fair rent increases, particularly in London, were very large, with a knock-on effect on MPs' postbags. Some of the largest increases affected middle-class tenants living in mansion blocks in central London. New Labour made it very clear, however, that they had no intention of introducing rent controls in the deregulated privately rented market. A well-functioning, market rented sector aimed at younger and mobile households was seen as a central part of New Labour's housing policy.

Second, as promised in the manifesto, a mandatory system of licensing for houses in multiple occupation will be introduced, when parliamentary time allows. Landlords will be legally required to buy a license from their local authority in order to let multi-occupied accommodation. They will only be able to do so if their property meets certain minimum standards in terms of its condition and the way it is managed. In this way, it is hoped to ameliorate some of the worst conditions at the bottom end of the private housing market. A permissive power to introduce licensing already exists in Scotland and has been implemented by city councils such as Edinburgh and Glasgow.

Third, New Labour has begun to explore ways of ensuring that private landlords do not unfairly refuse to return tenants' deposits. Tenant and consumer groups have campaigned for measures to protect tenants such the introduction of an independent rent deposit board (Phelps, 1998). However, so far – in line with its more market-friendly approach – the government has encouraged the letting industry to introduce a voluntary, self-regulated scheme. Legislation will only be introduced if self-regulation does not work.

Likewise, New Labour envisages only minor reforms in the owner-occupied housing market and these are largely aimed at making the market work more effectively in the interests of consumers. The government has published proposals aimed at speeding up the house-buying process and reducing some of the uncertainty for buyers. Legislation to remove the scope for exploitation of long leaseholders is also to be introduced. Neither measure is likely to have public expenditure implications.

New Labour, like all previous Labour governments, favours owner-occupation, but, unlike the Conservatives under Mrs Thatcher, not obsessively so. Hilary Armstrong has said that she is 'in favour of home ownership where it meets individual or family aspirations and where they can afford it' (Armstrong, 1998, p7). Despite the latter qualification, no mention was made of ending the very substantial subsidy to council tenants purchasing their home under the right-to-buy legislation, in which the sale price can be reduced by up to 60 per cent of its market value in the case of houses and up to 70 per cent in the case of flats. The Scottish Green Paper, however, did propose to reconsider these discounts. It also criticised the former government's 'almost exclusive concern with the expansion of owner-occupation' and, while supportive of the tenure, stated that the government had no wish 'to encourage into owner occupation households whose incomes are too low or too irregular to meet the costs involved' (Scottish Office, 1999, paras 2.74 and 2.75).

Neither in Armstrong's speech nor in the Scottish Green Paper was there any mention of reversing the cuts in income-support mortgage interest payments introduced by the Conservatives in October 1995. Instead, there was only talk of the need for flexible repayment arrangements for home buyers 'when times get tough' and the need for an industry-wide standard for mortgage protection policies. Neither measure has public expenditure implications and both rely on voluntary cooperation by the mortgage lenders and insurers.

Research has consistently indicated, however, that there is a significant degree of 'market failure' in respect of mortgage protection payment insurance (MPPI) policies. Most of the households that are likely to need MPPI do not take out such policies and some of those that do find themselves without assistance owing to the numerous exclusions included in such policies (Ford *et al.*, 1995; Ford and Kempson, 1997; Burchardt and Hills, 1998). Moreover, MPPI policies do not cover some of the main causes of mortgage arrears and possessions, such as relationship breakdown and sharp falls in earnings. Since 1990, over 450,000 households (containing more than 1.3 million adults and children) have experienced the trauma of having their mortgaged home possessed by the lender. Although the number of possessions in Britain has fallen in recent years, it is still running at a rate of 650 per week (Nettleton and Burrows, 1998). Tackling this problem effectively would probably require introducing compulsion to take out MPPI and perhaps improved state support for owner-occupiers in financial difficulty – neither of which accords with the ethos of New Labour. However, mortgage interest relief (MIRAS) – a universal home-owner subsidy not related to financial need – is being phased out, continuing a process begun under the Conservatives. Critics had argued that the saving of around £2 billion from abolishing MIRAS should be used to fund an income-related mortgage benefit scheme (Webb and Wilcox, 1991).

If New Labour is keen on owner-occupation and relaxed about private renting, where does council housing fit into its new, 'making the market work' philosophy? Hilary Armstrong made it clear that, unlike the Conservatives, who sought to coerce local authorities into transferring their housing stock to alternative providers, the new government's approach was not ideologically driven, and was neither dogmatically for nor against transfers. Instead, New Labour had a pragmatic approach to the transfer of local authority housing, based on whatever was practically possible and necessary to raise the quality of the housing stock: 'If it works, and it is what tenants want, transfer may be an appropriate option. What matters is what works', is how the Minister for Housing and Local Government in England put it (Armstrong, 1998, p4).

Nevertheless, separating out local authorities' strategic role from their housing management function was 'a key step', according to Armstrong, in this what-matters-is-what-works approach. Thus, while not ideologically driven for or against stock transfers, New Labour apparently favours transferring housing management if not necessarily the stock itself. In fact, New Labour appears to be ambiguous about how strongly it favours stock transfers to alternative landlords in England. Various consultation papers have hinted that local councils may decide to transfer the ownership or management of their houses to alternative landlords, but at present neither stock transfer nor outsourcing housing management services is official government policy.

In Scotland, there is no such ambiguity over the demunicipalisation of rented housing. The Scottish Office Housing and Local Government Minister, Calum MacDonald, has made it clear that he wishes to encourage councils to transfer their stock. The £300 million additional expenditure allocated to housing in Scotland following the CSR has been devoted to the establishment of New Housing Partnerships. A key feature of these new partnerships is the transfer of council housing to 'community ownership' housing associations. These non-profit landlords will be collectively owned and run by management boards comprising tenants, councillors and others drawn from the local community (Scottish Office, 1998).

This demunicipalisation policy was confirmed in the Green Paper on housing policy in Scotland, which argued that 'The time has come to move beyond . . . the "municipal paternalism", which resulted in large single tenure estates' (Scottish Office, 1999, para. 7). The main focus of the Green Paper is the possible transfer of council housing to non-profit, community ownership landlords. There has been considerable controversy in Scotland over the fact that Glasgow and other city councils are considering bidding for the New Housing Partnership money and transferring their entire stock to community ownership organisations, a proposal that has been described by public sector unions and some tenant activists as 'privatisation' to private landlords. The Green Paper stressed that community ownership 'most certainly does not involve "privatisation" with the housing being sold into private ownership to companies operating purely on a "for-profit" basis' (Scottish Office, 1999, para. 3.7). Housing would be transferred to non-profit social landlords, and only if the tenants consented to it via a secret ballot. Community ownership landlords, it argued, would be able to borrow money to finance much-needed repair and modernisation work that would not be possible (because it would constitute public expenditure) if the housing were retained by local councils.

Managerialism and social housing

Whatever the future of individual local authority housing portfolios, it is clear that the stock that remains in the council sector will continue to be subject to new public management techniques of the sort introduced by the Conservatives (Pollit, 1990), albeit in a different form. There are three main elements to New Labour's strategy for improving the efficiency and effectiveness of social rented housing:

● The new Best Value in housing regime
● The new Housing Inspectorate
● A new financial accounting system

Firstly, New Labour is replacing compulsory competitive tendering (CCT) of housing management and other local government services with a new regime called Best Value (Department of the Environment, Transport and the Regions (DETR), 1998a). The aim behind this new regime is to ensure that there is a year-on-year improvement in service delivery. To this end, local authorities will be required to introduce a process of annual planning, target setting, monitoring and performance review. Aware that, by itself, Best Value will not necessarily achieve improved efficiency, effectiveness and service quality, this new regime will be accompanied by a variety of carrots and sticks (discussed below), or what the English Minister for Housing and Local Government referred to as a system of 'reform and reward' (Armstrong, 1998, p13).

Secondly, the Audit Commission is to set up a Housing Inspectorate (within the Commission's Standards Inspectorate) to monitor local councils' progress towards improved service delivery. This Housing Inspectorate is akin to the system of inspection in schools established under the Conservatives and retained by New Labour. In order to encourage councils to work towards improved performance, their capital spending allocations will be linked to service reviews. Authorities that perform well will be rewarded with higher spending allocations, while poor performers will be penalised by having lower allocations. If these new incentives prove to be insufficient, the government will reserve powers to take over the management and delivery of services from 'failing local authorities'. Again, this bears close similarity with the government's powers in education.

Thirdly, the government is proposing to introduce a new financial framework for local authority housing. Under the proposed arrangements local authorities will be required to use a resource accounting method in order to put their housing stock on a 'more business-like footing' and enable them to take 'better decisions about the use of their housing assets' (DETR, 1998b). Currently, local authority housing revenue accounts are largely calculated on an historic cost basis. Local authorities which retain a housing stock will also be required to draw up an annual business plan for their housing revenue account. Resource accounting will make it possible to clearly identify the value of the housing assets owned by the local authority and the cost of maintaining them. The consultation paper setting out the proposed new resource accounting framework suggests that it should 'assist authorities to consider moving to a more arms-length management of council housing' (DETR, 1998b, para. 3.4). Thus, the move to resource accounting could help to pave the way for the transfer of housing management or even the stock itself.

Empowering tenants

As well as encouraging those councils that retain a housing stock to be better performers, New Labour will also be requiring them to take greater account of consumer's views, preferences and aspirations. The government promised to 'restore choice and power, self-reliance and personal responsibility to the social housing tenant' (Armstrong, 1998, p9). The main way in which this shift towards empowering tenants will be put into effect is through the introduction of Tenant Participation (TP) Compacts. These compacts will set out minimum and common standards for tenant participation in the management of council housing. Likewise, the Housing Corporation will be encouraged to strengthen its policies on tenant involvement in the running of housing associations. In Scotland, the Scottish Office has proposed a National Strategy for Tenant Participation and has floated the idea of a statutory right to participation.

In England, the government's Consultation Paper on TP Compacts (DETR, 1999) states that tenants will themselves decide at the local level how they wish to be involved in running the housing service. This participation could range from meetings between officials and residents' associations, through service level agreements to tenant management organisations. Whatever level of involvement tenants opt for, the Consultation Paper envisages that TP Compacts will apply to the whole range of housing management services, including, for example, developing the council's housing policy and strategy, drawing up the council's capital spending and renovation programmes, budget setting, rent setting, allocations and lettings policies, tenancy conditions and agreements, customer care, anti-social behaviour policies, performance monitoring, environmental works, the management of housing services, and neighbourhood issues. If TP Compacts involve tenants to a significant extent in such a wide range of housing services, it could offer the possibility of dissolving some of the distinctions between landlord and tenant in council housing.

Thus, it is clear that New Labour are committed to empowering tenants through enabling them to be involved in virtually every aspect of the housing service. TP Compacts represent a major shift towards a consumer-oriented approach to council housing and away from a producer-oriented one. However, this greater involvement also represents a partial off-loading of responsibility from councils to tenants. As such, it is fully consistent with New Labour's emphasis on responsibilities and not just rights within the welfare state. It is not enough for council tenants simply to pay the rent in order to get the service they require; they are now expected to spend their spare time and energy in helping to provide that service themselves. Hence, the new emphasis on tenant participation could prove to be something of a two-edged sword for council tenants. It offers them new opportunities to determine housing management policy and practice, but equally, if these are taken up, will present them with new responsibilities and duties to perform.

Strengthening communities

Perhaps the most important of the four cornerstones, at least in terms of new public expenditure, is the duty to strengthen local communities. In policy terms, this refers to New Labour's well publicised commitment to tackle 'social exclusion' in the most deprived housing estates. Whereas the Conservatives' 1987 housing White Paper (DoE, 1987) seemed almost to blame the social and economic problems of deprived housing estates on the very fact that they were mostly owned and managed by local councils, New Labour recognises that the problems have much more deep-seated and multiple causes. The SEU's (1998b) report on what it called the 'worst estates' argued that the problems from which they suffer can only be tackled effectively if urban regeneration, housing and other social policies are brought together in a coordinated ('joined up') way and sustained over a considerable period of time.

The CSR committed £800 million of public expenditure to the New Deal for communities (NDC) in England over the three years from 1999–2000. The NDC will bring together housing and urban regeneration spending in order to improve neighbourhood management and service delivery, and to improve economic opportunities for local people. The action will not be confined to local councils, but will include housing associations and other voluntary and private sector organisations working in partnership.

The NDC forms part of the national strategy for neighbourhood renewal outlined in the SEU's report, *Bringing Britain Together* (SEU, 1998a). Apart from the NDC, the national strategy for neighbourhood renewal will involve the transfer of the Single Regeneration Budget from central government to new Regional Development Agencies, and the targeting of employment, education and Health Action Zones on areas of severe social exclusion. In addition, an intensive programme of policy development has been set in train, involving eighteen cross-cutting 'policy action teams' drawn from ten Whitehall departments and involving experts from outside government including people with experience of deprived neighbourhoods. The intention is that this accelerated policy development will result in the production of a 'coherent national strategy' for England which, over a ten- to twenty-year period, will result in significant progress towards tackling spatial concentrations of social exclusion. In Scotland, a number of Social Inclusion Partnerships (SIPs) are being set up, including area-based SIPs in communities facing the greatest hardship and thematic SIPs to promote social inclusion amongst particularly vulnerable groups, such as homeless young people, care leavers and prostitutes.

Conclusions

During their eighteen years in power, the Conservatives introduced a string of new initiatives which helped to produce radical changes in housing policy and provision, and which helped to transform the ways in which the housing question was debated. While New Labour also aspires to be a radical, reforming government, there are still a number of important, unresolved issues, such as the relationship between social housing rents and housing benefit. New Labour seems to be finding it hard to take some of the difficult decisions that are inevitable if radical changes are to be implemented.

What is clear, though, is that New Labour has had to come to terms with the terrain carved out by the Conservative governments of 1979–97. Not only that, but they also appear to have accepted much of the previous governments' critique of council housing. New Labour has embraced market-based provision more wholeheartedly than before. Apart from owner-occupation, New Labour has accepted that privately rented housing can provide an important role for certain types of household and that the sector needs to be nurtured rather than regulated into submission or decline. Although New Labour still accepts that intervention in the market may be required, this is now to be limited in scope and necessary only where self-regulation fails; confined to tidying up the corners of the marketplace rather than shaping it.

Equally, since the market is seen to be largely working well and intervention is to be limited, the real problems have been defined as lying in the non-market housing sector, in the 'worst neighbourhoods' and low-demand estates (most of which are owned and managed by social housing landlords, though some are areas of private housing). In this way, New Labour has largely accepted the Conservatives' reprivatisation discourse, but without the ideological posturing. 'What matters is what works' – and that is the market, but not, at least in its present form, council housing. More ambiguously in England than in Scotland, the government seems intent on demunicipalising rented housing. This strategy is being pursued partly for financial reasons (as borrowing by non-municipal landlords is not counted as public expenditure) and partly because New Labour seems to have lost faith in this mode of provision.

The housing question has been defined as largely being a problem of social (particularly council) housing estates and connected to the wider complex of problems of 'social exclusion'. However, this redefinition overlooks a significant element of market failure in respect of MPPI policies and the problems of low-income owner-occupiers who have fallen on hard times. New Labour appears unwilling either to introduce compulsory MPPI in the private housing market (which would have to be organised or regulated by government) or to improve state support for low-income owner-occupiers (which would involve increased public expenditure). Yet, with owner-occupation accounting for about seven out of ten households, the shift to a low-inflation economy, the development of a more flexible, post-industrial labour market and the growth of lone parenthood, the need for effective financial provision for owner-occupiers who get into financial difficulty will not go away.

So far as the remaining stock of council housing is concerned, New Labour is pushing ahead with a modified managerialism. Although the government has dropped CCT, the new Best Value regime is another public management technique for squeezing improvements in service delivery out of council housing. Like CCT, Best Value reflects a fundamental belief, not necessarily unfounded, that in the absence of market mechanisms, social housing providers have to be coerced or cajoled into providing value for money. Similarly, the proposals to establish a Housing Inspectorate and to reserve powers where councils 'fail' also represent extensions of the managerialist and centralising tendencies exhibited by the Thatcher and Major governments. TP Compacts offer the potential to give the consumers of council housing the opportunity to influence service provision in a more direct way than hitherto. Again, they reflect a conviction that council housing, left to itself, will not necessarily provide a responsive service delivered in the interests of consumers rather than producers.

Where a new approach can be seen is in respect of New Labour's determination to tackle the problems of social exclusion, including rough sleeping and the 'worst estates'. Additional resources and a host of new policy initiatives are being developed as part of the national strategy for neighbourhood renewal. Thus, the shift of focus away from the problems of the private market and towards social rented housing has been accompanied by a redefinition of housing policy as merely one element of a wider complex of problems under the heading of 'social exclusion'.

Acknowledgements

I should like to thank the editors and Dr Joanne Neale for helpful comments on the first draft of this paper.

References

Armstrong, H. (1998) 'Speech by Hilary Armstrong', presented to the Annual Conference of the Chartered Institute of Housing, June, Harrogate.

Ball, M. (1983) *Housing Policy and Economic Power,* London, Methuen.

Blake, J. (1998) 'Question time', *Roof,* September/October, pp19–21.

Burchardt, T. & Hills, J. (1998) 'From public to private: the case of mortgage payment insurance in Great Britain', *Housing Studies,* vol. 13, pp311–323.

Cullingworth, J. B. (1979) *Essays on Housing Policy,* London, Allen & Unwin.

DoE (1977) Housing Policy: *A Consultative Document,* London, HMSO.

DoE (1987) *Housing: the Government's Proposals,* London, HMSO.

DETR (1998a) *Modernising Local Government. Improving Local Services Through Best Value,* London, Department of the Environment, Transport and the Regions.

DETR (1998b) *A New Financial Framework for Local Authority Housing,* London, Department of the Environment, Transport and the Regions.

DETR (1999) *Tenant Participation Compacts. A Consultation Document,* London, Department of the Environment, Transport and the Regions.

Ford, J. & Kempson, E. (1997) *Bridging the Gap: State and Private Safety-nets for Mortgages,* York, York Publishing Services.

Ford, J., Kempson, E. & Wilson, M. (1995) *Mortgage Arrears and Possessions,* London, HMSO.

Forrest, R. & Murie, A. (1988) *Selling the Welfare State,* London, Routledge.

Fraser, N. (1989) *Unruly Practices: Power, Discourse, and Gender in Contemporary Social Theory,* Minneapolis, MN, University of Minnesota Press.

Harloe, M. (1995) *The People's Home: Social Rented Housing in Europe and America,* Oxford, Basil Blackwell.

Hills, J. (1998) 'Housing: a decent home within the reach of every family?', in H. Glennerster & J. Hills (eds) *The State of Welfare,* 2nd edn, Oxford, Oxford University Press.

Kemp, P. A. (1989) 'The demunicipalisation of rented housing', in M. Brenton & C. Ungerson (eds) *Social Policy Review 1988–9,* London, Longman.

Kemp, P. A. (1998) *Housing Benefit: Time for Reform,* York, Joseph Rowntree Foundation.

Kemp, P. A. (1999) 'Housing policy under New Labour', in M. Powell (eds) *New Labour, New Welfare State?,* Bristol, Policy Press.

Malpass, P. (1986) 'From complacency to crisis', in P. Malpass (ed.) *The Housing Crisis,* Beckenham, Croom Helm.

Malpass, P. (1990) *Reshaping Housing Policy,* London, Routledge.

Malpass, P. (1998) 'Housing policy', in N. Ellison & C. Pierson (eds) *Developments in British Social Policy,* Basingstoke, Macmillan.

Malpass, P. & Murie, A. (1994) *Housing Policy and Practice,* 4th edn, Basingstoke, Macmillan.

Merrett, S. (1979) *State Housing in Britain,* London, Routledge & Kegan Paul.

Mullins, D., Niner, P. & Riseborough, M. (1995) *Evaluating Large Scale Voluntary Transfers of Local Authority Housing,* London, HMSO.

Nettleton, S. & Burrows, R. (1998) 'Mortgage debt, insecure home ownership and health: an exploratory analysis', *Sociology of Health and Illness,* vol. 20, pp731–753.

Phelps, L. (1998) *Unsafe Deposit: CAB Clients' Experience of Rental Deposits,* London, National Association of Citizens Advice Bureaux.

Piven, F. F. (1986) 'Cities, housing, and the rise of "hyper-capitalist" regimes', paper presented to the City Renewal Through Partnership Conference, May, Glasgow.

Pollit, C. (1990) *Managerialism and the Public Services,* Oxford, Basil Blackwell.

Prescott, J. (1998) *Housing and Regeneration Policy: A Statement by the Deputy Prime Minister,* London, Department of the Environment, Transport and the Regions.

Scottish Office (1998) *New Housing Partnerships,* Edinburgh, Scottish Office.

Scottish Office (1999) *Investing in Modernisation – An Agenda for Scotland's Housing,* Edinburgh, The Stationery Office.

SEU (1998a) *Rough Sleeping – Report by the Social Exclusion Unit,* London, The Stationery Office.

SEU (1998b) *Bringing Britain Together: A National Strategy for Neighbourhood Renewal – Report by the Social Exclusion Unit,* London, The Stationery Office.

Taylor, M. (1998) 'Ten years of stock transfers', *Scottish Housing Review 1988–1998,* Edinburgh, Scottish Homes.

Whitehead, C. (1998) 'Knowing what to do is not knowing how to do it', *Parliamentary Brief,* Housing Supplement, November, pp11–12.

Webb, S. & Wilcox, S. (1991) *Time for Mortgage Benefits,* York, Joseph Rowntree Foundation.

Wilcox, S. (1997) *Housing Finance Review 1997/98,* York, Joseph Rowntree Foundation.

10 Dismantling the Berlin Wall: developments at the health–social care interface

Bob Hudson

Since the inception of state welfare intervention in Britain in the nineteenth century through to the way in which 'partnership' has become the Zeitgeist of the 1997 Labour government, ideas about working together have been important in public policy in general, and in health and social care relationships in particular. It would, however, be a mistake to think that a policy exploration of such ideas will reveal an increasingly sophisticated understanding of successful joint working alongside an expanding record of collaborative achievement. Far from it. Indeed, although the problems created by fragmentation are now more widely recognised, and the need for a shared approach is deemed more necessary than ever, the reality is that policies have tended to be half-hearted and achievements correspondingly negligible. These experiences raise some critical policy questions for the new millennium: how deep-seated is fragmentation? In what ways does the Labour government have a new approach? And what is the likelihood of the effectiveness of this approach?

The nature of the collaborative problem

Precision or agreement about the meaning of terms such as collaboration and partnership is rare – a confusion which is deepened where authors use the same or similar terms, but attach their own definitions to them. Most serious conceptual explorations or policy applications take this confusion as the starting point. Aiken *et al.* (1975), for example, describe 'coordination' as a term which is 'overworked, underachieved and seldom defined' (p6), but others do make a stab at defining terms.

Warren *et al.* (1974) define coordination as:

> a structure or process of concerted decision-making wherein the decisions or action of two or more organisations are made simultaneously in part or in whole with some deliberate degree of adjustment to each other. (p16)

Although this sort of definition is at a very high level of generality, and therefore in danger of appearing somewhat trite, it does contain the crucial ingredient that separate but related organisations adjust their behaviour in some way that takes account of each other's interests. Exactly why and how they should do so is the meat on the collaborative bone.

While definitions are unclear, there is no lack of clarity about the need for some sort of joint approach to many problems in health and social care. Organisational autonomy has been increasingly recognised to be inadequate in the face of complex problems which require multifaceted responses. Huxham and Macdonald (1992) identify four examples of what they term 'pitfalls of individualism':

- *repetition:* where two or more organisations carry out an action or task which need only be done by one;
- *omission:* where activities which are important to the objectives of more than one organisation are not carried out because they have not been identified as important, because they come into no organisation's remit or because each organisation assumes the other is performing the activity;
- *divergence:* the actions of the various organisations may become diluted across a range of activities, rather than used towards common goals;
- *counterproduction:* organisations working in isolation may take actions which conflict with those taken by others.

This chapter explores the application of these issues to the intersection between the National Health Service (NHS) and the personal social services.

Joint working: the post-war experiences

The main interest in social policy coordination has developed since the Second World War, but the creation of the NHS introduced elements of fragmentation which still affect relationships within the NHS, and relationships between the NHS and social services. Of particular significance was the compromise reached over administrative arrangements. In order to secure the support of the leaders of the medical professions it was necessary to take account of their vehement opposition to local government control of hospitals, and of their desire to maintain the independence of general practitioners (GPs). As a result of this, the NHS acquired a tripartite structure consisting of hospital authorities (to run all hospitals, including those which had previously been run by local authorities), executive councils (to administer the contracts of independent GPs) and local health authorities (responsible for community-based health care services other than those provided by family practitioners). In addition, local education authorities retained their responsibility for the administration of the school health service. This amounted, in Ham's words, to 'a representation of what was possible rather than what might have been desirable' (Ham, 1992, p15). Instead of a unitary structure which could have facilitated the development of a more integrated approach to the delivery of health and social care services, this tripartite structure only served to reinforce divisions.

The 1974 reorganisation of the NHS is significant in the history of joint working for several reasons. First, it sought – through the creation of new Area Health Authorities (AHAs) – to bring the different health services under the same organisational umbrella. The main way in which it did this was by moving most of the local health authority services out of local government and into the NHS – a further and possibly final blow to hopes of a democratic and locally accountable NHS (Hudson, 1998). The list of transferred services was long, covering community health services for mothers and pre-school children, school health, vaccination and immunisation, home nursing, health visiting, domiciliary midwifery, family planning, health education, chiropody and ambulance services (Ottewill and Wall, 1990). GP services continued to be administered separately. Although this change was intended to secure a more integrated approach to the provision of health care services, it clearly also had the potential to further deepen the cleavage between health and social care services, as well as other local government services which contributed to health and well-being.

The amount of joint planning that resulted from the 1970s initiatives such as joint finance, Joint Consultative Committees (JCCs) and Joint Care Planning Teams was generally disappointing (Nocon, 1994). Part of the reason for this was argued to be the overemphasis on structural links and the failure to consider broader planning issues (Wistow, 1990). JCCs, for example, typically dealt with only the allocation of joint finance or operational matters that were causing problems, but not with strategic concerns, whilst joint finance itself did not give local authorities a sufficient incentive to engage in closer collaboration with AHAs and thereby give JCCs a proper role. Indeed, local authorities were often unable or unwilling to take on the long-term commitments implied by joint finance, sometimes seeing it as a 'bribe' to incur unwarranted expenditure (Davies et al., 1990).

The seeming inability of health authorities and local authorities to work together began to attract political interest as the 1980s progressed, with two particularly critical reports about fragmentation in community care coming from the House of Commons Social Services Committee (1985) and the Audit Commission (1986). The analysis of the Audit Commission led it to the conclusion that the difficulties of inter-agency collaboration were such that it should be designed out of the organisational framework for community care as far as possible. Consequently it recommended the allocation of responsibility for particular client groups to separate agencies: mental health to the NHS, learning and physical disabilities to local government, and elderly people to a single manager supervised by a joint board of health and local authority representatives (para. 174). The Commons Select Committee had advocated a similar course for mental health and learning disability services the previous year. Thus, from being the leitmotif of the 1960s and 1970s, within a decade collaboration had become an elusive chimera.

The introduction in the early 1990s of quasi-markets based upon the separation of previously conflated purchasing and providing roles posed a fundamental dilemma: while collaboration has long been recognised as the essence of effective service delivery in health and social care, the essence of markets is competition. Wistow and Hardy (1996a,b) argue that the issue is whether the collaborative imperative is compatible with the competitive imperative. There is little doubt that the Conservative government of the time did not see the two as mutually exclusive. For example, the then Minister of Health, Brian Mawhinney, was highly critical of early approaches to so-called 'macho' purchasing in the NHS based upon 'stand-off' relationships between purchasers and providers. Rather, he argued for relationships built upon partnership and long-term agreements (Mawhinney, 1993). Under the 1990 NHS & Community Care Act inter-agency working was given a more extensive statutory basis than previously – for example, the Secretary of State was given enhanced powers of direction, inspection, inquiry and default, and local government social services departments (SSDs) were required to publish community care plans annually, and to consult with health and other agencies on their content. However, a more significant push for collaboration arose from the transfer of responsibilities and funds from the social security system to SSDs – a move which greatly reduced the opportunities for unilateral action by the NHS in discharging people from both acute and long-stay hospitals because of the need to persuade SSDs of the appropriateness of a state-funded placement in residential or nursing home care.

Wistow and Hardy (1996a,b) suggest that collaborative purchasing (or 'joint commissioning', as it became known) was necessary to ensure the integration or compatibility of contracts with providers in order that services could be integrated at the level of individual users. So far as competition between purchasers goes, there also remained a need to counteract the continuing incentive to 'minimise market shares' – or 'cost-shunt' responsibilities by attempting to pass on responsibility (and thereby funding) to other agencies. They further argue that markets add new complexities to collaboration by requiring health and local authority purchasers to manage relationships with a larger number of providers, including their own 'in-house' suppliers. However, while the collaborative imperative dictated that these purchaser–provider relationships should be based upon long-term, trusting relationships, the competitive imperative required the maintenance of competition between providers – a difficult balancing act to achieve.

In general during the 1990s, the boundary between health and social care still threatened to be a focus for competition and conflict between agencies and professions, rather than for cooperation and collaboration. It was not clear whether the introduction of assessment and care management would remove the differences in professional perspectives and status which had bedevilled multidisciplinary working in the past, particularly since SSDs had no power to require the involvement of any other agency or profession in the process. In the absence of a single health and social care budget, individual care managers were no more able to commit resources for a unified package of care than their predecessors. In addition, the distinction between health and social care responsibilities was particularly unclear in relation to the purchase of continuing care. The 1989 White Paper, *Caring for People* (Department of Health (DH), 1989), stated that NHS responsibilities were unchanged by its proposals, and that health authorities were still expected to purchase continuing health care alongside the new responsibility of SSDs for purchasing nursing home care. In parallel with this, Acute Trusts were under pressure from the DH to reduce waiting lists and increase throughput, as a result of which the prospect of 'bed-blocking' due to a shortage of social care facilities in the community became a contentious issue. Even where agencies were prepared to work together much more closely, there remained legal ambiguities which could restrict them. All of this proved to be fertile ground for conflict and confusion.

New Labour, new partnerships?

The Labour government came to power in May 1997 with a clear view that the quasi-market approach to health and social services had been a failure, and that the key to effective service planning and delivery lay in the development of 'partnerships'. Health ministers talked incessantly about breaking down the 'Berlin Wall' between health and social services, and managers of both services were warned that collaboration was no longer an optional extra (Hirst, 1998). The shift in emphasis seemed to be clear; collaboration was not simply back on the agenda, but was at the very heart of new policies on health and social care in the shape of 'partnership'. This renewed emphasis is evident in four key areas of policy:

1. Reform of the NHS
2. Policies on public health
3. Reform of the personal social services
4. Reform at the health–social services boundary

Reform of the NHS

The government announced its proposals for change in the NHS in a 1997 White Paper (DH, 1997), parts of which carried important implications for relationships with SSDs. Perhaps most significantly, the dismantling – or at least the modification – of the NHS internal market (cf. Chapter 6 above) signalled a return to coterminosity of organisational boundaries, but not – as has traditionally been the case – between health authorities and local government, but rather between the new Primary Care Groups (PCGs) responsible for commissioning NHS services for populations of around 100,000 and local SSDs. The White Paper makes it plain that PCGs will be expected to work closely with social services on the planning and delivery of services, and that arrangements should 'develop around natural communities, while also taking account of the benefits of coterminosity with social services'. The suggestion that PCGs will typically serve populations of around 100,000 means that for smaller local authorities there will be 'whole organisation coterminosity', whereas larger local authorities may have up to ten PCGs in or on the borders of their area. The White Paper also stated that the local government chief executive would participate in meetings of the health authority, and that PCG governing bodies would include social services membership.

Section 10 of the 1973 NHS Act placed health and social services under a statutory duty to cooperate with each other, but this duty was general rather than specific, and was not supported by formal accountability arrangements. The 1997 NHS White Paper revisits this type of legislative partnership and proposes a new statutory 'duty of partnership' to require NHS bodies and SSDs to 'work together for the common good'. A prime vehicle for this duty will be the joint development of a Health Improvement Programme (HImP) in each local area. These will be the means to deliver national targets in each health authority area, and although the health authority will have lead responsibility for drawing up a local HImP, the process is portrayed as an inter-agency activity. The NHS White Paper, for example, states that 'in the new NHS, all those charged with planning and providing health and social care services for patients will work to a jointly agreed HImP' (para. 2.11), but it is not clear how far this might restrict the autonomy of non-NHS partners.

Policies on public health

Alongside the NHS White Paper, the Labour government also published a Green Paper on public health (DH, 1998a) which contains rather similar collaborative proposals. It recognises, for example, that local government authorities – with their responsibilities for social services, education, transport, housing and the local environment – have the capacity to make a big impact on the health of local communities. To reflect this role, it proposes to place upon them a new duty to promote the economic, social and environmental well-being of their areas – something which requires a close relationship with NHS agencies. The Green Paper also encourages local government participation in health authority planning activities, with reciprocal arrangements for Directors of Public Health to attend relevant local government meetings.

A second area of public health policy with a strong collaborative dimension has been the creation of Health Action Zones (HAZs). In April 1998, eleven areas were designated HAZs by the DH and allocated £34 million for setting up costs and for joint spending between participating agencies. HAZ status will be retained for between five and seven years, and a further wave of pilots began in April 1999. One of the key expectations of HAZ sites is that inter-agency partnerships will lead to improvements in people's health and relevant services – indeed, HAZ bids could only be submitted where there was explicit support from a consortium of local bodies prepared to share goals, resources and a 'whole systems' approach to managing change. Politically, much seems to be expected of the HAZ pilots, with ministers describing them as 'the trailblazer for a new approach to more integrated care' and able to 'cut through red tape barriers between health and social care' (DH Press Release 97/312).

Reform of the personal social services

In November 1998 the government published its long-awaited White Paper on the future of the personal social services, *Modernising Social Services* (DH, 1998c). Six areas of difficulty are identified – protection, coordination, inflexibility, clarity of role, consistency and inefficiency – and joint working is clearly something which has a bearing on all of these. The collaborative imperative is certainly at the heart of the overall framework for change. It is argued that:

> When people get passed from pillar to post it is a great cause of grievance and frustration. It is for agencies to collaborate to ensure that an approach to one will automatically trigger contributions from partner agencies as required. (para. 2.52)

A significant part of the White Paper is concerned with the regulation and inspection of care, and one practical measure aimed at better harmonising these activities is the proposal to establish eight Regional Commissions for Care Standards to replace the existing 250 registering authorities. The Commissions will cover both residential and nursing homes, as well as domiciliary care, thereby fusing the previously separate roles of SSDs and health authorities in this respect.

Unlike previous collaborative initiatives, the White Paper recognises the need to link joint working with access to resources. Accordingly the additional money for the personal social services which emerged from the Comprehensive Spending Review (amounting to £1.3 billion) has a number of collaborative strings attached to it. The main example is the proposed creation of a 'Promoting Independence Partnership Grant' of £647m 'to foster partnership between health and social services in promoting independence as an objective of adult services' with local expenditures needing to be agreed between the two agencies.

Reform at the health–social services boundary

The Discussion Document, *Partnerships in Action,* specifically addresses the interface between the NHS and social services – both the nature of the problems and the ways in which they might be overcome (DH, 1998b). In his foreword to the document, the Health Minister issues a stern warning about the sterility of boundary disputes:

> All too often when people have complex needs spanning both health and social care, good quality services are sacrificed for sterile arguments about boundaries. When this happens people . . . and those who care for them, find themselves in the no-man's land between health and social care services. This is not what people want or need. It places the needs of the organisation above the needs of the people they are there to serve. It is poor organisation, poor practice, poor use of taxpayer's money – it is unacceptable.

This is certainly the strongest political warning to the two agencies which has ever been issued in an official publication, and although it conveys a feeling of 'drinking in the last chance collaborative saloon', the alternative of a further reorganisation seems to be ruled out:

> Major structural change is not the answer. We do not intend to set up new statutory health and social services authorities. This would involve new bureaucracy, and would be expensive and disruptive to introduce.

For the foreseeable future, then, the answer to fragmentation is not unification but collaboration: separate organisations must somehow be persuaded to work together. Given the disappointing past record of achievement in this respect, what new ingredients are proposed in *Partnerships in Action?* The first answer to the question – and one which is easier said than done – is to view the problem holistically. It is noted that:

> We must deal with every link in the chain, from the strategic planners to people accessing services in their local communities. Past efforts to tackle these problems have shown that concentrating on single elements of the way services work together . . . without looking at the system as a whole, does not work. (p5)

Three levels where joint working is needed are identified:

1. *Strategic planning:* at this level, agencies will need to plan jointly for the medium term, and share information about how they intend to use their resources towards the achievement of common goals. The means for doing this are identified as HAZs, HImPs and Joint Investment Plans. The latter (the framework for which was in place by April 1999) are based upon a joint assessment of need and shared objectives, initially for older people.

2. *Service commissioning:* here it is expected that, when securing services for their local populations, agencies will have a common understanding of the needs they are jointly meeting, and the kind of provision likely to be most effective. The move to PCGs (in England) is seen as providing 'a unique opportunity for the key partners to test new approaches to joint commissioning' (p14), and yet more guidance on good practice from local joint commissioning initiatives will be issued.

3. *Service provision:* regardless of how services are purchased or funded, the key objective is that the user receives a coherent integrated package of care, and this is the third identified level of joint working. The Discussion Document sees several fresh opportunities at this level: the emerging Primary Care Trusts, the Primary Care Act pilot schemes and the experiences gained from special initiatives such as the Winter Pressures money. In the particular case of older people, the government further required that by 1999 a framework was in place for multidisciplinary assessment in community health and acute care settings, with local authorities required to spend part of their funding in support of rehabilitation and recuperation facilities.

Much of this seems similar to many previous attempts at collaboration through exhortation, even if the exhortation is more systematic and the tone more strident. However, there is a recognition in *Partnerships in Action* that more needs to be done. Three new types of action are accordingly proposed: the removal of constraints to joint working; the introduction of new incentives; and closer monitoring of achievements.

Removing constraints

Three proposals for allowing more flexibility between agencies are made. First, the legalisation of *pooled budgets* to allow health and social services to bring resources together to commission and provide services in a way that would be accessible to both partners in the joint arrangements – the sort of arrangement which was ruled illegal in Lewisham in the early 1990s. Unlike the current position, the pooled resource would lose its health or social services identity and be available for either type of support. Of course, where there is mistrust between agencies, and a fear of 'cost-shunting', then there could also be an unwillingness to commit budgets to the pool. Greater legal flexibility is no panacea for a basic lack of trust! The second flexibility is that of *lead commissioning,* where one authority is permitted to take the lead in commissioning the range of services for a particular group on behalf of both agencies. Learning disability and mental health are cited as examples where this could be usefully applied. Again, such an arrangement could only flourish in a collaborative relationship already characterised by a high degree of mutual respect and trust. Finally, there is the suggestion of permitting more *integrated provision* by allowing health and social services agencies to take on at least some of each other's functions.

Introducing incentives

Past incentives to joint working have concentrated mainly on additional financial incentives from central government, with local agreement between NHS and local authorities serving as a requirement for access to the funds. Joint finance, hospital discharge agreements and Winter Pressures money (aimed at reducing waiting lists over the winter period) are all examples of this approach. However, the Discussion Document states that the government 'wants to see joint working as a true part of core business' (p30) and proposes greater flexibility for authorities to transfer mainstream funds between each other. This involves extending the current capacity of NHS agencies to transfer money to SSDs (under S28A of the NHS Act 1977) and – for the first time – to allow SSDs to reciprocate. Joint finance, which for so long has been seen as the core of financial collaborative incentives, will be abolished, and incorporated into mainstream budgets. The statutory requirement to have a Joint Consultative Committee will also be relaxed. The use of these new powers will, however, be at the discretion of local agencies.

Closer monitoring

For the first time, the government has issued national priorities guidance for both the NHS and social services (DH, 1998d), setting out the key priorities for 1999–2000 to 2001–02. These identify some areas which have a social services lead (children's welfare, regulation and inter-agency working), some with a health lead (waiting lists/times, primary care, coronary heart disease and cancer) and others with a 'shared lead' (cutting health inequalities, mental health and promoting independence). Alongside joint national priorities guidance will be a growing list of National Service Frameworks which will set national standards and define service models for a specific service or care group, and which will inevitably require multi-organisational responses. The first two will be for coronary heart disease and mental health, with one new topic being developed annually (NHS Executive, 1998). Joint working will also be part of the performance frameworks being established for the two agencies, with progress being jointly monitored by the NHS and Social Care Regional Offices. *Partnerships in Action* acknowledges that there are still 'far too many areas where health and social services are not working well together', and these proposals on closer monitoring might be seen as the iron fist in the velvet glove. It is obviously too early to assess the impact of these proposals, but it is important to recognise that effective collaboration is based upon a stable and trusting relationship between two or more autonomous parties. Such a relationship cannot be properly produced through either the availability of more flexibilities or the threat of external monitoring, although these may well provide an environment in which it is more likely to happen.

Discussion: optimism or realism?

What is evident from the approach to joint working by the Labour government is the shift in emphasis from an 'optimistic' to a 'realistic' model of collaboration. Booth (1988) identifies two key premises of the optimistic model: the presumptions of rationality and altruism respectively. The presumption of rationality is the belief that organisations will collaborate where it can be shown that they can achieve the same ends more efficiently by working together rather than separately. The presumption of altruism is the belief that organisations will collaborate purely for the good of the community they serve. In this circumstance, 'system-gain' (e.g. the greater good of the client or community) will be readily identified by all and will serve as a sufficient reward for the achievement of consensus. Taken together, these two elements of the optimistic model of collaboration constitute a position which tends to be prescriptive, self-confident about achieving desired change and gives pride of place to long-term considerations.

Wistow and Whittingham (1988) identify the following features of this model:

- a systems-wide view of need and service interdependencies, rather than a perspective limited by the boundaries of a single organisation or its subsections;
- a well-developed analytical capacity for identifying need, gaps in provision and alternative means of filling them;
- a shared set of values and a broadly based consensus around means and ends, the most important element of which is a shared commitment to maximising client – rather than provider – benefit;
- sufficient goodwill, trust and altruism to allow providers to sacrifice territory, resources and service models in order to serve the higher goal of meeting service users' needs;
- the concurrence of all these conditions at an appropriate place and time.

As the authors note, 'merely to spell out these assumptions is to indicate what a hugely optimistic view of planning the rational synoptic model is based upon' (pp19–20). The required degree of optimism inherent in this model was not, however, a deterrent to policy formulation on relationships between health and social services for most of the post war period. The emphasis on the part of central government was initially on pointing out the benefits to individuals and communities that would arise from closer inter-agency working, and accordingly exhorting agencies to improve their collaborative practice. Where (as was usual) this was insufficient, the next step tended to be the production of detailed guidance or resource packs, as, for example, in the case of joint commissioning (DH, 1995). Such publications were based on the assumption that the optimistic model was still robust, but was floundering on the lack of 'technical' know-how about the best way to undertake the activity (Hudson, 1995).

The general lack of success of the optimistic model seems to have registered with the Labour government. Exhortations to agencies to be decent about joint working have been replaced by the panoply of sanctions, incentives and threats described above, and amount to the adoption of a very different collaborative model – the 'realistic model'. The basic assumption here is that individual and group interests are multiple and divergent, and that the net result is competition, bargaining and conflict. In answer to the question 'why does collaboration take place?', the answer is that it is in the self-interest of the organisations (and the individuals who work in them) to do so. Self-interest may not be the only thing which motivates public servants, but it is a significant motivation. The model therefore is characterised by three essentials: organisational life is an ongoing struggle to obtain, enhance and protect interests; collaboration is one of the means by which organisations seek to manage their own survival; and collaboration will accordingly only be entered into where there is some mutual benefit to be derived from doing so. This perspective is not one which sees inter-agency collaboration as unattainable, but it does see successful attempts to do so being rooted in hard-headed deals which seem to promise mutual gain.

Challis *et al.* (1988) pull out the following underlying elements of the realistic model.

- collaboration is problematic;
- organisations may not perceive a need for interaction, or may avoid interaction;
- interaction through exchange is most likely when organisations perceive mutual benefits, and lowest when neither perceives a benefit;
- interaction is wholly determined by perceived costs and benefits, and not by system-wide thinking or altruism;
- interaction is conditional, and therefore likely to be sporadic and inconsistent;
- interaction is locally determined and negotiated rather than externally imposed or mandated, but the structuring of local environments by superordinate bodies is a crucial influence on both the likelihood and nature of interaction;
- professional domain considerations may be offset when the other benefits of interaction are distinctly positive, but they are a crucial limiting factor when the benefits are marginal or uncertain;
- mutual resource scarcity may foster collaboration designed to increase the efficiency with which existing resources are used;
- an overall position of scarcity combined with the availability of some flexible or additional resources is mot likely to facilitate collaboration;
- additional resources can act as a major incentive for interaction if they are made conditional on the achievement of collaboration.

It remains to be seen whether the more strident approach to collaboration of the Labour government, rooted in an understanding of the 'realistic model', can be successfully implemented. The generally poor track record of joint working should serve as a warning against undue optimism and act as a reminder of some of the long-established fragmentary forces. A striking feature of the literature is this focus upon barriers to collaboration and the failure to overcome them. Hardy *et al.*

(1992), for example, have identified five categories of barrier, shown below.

Structural
- fragmentation of service responsibilities across agency boundaries, both within and between sectors
- inter-organisational complexity
- non-coterminosity of boundaries

Procedural
- differences in planning horizons and cycles
- differences in budgetary cycles and procedure

Financial
- differences in funding mechanisms and bases
- differences in the stocks and flows of financial resources

Professional
- competitive ideologies and values
- professional self-interest and autonomy
- inter-professional competition for domains
- threats to job security
- conflicting views about user interests and roles

Status and legitimacy
- organisational self-interest and autonomy
- inter-organisational competition to acquire domains
- inter-organisational competition to relinquish domains
- differences in legitimacy between elected and appointed agencies

The extent to which the Labour government's partnership proposals recognise the embeddedness of these barriers is variable. Generally a great deal of emphasis is put upon addressing structural, procedural and financial barriers, though as Henwood and Wistow argue, some of these remain optional rather than mandatory, raising concerns that the emphasis on accountability and performance management is not matched by a sufficient array of incentives and rewards (Henwood and Wistow, 1998). Less attention is paid to issues of inter-professional fragmentation, although it is here that the impact can be sharpest upon individual patients, users and carers.

Of course, 'partnership' or collaboration is not the only answer to fragmentation. The main alternative is some form of integration or unification, and it is an idea which has been around for many years and stubbornly refuses to die. Some see the whole problem of the health–social care boundary stemming from the failure to bring the NHS within the ambit of local government at the outset. Writing of Bevan's role in the creation of the NHS, for example, Campbell (1987) concludes:

> All the fundamental criticisms of the NHS can be traced back to the decision not to base services on local authorities. The various medical services were fragmented instead of unified, the gulf between the GPs and the hospitals widened instead of closed; there was no provision for preventive medicine; there was inadequate financial discipline and no democratic control at local level. In retrospect, the case for the local authorities can be made to look formidable. (quoted in Powell, 1994, p177)

Fifty years later, somewhat similar arguments have been put forward by the Health Select Committee (1998) in its examination of the relationship between health and social services. The Northern Ireland model made a sufficiently big impression on the Health Select Committee for it to recommend an integrated model for England also, though not necessarily under the control of local government. The Committee concluded that:

> We consider that the problems of collaboration between health and social services will not be properly resolved until there is an integrated health and social care system, whether this is within the NHS, within local government or within some new, separate organisation' (para. 68).

So for the Health Select Committee, the answer to fragmentation is not collaboration but unification – an opinion which is out of step with that of the Labour government and which casts doubt upon the attainability of 'partnership'. Of course, such a move would raise many problems. The Committee itself acknowledges that it would still leave other intersections (such as those with education and housing) untouched. Perhaps more significant, it would create huge political difficulties, with none of the NHS and social services agencies wanting to be 'taken over' by each other. The fact that the Committee felt unable to make specific recommendations on which organisation (if either) should have overall responsibility is an indication of the scale of political sensitivity.

It is likely that over the coming years, significant moves towards integrated services will take place, but at a different pace and of a different nature across localities. The proposals contained in *Partnerships in Action* will, in effect, encourage pilots on integration, and this will tie in with some of the models around the transition from Primary Care Groups to Primary Care Trusts. Although the official end point in this respect is 'Level 4' in which NHS commissioning and providing roles are integrated, it is not fanciful to envisage calls for a 'Level 5' in which social care is slotted into the Primary Care Trust structures. The extent to which this happens will depend greatly upon whether 'partnership' can be made to work. 'Partnership', serving as one of the essential features of Blair's 'Third Way', is truly at the crossroads.

References

Aiken, M., Dewar, R., Di Tomaso, N., Hage, J. & Zeitz, G. (1975) *Co-ordinating Human Services,* San Francisco, Josey-Bass.

Audit Commission (1986) *Making a Reality of Community Care,* London, HMSO.

Booth, T. (1988) *Developing Policy Research,* Aldershot, Gower.

Campbell, J. (1987) *Nye Bevan and the Mirage of British Socialism,* London, Weidenfeld & Nicolson.

Challis, L., Fuller, S., Henwood, M., Klein, R., Plowden, W., Webb, A., Whittingham, P. & Wistow, G. (1988) *Joint Approaches to Social Policy: Rationality and Practice,* Cambridge, Cambridge University Press.

Davies, B., Bebbington, A. & Charnley, H. (1990) *Resources, Needs and Outcomes in Community Based Care: A Comparative Study of Welfare for Elderly People in Ten Local Authorities in England and Wales,* Aldershot, Avebury.

DH (1989) *Caring for People,* Cm 849, London, HMSO.

DH (1995) *Practical Guidance on Joint Commissioning for Project Leaders,* London, Department of Health.

DH (1997) *The New NHS: Modern, Dependable,* Cm 3807, London, The Stationery Office.

DH (1998a) *Our Healthier Nation: a Contract for Health,* Cm 3852, London, The Stationery Office.

DH (1998b) *Partnerships in Action,* London, Department of Health.

DH (1998c) *Modernising Social Services: Promoting Independence, Improving Protection, Raising Standards,* Cm 4169, London, The Stationery Office.

DH (1998d) *Modernising Health and Social Services: National Priorities Guidance 1999/00–2001/02.* London, Department of Health.

Ham, C. (1992) *Health Policy in Britain,* 3rd edn, London, Macmillan.

Hardy, B., Turrell, A. & Wistow, G. (1992) *Innovations in Community Care Management,* Aldershot, Avebury.

Health Select Committee (1998) *The Relationship Between Health and Social Services,* vol. 1, London, The Stationery Office.

Henwood, M. & Wistow, G. (1998) 'Responsibility and accountability in community care', paper presented to Royal Commission Research Seminar.

Hirst, J. (1998) 'Inequalities could outlive the Berlin Wall', *Community Care,* May 7–15.

House of Commons Social Services Select Committee (1985) *Community Care,* Second Report, Session 1984–5, HC13, London, HMSO.

Hudson, B. (1995) 'Joint commissioning: organisational revolution or misplaced enthusiasm?', *Policy and Politics,* vol. 23, no. 3, pp233–250.

Hudson, B. (1998) 'Circumstances change cases: local government and the NHS', *Social Policy and Administration,* vol. 32, no. 1, pp71–86.

Huxham, C. & Macdonald, D. (1992) 'Introducing collaborative advantage', *Management Decision,* vol. 30, no. 3, pp50–56.

Mawhinney, B. (1993) *Purchasing for Health: A Framework for Action,* Leeds, NHS Management Executive.

NHS Executive (1998) *National Service Frameworks,* HSC 1998/074, Leeds.

Nocon, A. (1994) *Collaboration in Community Care in the 1990s,* Sunderland, Business Education Publishers.

Powell, M. (1994) 'The forgotten anniversary? An examination of the 1944 White Paper, 'A National Health Service', *Social Policy and Administration,* vol. 28, no. 4, pp333–344.

Ottewill, R. & Wall, A. (1990) *The Growth and Development of the Community Health Services,* Sunderland, Business Education Publishers.

Warren, R., Rose, S. & Bergunder, A. (1974) *The Structure of Urban Reform,* Lexington, MA, Lexington Books.

Wistow, G. (1990) *Community Care Planning: A Review of Past Experiences and Future Imperatives,* Caring for People Implementation Documents, CC13, London, Department of Health.

Wistow, G. & Whittingham, P. (1988) 'Policy and research into practice', in D. Stockford (ed.) *Integrating Care Provision: Practical Perspectives,* London, Longman.

Wistow, G. & Hardy, B. (1996a) 'Balancing the collaborative and competitive imperatives', paper presented to the European Health Management Association Conference, University of Leeds, Nuffield Institute for Health.

Wistow, G. & Hardy, B. (1996b) 'Competition, collaboration and markets', *Journal of Inter-Professional Care,* vol. 10, no. 1, pp1–6.

11 Putting crime in its place: the causes of crime and New Labour's local solutions

Dee Cook

Introduction

In terms of British politics, Tony Blair's promise to be 'tough on crime and tough on the causes of crime' may prove one of the most memorable soundbites of the 1990s. The purpose of this chapter is to examine how his promise, made in opposition, is being fulfilled by the New Labour government. This examination involves unpackaging what are perceived as the 'causes of crime' and looking at the ways in which criminal justice and social policies are (or are not) effectively addressing these causes.

As I have argued at length elsewhere (Cook, 1997), when it comes to identifying the 'causes of crime' there is, broadly speaking, an explanatory continuum – ranging from purely individual to purely social explanations – along which a range of theories are located. Those theoretical positions, in turn, largely determine the focus of policy responses to crime. For instance, at one extreme, if crime is seen as simply a matter of 'right and wrong', then individuals must be held responsible for their actions. Consequently, society should respond to crime not by trying to understand or excuse it, but by seeking to condemn, deter and punish it more effectively. At the other extreme, if crime is seen as a product of social factors (notably deprivation), then the individual is not entirely to blame. Policy solutions should thus be geared to tackling the 'root causes' of poverty and reducing social inequality to give individuals a sense of social, as well as criminal, justice.

Criminal justice and social justice

Invariably, any analysis of policies geared to be tough on crime and its causes is bound to raise the thorny issue of the nature of the relationship between criminal justice and social justice – to be tough on crime evokes the former, to be tough on its causes evokes the latter. It also raises the question of whether government policies in the 'criminal' and 'social' realms are reconcilable and mutually supportive. Ideally, in a 'just society' this would not be problematic because criminal justice and social justice would be part of the same 'two-way street' (Reiman, 1990; Cook, 1997). But, while musing about precisely what this just society would consist of, we should remain wary of any idealised or disembodied notion of 'justice' because

> To imagine that penal policy can be formulated or implemented according to abstract legalistic notions of justice, fairness or seriousness is . . . a nonsense. It is, after all, impossible to punish crimes, we can only punish people. (Hudson, 1993, p73)

What groups of people are currently most likely to be the subjects of such punishment? The answer is revealed in the most cursory analysis of the social profile of our current prison population, which sadly reflects Barbara Hudson's view (held more than a decade ago) that 'by and large the criminal law is imposed by whites on blacks; by the advantaged classes on the disadvantaged; by the elderly on the young, and by men on women' (Hudson, 1987, p95). The issues at stake when addressing issues of criminal justice are, at the same time, highly individualised and social; juridical as well as generic.

Crime and the poorest neighbourhoods

It is important to recognise that crime and its causes are, in both political and popular discourse, seen to be firmly located in particular places. As I go on to discuss, New Labour has targeted its twofold crime reduction strategy on those places where the consequences of crime are most apparent and on those groups who are defined as most prone to offending. Firstly, the national Crime Reduction Strategy aims to tackle crime by investing in neighbourhoods with disproportionately high crime rates and in engaging with groups most likely to offend. Secondly, the Crime and Disorder Act (CDA) 1988 (discussed in detail below) requires all local authorities to audit crime and disorder problems – down to the level of 'hotspots' – and to devise and implement community safety strategies to tackle them.

This emphasis on crime-prone localities and crime-prone groups is not only central to New Labour's criminal justice policies, but also underlies a range of social policies too: the interconnections between criminal justice and social policies are implicit in the remit of the Social Exclusion Unit (SEU), which seeks to 'develop integrated and sustainable approaches to the problems of the worst housing estates, including crime, drugs, unemployment, community breakdown and bad schools etc.' (SEU, 1998).

The SEU seeks to succeed, where earlier initiatives from the 1960s on have failed, in 'setting in motion a virtuous circle of regeneration, with improvements in jobs, crime, education, health and housing all reinforcing each other' (ibid., p9).

A key policy theme in both policy spheres is the notion of (welfare) dependency, which is held to constitute both a cause and a consequence of crime and social exclusion. Successive ministerial pronouncements have drawn heavily on the notion of welfare dependency as both symptom and cause of these 'sink estates'. For example, Tony Blair referred to the SEU's New Deal for communities project in terms of a plan 'to turn round poor neighbourhoods, to reduce dependency, and empower local communities to shape a better future for themselves' (ibid., p8). At the same time, in promoting his Crime Reduction Strategy, the Home Secretary, Jack Straw, stated that

> we also need to tackle the culture of crime and the conditions in which it breeds. That means adopting a range of social and economic policies designed to promote opportunity, responsibility and to eradicate dependency. (Straw, 1998)

Strategies for community regeneration and those to combat crime and disorder thus share the same goal, because the 'fight against crime is at the centre of this Government's commitment to make Britain a better place to live' (Home Office, 1999, p2). It is within this discursive context that New Labour has placed the notion of community safety firmly at the heart of its crime and disorder policies. In 'putting crime in its place', crime is defined as an essentially 'local problem, requiring local solutions' (Straw, 1998).

The emphasis on local solutions is also evident in the range of social policies establishing 'New Deals' for the young unemployed, for lone mothers and for the most disadvantaged communities in England. Both criminal justice and social policies are, therefore, ostensibly geared to providing genuinely 'joined-up policies' to tackle the (perceived) social causes of crime within specific 'problem' localities. This chapter examines the geopolitics of both 'workfare' and community safety strategies in order to assess the extent to which New Labour policies stressing local solutions offer a coordinated and effective response to tackling crime and its causes.

The causes of crime

A recent briefing paper on the Crime Reduction Programme confirms the Home Secretary's view on the causes of crime. In the paper, entitled *Reducing Crime and Tackling its Causes,* he asserts that: 'Individuals have to accept responsibility for their criminal behaviour, and we have to acknowledge that crime feeds on social exclusion and family breakdown.' Although Straw goes on to stress the importance of tackling those 'underlying causes' which go beyond individual responsibility, he is less clear on precisely what they are and how they should be tackled:

> For many years successive governments have focused too much on the effects of crime without trying to tackle these underlying causes of crime. But we can only make a long-term impact on crime by concentrating on both crime and its causes. (Home Office, 1999, p2)

What the Home Secretary terms 'underlying causes' appear here to relate to 'social exclusion and family breakdown'. But how are resources and policy geared to addressing these causes? The government's Comprehensive Spending Review signalled investment in the criminal justice agencies – the police, probation and prison services, and the Youth Justice Board. The Crime Reduction Programme, announced in July 1998, prioritised further investment in:

- Working with families, children and schools to prevent young people becoming offenders of the future.
- Tackling crime in communities, particularly high volume crime such as domestic burglary.
- Developing products and systems which are resistant to crime.

- More effective sentencing practices.
- Working with offenders to ensure they do not re-offend *(ibid.,* p3).

On the face of it, the majority of the programmes outlined thus far are directed to dealing with offenders, to situational crime prevention measures and to enhancing the effectiveness of the criminal justice system. It is far from clear how measures based on these themes would address the causes of crime – save those implicitly attributed to the failings of young people and/or their families. This political emphasis on systems and process was presaged by Crawford in his comments on the provisions of the (then) Crime and Disorder Bill that: 'much of the focus remains on the criminal justice *process*. The sections of the Bill which deal with *preventing* youth crime prefer to offer broad intentions' (Crawford, 1998b, p61; emphasis added).

Meanwhile, the rhetoric of 'tackling the causes of crime' goes on unabated, though it has been subsumed (and assumed to be effective) within the overarching process model of multi-agency working within an active and engaged 'community'. The assumption that 'more community equals less crime' is, however, deeply flawed: most low-crime, middle-class, suburban areas do not display the features of mutual support, identity and 'connectedness' which are commonly associated with 'community'. Following on from this observation by Crawford, another stumbling block is that

> . . . the central paradox exposed by a century of research into community crime prevention remains that community responses to crime are easiest to generate in exactly those areas where they are least needed and hardest to establish in those where the need is greatest. *(ibid.,* p159)

In spite of such difficulties, the Audit Commission, like the Home Secretary, proffers multi-agency, local solutions to problems of crime, though it offers a slightly more expansive list of the causes, noting that:

> Many factors, social and physical, contribute to crime. The availability of easy targets, low perceived risks of being punished if caught, a poor social situation and wrong internally-held beliefs and low abilities increase the chances of an offence being committed. A strategy to address crime must tackle all of these factors and requires action across government departments and between local agencies. (Audit Commission, 1998, p49)

In addition to individualised factors and failings, the notion of deterrence – of situational crime prevention and the criminal justice system – is central to such explanations of crime. But any consideration of the dynamic and subjective nature of 'social' factors is largely absent in such accounts, though it clearly emerges from the following summary offered by Jock Young:

> . . . the crime rate is affected by a large number of things: by the level of deterrence exerted by the criminal justice system to be sure, but also by the levels of informal control in the community, by patterns of employment, by types of child-rearing, by the cultural, political and moral climate, by the level of organised crime, by the patterns of illicit drug use etc. etc. And to merely add together all these factors is complicated enough but insufficient for it does not allow human assessment and reflexivity – the *perceived* injustice of unemployment, for instance, or the *felt* injustice of bad policing or imprisonment. (Young, 1997, p33; emphasis in original)

Few would argue with the issue of complexity surrounding the multiple and various causes of crime which clearly add up to more than the sum of its parts, nor with the argument that we must take human reflexivity in account. But it must be stressed that the deterrent effect exerted by the criminal justice system is not something we can be 'sure' of at all. Even if we are persuaded by the logic of deterrence, it may operate very variably in practice. Deterrence theory is rooted in a rational calculation of risks – risks of detection, prosecution and subsequent punishment. But such risks are not only perceived very differently by certain individuals and groups within our society; they are experienced very differently too. For example, one would expect that a young, unemployed, black male who admitted importing cannabis, cocaine and gay pornography from Amsterdam would feel the full force of the law in terms of swift, certain and severe punishment, but if these same crimes were committed by a member of the European Parliament (as in the case of Tom Spencer MEP) they may be written off merely as 'an act of extreme folly', deserving only a financial penalty of £550 (*The Guardian,* 1 February 1999).

In summary, to return to Hudson's earlier point, the law is applied in a profoundly unequal manner and this is bound to cast doubt on the assumption that crime may be reduced by the (rationally calculated) deterrent effect of the (apparently irrational and perverse) criminal justice system. At the same time, process-based models of crime prevention fail to take into account the (often negative) perceptions of the criminal justice system held by members of marginalised groups, who are most likely targets of its policy interventions.

An understanding of, and voicing of, the views of marginalised or socially excluded groups is essential if the logic of New Labour's 'community safety' approach is to be effectively pursued. Under the CDA 1998 (discussed in detail below), data from local crime audits form the basis of community safety strategies and local target setting to reduce crime and disorder. But these audits concentrate overwhelmingly on existing data, already gathered and available from local partner agencies. Although exhorted to obtain feedback on community safety issues from 'hard to reach groups', local partnerships conducting crime and disorder audits may end up seeking the security of 'hard data', regardless of its utility for crime reduction. In turn, this could lead to a tokenistic approach to community safety on the part of information providers who may simply 're-badge existing activity as crime reduction' (Allen, 1998, p10). It is to the complex issue of the community safety planning process that we now turn.

Community safety planning

New Labour's adoption of the 'community safety' approach signifies a broader policy perspective on crime prevention than hitherto. Building on the principles of the Morgan Report (1991), New Labour's strategy stresses the importance of a broad-based multi-agency approach in preventing crime and enhancing community safety – a term which itself encompasses the wider material and social impact of crime and the anxieties it causes. It follows from this broader definition that agencies other than the police are to be actively involved: echoing the Morgan Report, the CDA 1998 enshrines the (statutory) role of the local authority and criminal justice agencies in jointly leading the community safety policy-making process. This approach was evident in the Local Authorities Association manifesto for community safety, published before the May 1997 election. It commends

> a locally-based approach derived from a partnership bringing together the local authority, the police service, other statutory agencies and the voluntary sector offers the best means to tackle the crime suffered by local communities.

But it adds that 'if this community safety approach is to succeed, it requires local coordination and a sympathetic national framework within which to operate' (ACC/ADC/AMA, 1997).

Despite the post-election 'sympathetic' political climate, the problem in successfully implementing community safety strategies remains one of resourcing. The New Labour government has continued to argue (as its predecessors did) that the development of effective crime reduction and prevention strategies, coupled with putting crime and disorder considerations at the centre of a range of local authority business, will offer 'substantial savings for local authorities' (Home Office, 1997, para. 34). On the other hand, Local Authority Associations had countered that: 'Without adequate resources, the community safety approach supported by the proposals in this manifesto will not achieve the objective of reducing crime and levels of anti-social behaviour' (ACC/ADA/AMA, 1997).

Recent research conducted in the West Midlands confirms that resourcing is very much an issue for local partnerships charged with implementing community safety strategies (Cook and Roberts, 1998). The resource issue may also determine the scope of local crime audits, which will form the basis of community safety plans. There is evidence that local partnerships may be encouraged to adopt a 'cheap and dirty' approach to collecting audit information, because of constraints of police and local authority resources and expertise, and because of the need to work to extremely tight Home Office deadlines. Although the CDA only received Royal assent on 31 July 1998, all local partnerships are required to have conducted crime audits and have their subsequent three-year crime and disorder reduction strategies in place by April 1999. These timescales have arguably undermined the Act's requirement for consultation with local residents and voluntary groups who are, literally, best placed to inform the audit process.

The provisions of the CDA require a multi-agency approach to community safety, coupled with the joint leadership of the local authority and criminal justice agencies, to achieve genuine reductions in crime and disorder. Within its framework, local authorities are required to publish a local community safety strategy with details of:

● mechanisms for local consultation;
● analysis of crime and disorder in the area;
● long- and short-term targets for crime and disorder reduction;
● time scales for each element in the plan;
● identification of responsibility for delivery of targets.

As the crime audit, and its subsequent role in monitoring against crime reduction targets, is regarded as the cornerstone of community safety planning, it is essential to examine the extent to which local partnerships have the expertise to perform the audit and monitoring tasks. In this context, Hirschfield and Bowers (1998) pose four key questions:

- Does the team have the necessary technical and research skills available to undertake the tasks?
- Are appropriate data sharing arrangements in place between the police, local authorities and other agencies?
- Do the gatekeepers of the relevant data (including the police) have the ability to respond to requests for information?
- Are the necessary analytical tools available – crime pattern analysis and geographical information system?

Recent experience of crime audit research indicates that, as leading agencies, many police forces and local authorities do not possess all of these essential capabilities, and that technical issues concerning data availability, collection and compatibility (let alone those of data sharing) may pose significant problems. For example, the principal unit for the analysis of crime data is the 'police beat'. The quality of the data varies enormously between police forces – from digitally held and up-to-date information on beat boundaries, to crude and dated 'paper' maps, annotated by hand. Clearly, the ability of local partnerships to 'map' crime and disorder in their borough will depend on the quality of this police data.

At the same time, police forces vary in their attitude to data sharing: some are prepared to share 'command and control'-type data on all reported incidents, while others will only offer the 'filtered' data provided to the Home Office on 'recorded crime', which fails to reflect the 'lower level' offences and incidents which are commonly regarded as the crime and disorder problem. Despite the CDA emphasis on multi-agency working, one police force quoted the Data Protection Act when justifying its refusal to release to its partners the grid references for its crime data – so much for identifying local crime problems, and so much for multi-agency working!

Although the CDA offers a legislative framework within which local partnerships must operate, it does not prescribe the agendas or structures of those partnerships. The mantra 'local solutions to local problems' echoes in the Home Secretary's assertion that the Act represents 'the culmination of a long held ambition to empower local people to take control of the fight against crime and disorder in their area'. Although I would not disagree that local residents are often best placed to identify the problems which face them and to pose workable solutions, the extent to which this will happen on the ground is open to debate. To a great extent the success or otherwise of local 'empowerment' to tackle crime depends on factors outside the realm of community safety policy per se:

If the interaction with the community is going to have continuity, from information gathering through consultation about priorities to involvement in strategy implementation, then the mechanisms for it to take place need to be integral to the overall approach to community involvement in the area . . . [and] may well be a reflection of how well communities are involved in local affairs generally. (Warburton, 1998, p14)

The Home Secretary presents the legislative framework provided by the CDA as hard evidence of 'the strength of the government's commitment to tackling crime and its causes across the board' (Home Office, 1998). As already argued, questions about exactly what these causes may be and the ways in which they will be addressed by the Act are left unanswered. In addition, critics may argue that, whatever these causes may be, the CDA passes the responsibility for 'tackling crime and its causes across the board' to local authorities and their partners without:

● adequate resourcing;
● an understanding of the practical problems of multi-agency working;
● clear guidance on crucial aspects of the legislation – not least, what constitutes 'disorder'.

To take some practical illustrations: the CDA empowers local authorities and police to seek antisocial behaviour orders against those who 'alarm, distress or harass' and requires that they consult over orders to avoid duplication. But several questions may arise in implementing this provision in the local context, for example:

● What, if any, is the role of the community in defining, interpreting and reporting antisocial behaviour?
● How can the technicalities of the law in relation to proof and legal procedure best be explained to concerned residents?
● Are police and local authority planning mechanisms compatible with one another and are the links between them transparent?
● How are the protocols for cooperation and responsibility for applying for antisocial behaviour orders to be managed between these 'equal partners'?

Similar questions may arise in relation to partnership provision between health authorities, youth justice and probation services geared to implementing other CDA provisions (including youth justice service plans, youth offending teams and child curfew schemes). The aspiration for 'joined-up solutions' to the local problems of crime and disorder is a laudable one, but clearly poses significant challenges. In addition, the integral role of 'the community' in the community safety project itself represents a challenge in both identifying local problems and joining up (and evaluating) local solutions.

Nonetheless, optimism about the future of community safety policy does remain. For example, when launching the region's Community Safety Conference (22 June 1998), the West Midlands Chief Constable, Ted Crewe, was enthusiastic about the provisions of the CDA which, he asserted, were 'about seizing the opportunity to improve the lot of the people of the West Midlands'. In relation to the challenges posed in auditing crime and disorder and in the community safety planning process he declared that 'He who hesitates is lost' and that 'Who dares wins'! The combative rhetoric continued with another lead agency representative – from the probation service – declaring to the assembled conference that 'The war against crime can be won'. Significantly, local authority representatives were more circumspect, indicating the 'danger of raised expectations' and a need to be 'realistic' about what can be accomplished in relation to crime and disorder, given local authority priorities in other key initiatives about education, health, democratic renewal and the New Deal (discussed below).

Partnerships in action

Research on partnership working indicates that, above all, clarity of aims, commitment of purpose and accountability are essential for success. For instance, an (unpublished) local research project on youth justice partnerships conducted before the CDA indicated the features which successful partnerships should display:

● partnerships need to be clear about their membership/constitution, expectations and agendas;
● the work of partnerships must be clearly publicised and understood (for instance, by the publication of annual reports to record and disseminate information about their work);
● a clear focus on stated objectives and terms of reference strengthens partnerships, and counters the claim that some may be 'merely talking shops';
● efforts should be made to enhance a sense of commitment from those involved in the partnership – greater authority to shape and implement policy results from the presence of more senior staff;

- communication between partners could be enhanced by the greater use of initiatives such as in-service training, secondments, shadowing and work placements in other agencies.

Recent crime audit research in the West Midlands has additionally indicated that a more genuine sense of partnership needs to be fostered between those seen as 'outsiders' and/or 'experts' and the community which they serve – the need for a sense of community 'ownership' of safety-related initiatives is essential. In this instance, physical improvements to the locality, funded by a series of Single Regeneration Budget (SRB) grants, had led to material and qualitative improvements in the lives of residents, and these improvements were also accompanied by reductions in crime. However, residents' fears about 'what will happen when the money runs out?' gave rise to feelings of insecurity over the future safety of their area (Cook and Roberts, 1998).

These research findings are echoed in the work of Crawford, who, in relation to community safety partnerships, adds the specific question – 'Does governmental policy encourage conditions which will sustain joint and collaborative action?' (Crawford, 1998a). Clearly, in the provisions of the CDA the government is investing heavily in the idea of partnerships at local level, but practice may prove problematic: the managerial imperative (performance indicators and output measures) and the internal politics of collaborating agencies may well distort this ideal. In so doing, one cornerstone of community safety policy may be eroded. Conditions favouring sustained collaborative action also depend on political momentum and resourcing: only time will tell if, in relation to community safety, either (or both) is sustainable.

Joined-up policies?

In commenting on the implementation of New Labour's crime and disorder policy, representatives of the National Association for the Care and Resettlement of Offenders have stressed the importance of locating community safety strategies within a broader social policy context, noting that 'It will be particularly important to maximise opportunities afforded by initiatives in adjacent areas of public policy, health and education action zones' (Allen, 1998). The brief discussion of partnership working above indicates the difficulties of 'joining up' responses even at a local level; the challenge of joining up policies across government departments raises the political stakes to another level entirely.

The SEU's report acknowledges the difficulties of coordinating the eighteen different policy action teams whose work will put into effect the project *Bringing Britain Together – a National Strategy for Neighbourhood Renewal* (SEU, 1998). The four goals of this strategy epitomise the 'virtuous circle of regeneration' referred to earlier; namely, 'lower long-term unemployment and worklessness; less crime; better health; better qualifications' (*ibid.*, p78).

The remit of Action Team 17 is 'joining it up locally', in itself an acknowledgement of the pivotal role of local authorities in a range of social initiatives on health, education, democratic renewal and crime reduction. The aim is that 'all these different initiatives should be dovetailed so as to make local planning to tackle social exclusion the norm' (SEU, 1988, p76). But there is currently a sense of being 'zoned out' in those (many) local authorities who are involved in bids for funding a range of policy initiatives – such as Health Action Zones, Education Action Zones, the New Deal for communities and SRB. In such circum- stances, it is understandable that many local authorities are more circumspect than their police partners about their ability to 'deliver' on community safety. But, under the provisions of the CDA, local authorities are required to take into account issues of community safety in all aspects of their work, so that it is community safety which (theoretically, at least) is held to lie at the heart of their strategic planning process.

There is a risk that the apparent priority accorded to crime reduction under New Labour could have a distorting effect on social policy, both nationally and within localities. As Crawford argues, the undue emphasis given to 'crime prevention – as opposed to poverty prevention, for example – may result in social policy, its direction and funding being redefined in terms of its implications for crime' (Crawford, 1998b, p121). This argument may be carried further, to account for the relative absence of the 'p word' – poverty – in New Labour's social policy discourse. What passes for 'joined-up policy' in reality serves to obfuscate more fundamental issues of poverty and inequality in contem- porary Britain.

This tendency is apparent in the conflation of the (allegedly) twin problems of crime and dependency: for example, in references to 'safer more responsible communities' and in tackling the causes of crime through policies designed to 'promote opportunity and eradicate dependency' (Straw, 1998). The very specific conception of dependency operating here is that of welfare dependency. Policies to eradicate dependency referred to within such discourses do not, for example, address the economic dependency of many women on their male partners (which is instead valorised in a range of family and child support policies), nor the dependency of often poorly paid workers on their employers which is, paradoxically, construed within this discourse as 'independence' (Dean and Taylor-Gooby, 1992).

The conflation of welfare dependency and crime, so evident in Straw's comments, also serves to limit the usage of the 'p word' in favour of the softer 'e word' – exclusion. By means of this ideological and linguistic sleight of hand, the increasing levels of poverty and widening gap between rich and poor which have characteristised British society over the past two decades (Joseph Rowntree Foundation, 1995; Walker and Walker, 1997) are magically consigned to the discourse of politics past.

The discursive project: crime, dependency and workfare

> The real breaking point is when you find yourself having a whole new debate, with new terms. That's more important than legislative achievements. (Newt Gingrich, quoted in Peck, 1998, p135)

The shift to 'workfare' in the USA can be understood as an essentially discursive project (Peck, 1998). The importance of ideas, vocabularies and discursive strategies to the building of the 'workfare consensus' is clearly appreciated by the Republican Speaker of the House, Newt Gingrich. A consequence of this consensus, according to Peck, is the imperative

> to end welfare not poverty per se, the objective being to correct those individual behavioural dysfunctions – such as moral laxity, inadequate work discipline – which are seen as a cause of poverty but more importantly as a consequence of the welfare system. (p136)

What has this got to do with tackling the causes of crime? The workfare and the crime reduction discursive projects share many common features: first and foremost, a firm belief in 'local solutions'. Additionally, they adopt remarkably similar frames of reference (in terms of locations and targeted groups) and share keenness for disseminating 'what works elsewhere'. Peck notes, too, that the language of poverty research and political commentary is framed largely in terms of ETM – the economistic–therapeutic–managerial model. The same may be argued for crime reduction strategies. The classic workfare experiments of Wisconsin and Massachusetts are hailed as exemplars of good practice in reducing the welfare rolls in the USA and their lessons have been (relatively uncritically) imported into the UK.

In a similar vein, the 'zero tolerance' approach of New York Police Chief William Bratton was hailed in the mid-1990s as the way forward for urban policing in England and Wales. But, in a persuasive critique of zero tolerance strategies, the Chief Constable of Thames Valley Police, Charles Pollard, argued that the adoption in the UK context of this New York approach 'characterised by aggressive policing, confrontational management, opportunistic short-termism and undue emphasis on "the numbers game" poses an enormous threat to the future' of policing and police–community relations (Pollard in Bratton, 1997). More recently, many of the empirical case studies which are drawn upon in the Home Office's paper *Reducing Offending* (itself the centrepiece of the Crime Reduction Programme) are based on US 'experiments'. The extent to which these are robust, reliable and relevant in the UK context is open to debate (Fraser, 1998).

The extensive Home Office guidelines on implementing the CDA (Home Office, 1998) are largely made up of similar 'what works' case studies from a range of UK pilots and locally based community safety programmes. They may suffer from the same criticism made by Peck of workfare experiments and exemplars in the USA – that they are 'disembedded' and lead to the tendency to construct policy on the basis of 'facts from nowhere', or at least form somewhere else (Peck, 1998, p141). He persuasively argues that in the USA poverty and welfare dependency have been conceptualised as largely inner-city problems, but the 'local solutions' posed, especially the workfare solution, have come from very different places, notably 'rural' areas of Wisconsin and Riverside in California. What he terms this 'profound spatial disconnect' is 'largely buried under the decontextualised pseudo-science of workfare advocacy' (*ibid.*, p141).

It could similarly be argued that guidance on 'model' community safety practice is disconnected and decontextualised. The notion of learning from 'best practice' (in terms of local solutions to local problems) is evident in the Home Office CDA guidelines, which offer 'boxed' exemplars of 'what works elsewhere' in terms of enhancing community safety. While acknowledging the value of sharing ideas on effective practice, it is also important to recognise the uniqueness of 'place' and localities in the development of community safety strategy. Moreover, if good practice guidelines were seen as a 'short cut' and adopted wholesale, they may also undermine one of the cornerstones of the CDA – community consultation – and could be seen to run counter to the 'down-up', community empowerment, partnership model which lies at the heart of the community safety project itself. In the realm of crime reduction, as in that of workfare, 'sub-national experiences leaving a strong imprint on national debates' in the sense that we may feel we know what works, but are unsure if/where else it will work. In relation to both crime reduction and workfare, effectiveness is 'contingent on local conditions', not least local (flexible?) labour market conditions (ibid.).

In the sense that workfare addresses the politics of poverty, not its roots, I would argue that New Labour's Crime Reduction Strategy addresses politics of crime rather than its root causes. Just as the 'fuzzy language' of workfare facilitates the discursive project by holding together a wide range of contradictory political views, so the language of 'community safety' and 'local solutions' is sufficiently benign to serve a similar ideological function. In both instances, deep-rooted issues of inequality are thereby concealed, and (macro-) economic interventions are eschewed:

> If we wish to achieve real, and effective, changes to problems of unemployment and inequality in modern society, we have to take a broader policy perspective, and focus policy intervention earlier in the economic cycle. . . . To put this in more practical terms, changing incentives and encouragement for the unemployed will not provide them with jobs, still less adequately paid ones. (Alcock, 1997)

Alcock goes on to suggest interventions such as investment planning, job creation strategies and labour market regulation (minimum and maximum wages!), and rightly identifies that, despite the political focus on moral responsibility, issues of 'collectivism and redistribution keep creeping back on to the agenda' (*ibid.*, p58). Peck (1998) similarly indicates the need for a broader policy framework for dealing with issues of unemployment, which both takes account of the realities of 'flexible' labour markets and does not rule out increased taxes for the rich.

This critical perspective does not accord with current New Labour policies: the Trade and Industry Secretary Stephen Byers recently declared that 'wealth creation is now more important that wealth redistribution' and went on to echo Nigel Lawson's (much decried) 'trickle-down theory':

> I firmly believe that the best way to address inequality and social exclusion is to create a more affluent, more successful Britain with opportunities for everyone to fulfil their potential. (Byers, quoted in *The Guardian*, 2 February 1999)

If poverty is to be regarded as a source, if not a cause, of crime (Cook, 1997), then by putting crime 'in its place', New Labour has effectively sidestepped the 'source' problems of economic conditions and inequalities at local, regional and national levels. Tackling the causes of crime would also involve addressing a range of issues around the perceived legitimacy of the criminal justice system – after all, if people are to obey the law, then the law itself must be seen to be just and to be fairly applied to all. In the wake of the MacPherson enquiry, following six years on from the death of Stephen Lawrence, the question of such legitimacy remains a vital one.

In pursuit of noble causes

In his first pronouncement as Prime Minister on the steps of 10 Downing Street, Tony Blair promised 'practical measures in pursuit of noble causes'. While social justice is regarded by many as the noblest of causes, there seemed reluctance on the part of New Labour to spell out the ideological commitment which would underlie such measures. Immediately after the May 1997 election victory, former Deputy Leader Roy Hattersley expressed frustration that New Labour lacked an identifiable 'ideal to live by' He perceptively noted that the promise of practical measures was all very well, but 'the problem with pragmatism is nobody ever died for it ' (*The Guardian*, 14 May 1997). At the infamous 'relaunch' of a raft of New Labour policies in January 1999, political commentators were still calling out for 'the big idea' which would underpin and guide the range of programmes being (re)announced:

> The Government needs to generate the one commodity that has so far eluded it: a single, coherent idea which might connect the whole. Without that over-arching logic, the rash of schemes and projects to be rolled out this week will still seem like a shopping list, not a vision. (*Guardian* editorial, 12 January 1999)

Current criminal justice and social policies ostensibly geared to tackling crime and its causes seem more like a shopping list to me. Without a clear vision or sense of what 'community' actually means in disparate localities, it is unlikely that 'community safety' will prove a big enough idea around which to construct both the criminal justice and social policies required to combat crime and its causes. Without a 'bigger' and clearer vision of justice itself, the task is an impossible one.

Recent years have seen a series of setbacks to the notion of 'criminal justice', the most recent, and possibly most significant, being evident in the findings of the MacPherson Report. As stated at the beginning of the chapter, social and criminal justice are interdependent and part of the same 'two-way street' (Reiman, 1990). The establishment of the SEU and its focus on bringing together a range of social policy intiatives – in relation to crime reduction, health, education, training and local democracy – does signal New Labour's intention to generate coherent policies to tackle 'social exclusion' in the local context. However, the 'two-way street' approach would also mean New Labour going 'back to basics' in stating a firm and overarching commitment to reducing the economic and social inequalities which are a source both of crime and of injustice. It would mean challenging the Treasury view of Stephen Byers, in an acknowledgement that wealth redistribution (and notably increased taxation) is not beyond the pale for New Labour. I would argue, therefore, that the 'coherent idea' which New Labour needs to establish is that criminal justice and social justice are interconnected ideals to which the government is equally committed.

References

ACC/ADA/AMA (1997) *Crime: the Local Solution Manifesto,* London, Association of County Councils, Association of District Councils, Association of Metropolitan Authorities.

Alcock, P. (1996) 'Welfare and self-interest', in F. Field (ed.) *Stakeholder Welfare,* London, Institute of Economic Affairs.

Allen, R. (1998) 'Partnership, prevention and powers: the crime and disorder act 1998', *Safer Society,* no.1, October.

Audit Commission (1998) *Misspent Youth '98: The Challenge for Youth Justice,* London, Audit Commission.

Bratton, W. (1997) *Zero Tolerance: Policing a Free Society,* London, Institute of Economic Affairs.

Cook, D. (1997) *Poverty, Crime and Punishment,* London, Child Poverty Action Group.

Cook, D. & Roberts, M. (1998) 'The Wren's Nest crime audit', unpublished report for Wren's Nest Safety Partnership and Dudley MBC.

Crawford, A. (1998a) 'Delivering multi-agency partnerships in community safety', in A. Marlow & J. Pitts (eds) *Planning Safer Communities,* Lyme Regis, Russell House Publishing.

Crawford, A. (1998b) *Crime Prevention and Community Safety,* London, Longman.

Dean, H. & Taylor-Gooby, P. (1992) *Dependency Culture: the Explosion of a Myth,* Hemel Hempstead, Harvester Wheatsheaf.

Fraser, P. (1998) 'Reducing offending', *Safer Society,* no.1, October.

Hirschfield, A. & Bowers, K. (1998) 'Monitoring, measuring and mapping community safety', in A. Marlow & J. Pitts (eds) *Planning Safer Communities,* Lyme Regis, Russell House Publishing.

Home Office (1997) *Getting to Grips with Crime: a New Framework for Local Action,* Consultation Document, London, Home Office.

Home Office (1998) *Crime and Disorder Bill (1998): Guidance on Statutory Crime and Disorder Partnerships,* London, Home Office.

Home Office (1999) *Reducing Crime and Tackling its Causes: Briefing Note on the Crime Reduction Programme,* London, Home Office.

Hudson, B. (1987) *Justice Through Punishment,* London, Macmillan.

Hudson, B. (1993) *Penal Policy and Social Justice,* London, Macmillan.

Joseph Rowntree Foundation (1995) *Inquiry into Income and Wealth,* vol. 1, York, Joseph Rowntree Foundation

Peck, J. (1998) 'Workfare: a geopolitical etymology', *Environment and Plannning: Societry and Space,* vol. 16, pp133–161.

SEU (1998) *Bringing Britain Together: a National Strategy for Neighbourhood Renewal,* Cm 4045, London, The Stationery Office.

Reiman, J. (1990) *The Rich Get Richer and the Poor Get Prison,* London, Macmillan.

Straw, J. (1998) Speech to Conference on The Renewal of Criminal Justice? New Labour's Policies in Perspective, Leeds University, September 1998.

Walker, A. & Walker, C. (eds) (1997) *Britain Divided: the Growth of Social Exclusion in the 1980's and 1990's,* London, Child Poverty Action Group

Warburton, F. (1998) 'Implementing crime and disorder reduction strategies: the Crime and Disorder Act 1998', *Safer Society,* no.1, October.

Young, J. (1997) 'Charles Murray and the American prison experiment: the dilemmas of a libertarian', in C. Murray (ed.) *Does Prison Work?,* London, Institute of Economic Affairs.

12 Retreat or reform? New US strategies for dealing with poverty

Robert I. Lerman

The realignment of US welfare policies over the 1990s is real, significant, but often misunderstood. From the publicity surrounding the passage of 1996 welfare law (the Personal Responsibility and Work Opportunity Reconciliation Act, or PRWORA), observers could reasonably conclude that the US was abandoning programmes for the poor, the ideology of self-reliance had run amok, and soon massive numbers of low-income families would be living on the streets. President Bill Clinton's willingness to sign the new law set off a wave of protests within his own party and even his administration. Senator Daniel P. Moynihan, the acknowledged Congressional expert on welfare, called the bill 'welfare repeal' not 'welfare reform' and '. . . the first step in dismantling the social contract that has been in place in the United States since at least the 1930s' (Moynihan, 1996). The *New York Times* (25 August 1996, p12) saw the bill as 'draconian'. Three high level officials in the Department of Health and Human Services (DHHS) resigned because of their strong distaste for the bill. Clinton's old friend and DHHS official, Peter Edelman (1997), wrote that signing the bill was 'The worst thing Bill Clinton has done'.

Reporters certainly exaggerated the notion that the President had '. . . ended six decades of guaranteed help to the nation's poorest children . . .' (*New York Times*, 25 August 1996, p1). Even under the former cash assistance programme, states rather than the federal government chose the benefit level paid to families with children. The federal government only matched state dollars, sometimes helping to pay minimal benefits. Under the new programme, states would continue to decide on benefit levels and receive federal dollars in return, albeit via a formula that might reduce state effort. From its inception, the nation's cash welfare programme was a federal–state system, but one that gave states plenty of authority to offer only minimal support.

Critics of the new bill properly cited the 'sticks' forcing low-income parents, especially lone parents, off cash assistance and into an inhospitable job market. But they took little account of the social policies that added 'carrots' to help those parents who went to work. The substantial expansion of the Earned Income Tax Credit (EITC), of childcare and of health insurance for low-income families is making work more rewarding just as cash welfare is becoming less hospitable. Moreover, while time limits now only apply to the receipt of cash assistance, low income families can supplement their wages indefinitely with food stamps, housing and medical assistance.

How, then, should we judge US welfare policies? Should we see the new law as a war on the poor? Or should we instead focus on changes in cash welfare in the context of other US social policies that maintain and in some ways expand the commitment to low-income families? Is there an underlying logic to this new approach to structuring benefit programmes? If so, are the early results promising or discouraging? What criteria should we use to judge the success or failure of the new policies?

The history in brief

Despite the rhetoric about abandoning the poor, the replacement of the nation's cash assistance for low-income families with children (Aid to Families with Dependent Children, or AFDC[1]) took place in the context of increasing spending on other antipoverty programmes. Federal spending on six major programmes rose most in percentage terms between 1965 and 1975, continued rising but at a slower rate between 1975 and 1990, and jumped significantly between 1990 and 1995 (Burtless *et al.*, 1997). The share of GDP going to these six programmes increased from 1.9 to 2.9 per cent during the first half of the 1990s. Federal and state spending on a more comprehensive list at income-tested programmes amounted to over 5 per cent of GDP in 1994. Expansions in spending have come almost entirely through programmes providing goods in kind, such as food stamps, housing assistance, medical assistance and childcare assistance (Committee on Ways and Means, 1996).

The passage of a significant welfare law in 1996 came about not because of a revolt against spending but because of near-universal dissatisfaction with the existing cash assistance programme and after many failed attempts at reform.[2]

By the mid-1990s, the time was right for a new set of reform initiatives. AFDC benefits had dramatically eroded with inflation, with income floors in the median state falling by 50 per cent between 1970 and 1996. While food stamp benefit levels increased with inflation, the combined income floor from AFDC and food stamps had declined by about 30 per cent. Still, AFDC rolls had recently ballooned to record levels, rising from 3.7 million families in 1989 to over 5 million in 1994; at that point, about 15 per cent of all families with children and over 60 per cent of poor children obtained support from AFDC (Committee on Ways and Means, 1996). The mild approach to requiring work and encouraging training embodied in the 1988 Family Support Act appeared ineffective. The welfare system was extremely unpopular not only with taxpayers but also with recipients. According to Edin and Lein (1996), few recipients received enough assistance to make ends meet. Yet going to work and reporting their earnings would do little or nothing to raise their incomes, since dollars earned would be offset by reductions in or total loss of benefits. The only elements of the system stimulating work were the relatively low benefits and the ability to earn small amounts of unreported income by working 'off the books'.

Inspired in part by Ellwood's plan for coupling expanded non-welfare benefits (such as assured child support and guaranteed jobs) along with time limits on cash assistance (Ellwood, 1988), President Clinton had run on a platform to 'end welfare as we know it'.

Meanwhile, Congress was increasingly animated over the continuing rise in the proportion of children born outside marriage. Between 1970 and 1995, non-marital births had increased from 11 to 32 per cent of all births in the USA. The percentage of children living with only one parent tripled from about 9 per cent in 1960 to over 27 per cent in 1995. Children living with the poorest group of lone parents – mothers who had never married – jumped from less than 3 per cent in 1980 to over 9 per cent in 1995. By 1995, only one in three black children lived with two parents and over 30 per cent lived with a mother who had never married (Committee on Ways and Means, 1996).

After the passage of the 1988 Family Support Act, the federal government liberalised policies that allowed states to waive selected provisions of the AFDC law. Policies embodied in state waivers helped pave the way for the passage of PRWORA. Although the waiver requests varied, they typically included such features as family caps (no increment in benefits for additional children born to families already on welfare), requiring mothers under age 18 to live with their parents to qualify for benefits and mandating benefit reductions to families whose children did not attend school or become immunised. States often liberalised rules to allow recipients to keep more of their earnings and to expand eligibility for low-income two-parent families. More significantly, several states adopted time limits on the receipt of cash benefits.

The legislative path to 'ending welfare as we know it'

Notwithstanding the popularity of welfare reform, the Clinton administration chose to begin with two components related to a non-welfare strategy for low-income families. The first, a major expansion of the EITC passed in 1993, would provide sufficient work-related cash subsidies so that working families would escape poverty even if the jobs paid low wages. Unlike most benefit programmes, the EITC subsidy rises as families earn more over an initial range of earnings, thereby encouraging work at least up to a threshold level. Between the initial threshold and an intermediate income level, families receive a constant credit. The credit then phases out as earnings rise beyond the second threshold. Under the expanded EITC, parents of two children receive a 40 per cent subsidy on their first $9,000 of annual earnings, a fixed amount of $3,600 per year for those with earnings between $9,000 and $12,000, and then a 21 per cent phase-out of benefits as income rises above $12,000. Aggregate benefits from the EITC jumped from about $7 billion in 1990 to nearly $26 billion in 1996.

The second component, a universal health insurance plan, would allow low-income families to leave welfare without losing access to medical care. The universal health insurance plan not only failed in Congress, but also paved the way for a Republican takeover of Congress in the 1994 election.

The Clinton administration unveiled its welfare reform legislation in mid-1994. The proposal called for restricting the years of cash assistance to families headed by young mothers, subsidised public jobs offered to those over the time limit and unable to find unsubsidised positions, expanded childcare funding, and tightened enforcement of child support. At the time, the administration bill was not far from the pending Republican alternative. However, opposition from liberal members of the relevant House subcommittee delayed the bill long enough to prevent passage in the 105th Congress (Ellwood, 1996). Then, in November 1994, the Republicans took over the majority in the House and Senate for the first time in forty years. From that point on, a new dynamic took hold that ultimately led to the passage of PRWORA.

The welfare bill becomes law

The Republican majority in the House of Representatives developed a stricter plan than the one proposed by President Clinton or even the Republican plan of 1994. After President Clinton vetoed two versions of the Republican plan, he weathered the harsh criticism of many fellow Democrats and signed the third version of a law that represented a dramatic shift in US welfare policy. The bill repealed AFDC but replaced it with an alternative cash assistance programme, Temporary Assistance for Needy Families (TANF).

The federal government ceded considerable authority to the state level. States can now choose which groups are eligible, how benefits vary with income, how long benefits can last, how quickly recipients must go to work, and which individuals are exempt from time limits. They are not bound by federal rules that give eligible applicants an unconditional entitlement to benefits. If a state runs out of money near the end of the year, they can simply tell otherwise eligible families to wait until the following year.

Oddly, while proponents of PRWORA were touting the authority it was handing over to states, Congress was imposing new federal mandates through this very programme. The new law required that recipients enter a work activity (which could involve subsidised jobs, job search or job readiness training) within two years of obtaining assistance and that states must have at least 25 per cent of single-parent families in work activities by 1997, rising to 50 per cent in 2002. It also placed a five-year lifetime limit on the receipt of federal welfare assistance. However, the law does allow states to exempt up to 20 per cent of their average monthly caseload from the time limit and to continue covering cash assistance for families who stay on welfare form for more than five years out of their own state revenues.

One of the most controversial changes was the shift in federal funding. Under AFDC, the federal government matched each dollar spent by states with at least one dollar in federal funds, thereby providing states with an incentive to spend more on welfare. PRWORA replaced this system with a fixed federal block grant for the TANF programme based on what states received in 1993 or 1994. The absence of a matching payment reduced the marginal incentive for states to raise benefits. Further, PRWORA repealed a provision that had prevented states from lowering their benefits below May 1998 levels. A common expectation was that states would respond to the fiscal incentives and to the long-time concern about migration to more generous areas by lowering payment levels. And, once one state moved to lower benefits, neighbouring states would do so as well, thus setting off a vicious cycle.

Budgetary savings were to come largely from aspects of PRWORA unrelated to the AFDC programme. Space does not permit a detailed analysis of these provisions, but they are worth mentioning. The largest policy changes involved reducing welfare benefits paid to immigrants, reducing food stamp benefits to non-working childless individuals (ages 18–50) and tightening eligibility for disability benefits for children.

Two other initiatives passed in 1997 improved the chances of recipients making a successful transition off welfare. One was the expansion of health insurance for children in low-income families. Although all children in poor families were already eligible for Medicaid benefits, Congress authorised an additional $24 billion over five years to expand health insurance coverage to children in families with incomes up to 200 per cent of the poverty line (Bruen and Ullman, 1998). Also in 1997, the President proposed and Congress passed an allocation of $3 billion beyond the TANF block grant to spend on moving the least-employable TANF recipients and non-custodial fathers of TANF children into long-term unsubsidised employment (Nightingale and Brennan, 1998). Coming on top of funds in the block grant formerly earmarked for employment assistance, the welfare-to-work grants have enabled states to provide significant funds for programmes emphasising direct job preparation, job placement and career advancement.

The underlying logic of the new benefit structure

Benefit programmes for the poor face inevitable trade-offs between assuring adequate benefits, providing reasonable incentives to work and limiting budgetary outlays. Targeting payments on those in need requires phasing out benefits with income, thereby reducing the financial gain from working. US benefit programmes have long followed the negative income tax algebra of an income guarantee (a maximum payment to those with the lowest incomes), a tax or benefit reduction rate (the decline in benefits per dollar of added income) and a breakeven point (an income level at which benefits phase out completely). Food stamps, housing benefits and cash assistance have all adopted this approach. Until recently, the combined impact of benefit programmes was to create a welfare trap, with benefit reduction rates reaching nearly 100 per cent. Recipients not working at all received virtually no additional income by going to work at low wages or working part-time. Lone parents leaving work for welfare lost little income and gained more time to care for their children. Partly as a result of this benefit structure, AFDC attracted not only the destitute who faced chronic and serious barriers to work but also lone parents with moderate earnings potential.

Given the diversity in the caseloads, advocates for the poor have long faced a difficult quandary in portraying non-elderly, non-disabled families on welfare. Were they just like everyone else but temporarily down on their luck? Or were they incapable of helping themselves because of so many social and physical barriers? Conservatives saw most recipients as capable but either trapped or willingly participants in a system that penalised work and rewarded divorce and non-marital childbearing. Both groups used research on the length of time families remained on welfare to justify their image of recipients. The evidence showed that most families entering welfare stayed for a short time, certainly less than two years. On the other hand, at least half the caseload at any point in time was made up of people staying on welfare for many years.

Under the new benefit structure, the two types of recipients are increasingly going separate ways. Recipients or potential recipients with a low-to-moderate capacity to earn money on their own are avoiding cash welfare and many are taking advantage of benefits under a kind of bridge system – one that provides benefits to low-wage workers until they achieve high enough incomes on their own. 'Hard-core' recipients with few skills and with physical or social barriers to work remain on welfare.

The implicit strategy is to cajole, threaten and encourage recipients (or potential recipients) to enter the job market, leave the welfare system or avoid enrolling in the first place, and then take advantage of non-welfare income supplements to achieve adequate incomes. Success in these steps reduces the welfare rolls and leaves states with more money per remaining recipient and thus more resources to deal with long-term, hard-core cases. In principle, the new approach can make both groups better off. Former recipients leaving (or not entering) welfare even for a full-time (35 hours), minimum wage ($5.15 per hour) job can attain an income level 10 per cent above the official poverty line by combining earnings with the EITC and food stamp benefits. With housing assistance (received by about 25 per cent of welfare families), working at the minimum wage would bring a family about 30 per cent above the poverty line. By working for part of their income and receiving supplements outside the cash welfare system, these low-income working families are more likely to gain pride in their accomplishments, less likely to experience the stigma of receiving welfare and more likely to participate in mainstream social insurance programmes (Solow, 1998).

Families with no one able to earn even a modest income often face serious educational or social problems (such as drug abuse or domestic violence) that were formerly ignored by the welfare system. Indeed, the inability to work at a minimum-wage job in the context of a high employment economy strongly suggests the presence of some non-economic barrier. With recipients under threat of ultimately losing cash benefits and with states concerned about what will happen to the children, states are trying harder to deal with these intractable problems.

The threats to non-working recipients come in the form of a five-year lifetime limit on the receipt of federal cash welfare and a requirement to take part in a work or training activity for at least 20 hours per week after two years. How many recipients lose benefits directly as a result of these rules will take years to determine. Estimates based on a world in which no time limits were in place indicate only about 23 per cent of recipients would have remained on the rolls for five consecutive years (Duncan *et al.*, 1997) and that less than 20 per cent of new recipients would have exceeded the time limit within eight years. Up to 20 per cent of recipients can receive federal dollars beyond five years and some states – including the two states with the largest caseloads, California and New York – are guaranteeing assistance beyond the five-year limit (Zedlewski *et al.*, 1998). New Jersey plans to extend benefits at state expense for at least a sixth year.

The financial elements of the income support system reinforce the pro-work message. Jobless families see stagnating benefits at a time when low-income working families have access to expanded support. Going to work no longer leads to sharp reductions in public benefits, partly because some states permit recipients to keep more of their cash welfare benefits when their earnings increase. Although the specifics vary by state and by whether a family must pay for childcare and/or receives child support or housing assistance, recipients who go to work at the minimum wage typically see reductions in benefits of only about 20–30 per cent of their earnings. In the median of thirteen states studied by Acs *et al.* (1998), a lone parent with two children would find her family income rise from about $730 per month to nearly $1,300 per month (18 per cent over the poverty line) by working 35 hours per week at the minimum wage. While such families would no longer be eligible for welfare in low-paying states, they would still manage to achieve an income above the poverty line. Today's low unemployment rates and availability of low wage jobs in most areas of the USA make the path above the official poverty line a realistic option.

Financial disincentives become more significant once mothers reach moderate wage levels. A full-time lone parent raising her wage from $5.15 to $9 per hour would increase her earnings by nearly $600 per month, but see only a $200 increase in income. Thus, serious financial disincentives arise only after families are somewhat above the poverty line.

Going to work moves recipients into a kind of 'bridge' system, which falls between primary reliance on welfare and full independence from government transfers. Like other low-income working families, former recipients supplement their earnings with the EITC, food stamps, childcare and health insurance. As workers, they are less subject to administratively costly and paternalistic requirements. They themselves and taxpayers begin to see the supplements as providing a helping hand to those willing to work and very unlike welfare payments paid mostly to families with no one working. In addition, child support payments become more important than when the family receives welfare. Recipients of AFDC gained little from support payments because dollars paid by non-custodial parents were counted as income to the family and thus reduced welfare payments nearly dollar for dollar (Bassi and Lerman, 1996). Once families leave welfare, they can keep over 70 per cent of these contributions from non-custodial fathers. While child support payments go to only a minority of former recipients, the improved incentives and more effective enforcement should make child support a more important income supplement in the future.

Problems in financing childcare and health insurance coverage are often cited as major barriers to employment among lone mothers. To cope with the added childcare burden, spending on childcare subsidies for low-income families increased substantially. Federal childcare funding rose by over 25 per cent (Long and Clark, 1997), and states are raising their spending on childcare as well.

Since welfare recipients automatically qualified for health insurance under the Medicaid programme but low-income workers were rarely eligible for Medicaid or employer-based health insurance, the potential loss of health insurance apparently discouraged families from leaving welfare (Moffitt and Wolfe, 1992). To mitigate this problem, Congress severed the link between welfare and Medicaid; under PRWORA, families who qualify on an income basis but no longer receive cash welfare still qualify for Medicaid. In addition, 1986 expansions of Medicaid are now providing coverage for low-income pregnant women and children born on or after 1 October 1983 (children sixteen years and under in 1999). Medicaid benefits are also available on a transition basis for up to two years after leaving welfare. Finally, as noted above, Congress added $24 billion over five years in federal funds for state health insurance for uninsured, low-income children in families with incomes too high to qualify for Medicaid but too low to afford insurance themselves (Weil, 1997). Again, the emphasis is on helping low-income working families, thereby improving their work incentives.

Overall, the tightening of work requirements and restrictions on long-term eligibility will reduce but far from end cash welfare in the USA. Historically, most welfare recipients would not be directly affected by the lifetime five-year limit. Nearly 20 per cent of welfare cases represent 'child-only' cases, in which children either are not living with a parent or are living with a parent not eligible for welfare. The parents may receive disability benefits, may be immigrants ineligible for welfare or may have been sanctioned. Welfare assistance is likely to continue for these cases, since no one in the unit is subject to the work requirement or time limit.

Early responses by recipients and states

Critics feared that the new welfare law would trigger a rise in poverty for four main reasons. First, states would ultimately lower benefits in response to competition from other states, to a funding formula that no longer provided federal matching payments and to the long-term decline in federal contributions. Second, because of the scarcity of jobs, large numbers of recipients would find themselves with no visible means of support once they reached the time limit. Third, even in areas of low unemployment, many recipients would be unable to find jobs because of their limited capacity to work. Fourth, the cut-off of benefits to immigrants would quickly worsen the level of economic deprivation among poor people who had not yet become citizens.

Surprisingly, despite the outrage against the new law voiced by advocates for the poor, welfare recipients were ambivalent about if not supportive of several of its most controversial provisions. In a survey taken by Public Agenda (Farkas with Johnson, 1996) and in focus groups in Boston, Chicago and San Antonio, a majority of recipients endorsed limitations on the amount of time people could spend on welfare, work requirements and family caps that deny added benefits to mothers having additional children while on welfare. Sometimes, the rhetoric of mothers on welfare mirrored the speech of advocates of reform. Time limits would force recipients to take control of their lives and avoid becoming trapped in the system, and would limit the abuse of the system by people not in need. At the same time, recipients voiced strong support for non-welfare assistance, especially childcare and health insurance, which allowed them to take and keep jobs. Overall, the recipients were more optimistic than the critics, but more pessimistic than supporters of the new law.

A race to the bottom?

Substituting a block grant for a matching formula means that states bear the full added costs of raising benefits and gain all the revenues from cutting benefits. So, the argument goes, once a few states respond to these incentives, other states will follow so as not to become more generous than their neighbours and possibly attract migrants from low-paying states (Peterson, 1995). The weak part of the argument is clear when one recognises that even under the matching formula, states allowed benefits to erode significantly. Moreover, the old system did less to encourage benefit increases than meets the eye. While the federal matching formula meant that each dollar increase in AFDC benefits would cost states at most half a dollar, states soon found that the increased eligibility for AFDC would lower federally financed food stamp benefits, raise Medicaid costs and thus end up costing states more than a dollar.

The second argument is that by 2002 – when the federal five-year time limit becomes effective – the fixed federal grant will be insufficient to cope with state caseloads. States will then have to cut back on job assistance and childcare, and/or lower benefits.

So far, the block grant has worked to encourage, not discourage, state spending on low-income families. Had the old matching formula been in place, federal spending would have declined with the decline in caseloads. Instead, the US General Accounting Office (1998) estimates that the shift to a block grant has meant a windfall for states of about 40 per cent of expected federal resources. Between 1996 and 1997, federal outlays per recipient jumped from nearly $1,200 to $1,650. The percentage gains were much higher in most states but somewhat smaller in the states with the largest caseloads. For example, Wisconsin saw its federal grant per recipient more than double from $1,310 to $3,170; in Massachusetts, the increase was from $1,542 to $2,336. The new law required states to maintain spending at about 75–80 per cent of prior levels. But with caseloads plummeting, states were able to reduce total state spending while leaving state spending per recipient constant, thereby allowing overall resources per recipient to increase by about 25 per cent.

With additional money available per recipient, it is not surprising that states have maintained benefit levels. In fact, by allowing recipients to earn more without losing benefits, many states have actually raised benefits paid to recipients with earned income. Some of the added money is spread across low-income families not on welfare. Many states are putting funds away for a future contingency, recognising that times are particularly good at the moment but that future increases in unemployment could expand the welfare rolls and strain state resources. For these reasons and perhaps because of the transitional first year of the new programme, states left $1.2 billion in federal dollars, or 9 per cent of their allocation, unspent in 1997 and remaining in their accounts.

Another way for states to avoid having heavy fiscal burdens in the future is to invest in improving the job capacities of recipients. Most states are expanding job placement, childcare, counselling and transportation assistance. Outlays on job preparation programmes rose by over 100 per cent in California, 39 per cent in Maryland, and almost 25 per cent in Louisiana and Michigan. New York and California each raised spending on childcare services by over $100 million. The broader availability of work-related benefits reinforces efforts to reshape the culture of the welfare office from processing cheques to helping recipients find jobs. Today's caseworkers must motivate recipients to seek work, judge their willingness to participate in programme activities, provide one-time grants for short-term needs to divert people from going on welfare and refer recipients to specialised services, including programmes dealing with drug abuse, mental health and domestic violence.

A serious recession that expands caseloads and cuts state tax revenues may cause states to cut cash assistance benefits in the way critics fear. So far, however, states are expanding rather than cutting benefits, assisted by the reductions in caseloads, the sharp increases in federal resources per recipient and the decisions by many state policy makers to invest today in order to avoid fiscal burdens tomorrow.

Availability of jobs

The concern over the shortage of jobs available to welfare recipients is widespread. Edelman (1997) sees the problem in stark terms, arguing:

The basic issue is jobs. There simply are not enough jobs now. Four million adults are receiving Aid to Families with Dependent Children. Half of them are long-term recipients. In city after city around America the number of people who will have to find jobs will quickly dwarf the number of new jobs created in recent years. (p52)

Another worry is that a massive inflow of welfare recipients into the job market will impose hardships on other workers in low-wage markets (Solow, 1998). As recipients expand the supply of low-skill workers, wages in the market will fall.

To gain perspective on the jobs issue, consider the national figures. Although welfare caseloads stood at 4 million in 1996, over 1 million were 'child-only' cases or otherwise exempt from work requirements. The best estimates suggest that welfare changes will add between 140,000 and 300,000 recipients per year to the job market, at most 0.2 per cent to the labour force of 135 million workers. At a maximum, the economy would have to absorb labour force growth of 1.3 per cent per year instead of the expected growth (absent welfare recipient inflows) of 1.1 per cent per year in order to have no increase in unemployment. Since the US economy sustained a growth rate of 2 per cent per year over a thirty-year period from 1960 to 1990, reaching this goal may not be difficult. Indeed, these added workers might be viewed as helping the economy attain slightly higher growth rates.

What about jobs for less-skilled workers? Certainly, the low education levels of many recipients pose a serious barrier to their employment options. Still, the national figures provide grounds for optimism. In the US job market, the educational advantage of new entrants over those leaving the workforce is so large that fewer less-educated workers are in the labour force each year. Between 1992 and 1998, the number of adult workers with a high school degree or less declined from 51 million to 50 million while the total labour force increased by 9 million (Lerman *et al.*, 1998; Pigeon and Wray, 1998).

The evidence thus far paints an optimistic picture. Between the first quarter of 1996 and the second quarter of 1998, about 741,000 additional never-married mothers entered the labour force and the economy generated enough jobs for these new entrants. The 33 per cent jump in the labour force of never-married mothers was matched by an astonishing 40 per cent rise in the employment of never-married mothers. This 40 per cent job growth dwarfed the 9 per cent increase in employment for the economy as a whole. Despite the rapid expansion in their labour force participation, never-married mothers experienced a decline in unemployment rates from 19 to 14.8 per cent.[3]

The trends strongly suggest that welfare reforms rather than the economy played the primary role in stimulating the entry of recipients and potential recipients into the job market. The rate of participation in the labour force jumped from 60 per cent in 1994 to about 74 per cent in 1998 among never-married mothers, but rose only slightly (from 69 to 70 per cent) for married mothers (Bishop, 1998). In fact, no other groups in the economy raised their participation rates nearly as fast as did unmarried mothers.

Surveys of employer attitudes about hiring recipients lend support to the favourable employment picture. In a recent national survey weighted toward small employers (Regenstein *et al.*, 1998), researchers found that a majority of employers (62 per cent) had hired someone who has been on welfare. Among those who had hired welfare recipients, 94 per cent reported their willingness to hire one again. Even among employers with no experience employing welfare recipients, 82 per cent expected to hire at least one in the coming year.

While these calculations at the national level suggest solid job prospects for welfare recipients, the national estimates do not tell the entire story, in part because welfare recipients are concentrated in select geographic areas. An analysis (Lerman *et al.*, 1998) of the effects of welfare inflows on local labour markets shows that recipients in New York, Los Angeles, Baltimore and St Louis will face a difficult time finding jobs.

As the worry over numbers of jobs has receded, opponents of welfare changes have come to emphasise the problem of low wages. It is certainly true that working at the types of jobs available to most recipients does not yield enough for a family to escape poverty. At the same time, low-wage heads of families can combine their earnings with various non-welfare income sources – including the expanded EITC, food stamps, childcare, child support and health insurance – and thereby move out of poverty. In any event, under the current benefit structure, the financial gains from taking a $10 per hour job over a $7 per hour job are modest.

Today's low national unemployment rate (4.5 per cent in late 1998) is no doubt largely responsible for the ability of the US economy to absorb hundreds of thousands of welfare recipients per year. The concern that many recipients will be less successful if and when unemployment rises is real. However, by obtaining jobs and work experience in good times, welfare recipients will have more of a chance of maintaining their positions even when the job market weakens.

Dealing with hard-to-serve cases

One remaining critical question is how states will deal with chronically poor families experiencing an array of intractable (or barely tractable) social problems. No one knows the precise number of recipients whose heavy drug, mental health, domestic violence or literacy problems prevent them from working. Estimates of the incidence of work-related disabilities, mental health and substance abuse range from less than 10 to almost 30 per cent of all welfare recipients. Those with extremely low basic skills or learning disabilities may make up 25–40 per cent of the caseload (Thompson *et al.*, 1998). About 3–4 per cent have children who cannot perform some age-appropriate activities (Loprest and Acs, 1995). Although a substantial number of recipients face one or more of these barriers to work, their impact on the ability to work is surprisingly modest. According Olson and Pavetti (1996), 57 per cent of recipients reporting a potentially serious barrier (other than low skills) reported working, a rate nearly as high as the job-holding rate among recipients who did not report such barriers.

States can choose to exempt up to 20 per cent of their caseloads from time limits and up to 50 per cent from work requirements. Nevertheless, time limits are increasing pressure on welfare agencies to attempt to face these barriers head on. Until recently, agencies could simply send these families a cheque indefinitely without worrying about why their poverty persisted. Now, they must help recipients deal with those barriers preventing them from finding and keeping even a minimum-wage job.

Strategies for coping with 'hard-to-serve' recipients vary. Some states actively assist severely disabled individuals to obtain benefits from the federal means-tested disability programme (Supplemental Security Income). Yet few appear to exempt recipients with moderate disability from work requirements. Model programmes have emerged selectively around the country (Pavetti *et al.*, 1996). Utah considers treatment for substance abuse treatment or mental health counselling as allowable work activities. The state has hired specialised professionals to work with families on these problems. In Oregon, welfare officials count participation in substance abuse or mental health treatment as meeting their work requirement. Mental health professionals sometimes locate out of welfare offices to assess recipients, to refer them for treatment and to monitor their participation. A programme in Chicago provides a structured General Educational Development degree (ostensibly equivalent to a high school diploma) and vocational training preparation, but also uses support groups to address domestic violence, parenting and depression.

It is by no means clear how well these rehabilitative activities will work to prevent hard-to-serve recipients and their children from becoming destitute and homeless. At one level, states want recipients to face the threat of losing benefits and income so that they participate in remedial activities and make every effort to earn as much as they can. On the other hand, they appear to recognise the need for a back-up set of benefits in cases in which ill or disabled recipients cannot cope with the new demands placed on them. While states will have to tread carefully in this area to avoid adding to homelessness and extreme poverty, their willingness to direct services toward families with chronic social problems is a hopeful sign.

Overall assessments and remaining challenges

It is still too early to declare victory for the new US welfare policies. The earliest year recipients will reach the federally mandated time limits is in late 2001 or 2002. The US economy remains strong, unemployment stands at 4.5 per cent and states are flush with resources. Still, it would be a mistake to discount the apparent success of the changeover so far. Hundreds of thousands if not millions of families are moving off welfare to take jobs that pay a low salary but come with a package of benefits. Access to health- and childcare for low-income working families has expanded significantly. Benefit levels have remained constant.

Assessments could remain ambiguous even after data on the experience of recipients unfold. For example, how should we assess the initiatives if they benefit 70 per cent of recipients or potential recipients and harm 30 per cent, especially when all those affected start out as poor or near-poor and when the losers are the poorest individuals?

Achieving further progress will require US policy makers to confront several challenges. Engaging non-custodial fathers in providing financial and other support for their children is critically important. As low-income mothers increasingly work and attain a degree of self-support, low-income non-custodial fathers may become increasingly marginalised. Until recently, government policies aimed at collecting additional child support, both through improved enforcement of existing support orders and establishing legal paternity more frequently. In the paternity area, government policies are finally bearing fruit. But now that people understand that most fathers of low-income children are themselves poor or near-poor (Sorensen and Lerman, 1998), public agencies are sponsoring employment and training services in an effort to raise fathers' earnings capacities. Under the Parents' Fair Share demonstration (Doolittle *et al.*, 1998), several local agencies attempted to combine peer support, training, job counselling and help in assuring visitation hours in order to promote active and constructive fathering and increase child support payments to children on welfare. The project raised child support payments, but had no effect on the earnings of non-custodial fathers. The challenge is to devise new ways to reach millions of low-income, non-custodial fathers.

Another challenge is to help families negotiate the new, complicated system more effectively. Working poor families often do not take up food stamp and other benefits for which they are eligible, partly because of high stigma and transactions costs and partly because of asset tests. Early indications are that families leaving welfare may believe they are no longer eligible for food stamps or medical benefits, when in fact most are. Under the EITC, low-wage, lone mothers often qualify for the maximum $3,600 per year, but typically receive the money in a lump sum after filing their tax return sometime between January and April. As a result, beneficiaries do not generally obtain the credits as they accrue nor do they integrate the money into their weekly or monthly budget. Helping recipients do so could increase their perception that added work pays off and could make family budgeting more rational.

Smoothing the transition from welfare to work also requires that low-income parents easily access the available health insurance and childcare assistance. Managing this process and making the programmes client-friendly will be a formidable administrative challenge.

Finally, widening the agenda to make work pay encourages recipients or potential recipients to work or to remain in mainstream programmes. One possibility is liberalising the eligibility rules for unemployment insurance (UI). An accessible UI would do more to limit income shortfalls of workers who become unemployed, while keeping their families in a mainstream programme and off welfare. Moreover, work becomes more rewarding for recipients since it allows for the build-up of eligibility for UI.

When President Clinton and the 1997 Republican Congress ended 'welfare as we know it', they were taking steps to build an alternative approach that promotes work but continues to assist low-wage workers heading families. So far, the results of this effort are promising for many but damaging for some.

Notes

1 Under AFDC, the federal and state government provided means-tested benefits to families with children in which at least one parent is no longer living in the home, is incapacitated or, in many states, is unemployed. Begun during the New Deal primarily to help widows and their children, the programme was to wither away as the survivors' insurance programme matured and widowed families qualified for its social insurance benefit. Instead, AFDC became largely a programme for low-income divorced, separated or never-married mothers and their children.

2 Even Edelman (1997) begins his harsh critique of the new welfare law with the comment, 'I hate welfare. To be more precise, I hate the welfare system we had until last August, when Bill Clinton signed a historic bill ending 'welfare as we know it.'

3 These numbers come from unpublished tabulations provided by the US Bureau of Labor Statistics.

References

Acs, G., Coe, N., Watson, K. & Lerman, R. I. (1998) *Does Work Pay? An Analysis of the Work Incentives under TANF,* Assessing the New Federalism Occasional Paper, Washington, DC, Urban Institute, July.

Bassi, L. & Lerman, R. (1996) 'Reducing the child support-welfare disincentive program', *Journal of Policy Analysis and Management,* Winter, pp89–96.

Bishop, J. (1998) *Is Welfare Reform Succeeding?,* Discussion Paper 98-15, Center for Advanced Human Resource Studies, New York School of Industrial and Labour relations, Cornell University.

Bruen, B. & Ullman, F. (1998) *Children's Health Insurance Programmes: Where States Are, Where They Are Headed,* New Federalism: Issues and Options for States No. A-20, Washington, DC, Urban Institute.

Burtless, G. R. Weaver, K. & Wiener, J. (1997) 'The future of the social safety net', in R. D. Reischauer (ed.) *Setting National Priorities,* Washington, DC, The Brookings Institution.

Clines, F. (1996) 'Clinton signs bill cutting welfare: states in new role', *The New York Times,* 23 August.

Committee on Ways and Means (1996) *Green Book: Background Material and Data on Programmes within the Jurisdiction of the Committee on Ways and Means,* Washington, DC, US Government Printing Office.

Doolittle, F., Knox, V., Miller, C. & Rowser, S. (1998) *Building Opportunities, Enforcing Obligations: Implementation and Interim Impacts of Parents' Fair Share,* New York, Manpower Demonstration Research Corporation, December.

Duncan, G. J., Mullan Harris, K. & Boisjoly, J. (1997) 'Time limits and welfare reform: new estimates of the number and characteristics of affected families', unpublished manuscript, Joint Center for Poverty Research, Northwestern University, 22 April.

Edelman, P. (1997) 'The worst thing Bill Clinton has done', *Atlantic Monthly*, March, pp43-58.

Edin, K. & Lein, L. (1997) *Making Ends Meet: How Single Mothers Survive Welfare and Low-wage Work*, New York, Russell Sage Foundation.

Ellwood, D. T. (1988) *Poor Support*, New York, Basic Books.

Ellwood, D. T. (1996) 'Welfare reform as I knew it: when bad things happen to good policies', *The American Prospect*, no. 26, pp22–29.

Farkas, S. with Johnson, J. (1996) *The Values We Live By: What Americans Want From Welfare Reform*, New York, Public Agenda.

Lerman, R., Loprest, P. & Ratcliffe, C. (1998) 'How well can urban labor markets absorb welfare recipients?', presented at 20th Annual Research Conference of the Association for Public Policy and Management.

Long, S. & Clark, S. (1997) *The New Child Care Block Grant: State Funding Choices and Their Implications*, New Federalism: Issues and Options for States No. A-12, Washington, DC, Urban Institute.

Loprest, P. & Acs, G. (1995) 'Profile of disability among families on AFDC,' unpublished manuscript, Washington, DC, Urban Institute, November.

Moffitt, R. & Wolfe, B. (1992) 'The effect of the Medicaid programme on welfare participation and labor supply', *Review of Economics and Statistics*, November, pp615–626.

Moynihan, D. P. (1996)'When principle is at issue', *Washington Post*, 4 August 1996, pC7.

Nightingale, D. & Brennan, K. (1998) *The Welfare-to-Work Grants Programme: A New Link in the Welfare Reform Chain*, New Federalism: Issues and Options for States No. A-26, Washington, DC, Urban Institute.

Olson, K. & Pavetti, L. (1996) *Personal and Family Challenges to the Successful Transition from Welfare to Work*, Washington, DC, Urban Institute.

Pavetti, L., Olson, K., Pindus, N., Pernas, M. & Isaacs, J. (1996) *Designing Welfare-to-Work Programmes for Families Facing Personal or Family Challenges: Lessons from the Field*, Washington, DC, Urban Institute.

Peterson, P. (1995) 'State response to welfare reform: a race to the bottom?', in I. Sawhill (ed.) *Welfare Reform: An Analysis of the Issues*, Washington, DC, Urban Institute.

Pigeon, M. & Wray, L.R. (1998) 'Did the Clinton rising tide raise all boats?', *Public Policy Brief*, No. 45, Jerome Levy Economic Institute of Bard College.

Regenstein, M., Meyer, J. and Hicks, J.D. (1998) 'Job prospects for welfare recipients: Employers speak out', Occasional Paper no 10, *Assessing the New Federalism*, Washington, DC, Urban Institute.

Solow, R. (1998) *Work and Welfare,* Princeton, NJ, Princeton University Press.

Sorensen, E. & Lerman, R. (1998) 'Welfare reform and fathers', *Challenge,* July–August, pp101–116.

Thompson, T., Holcomb, P. A., Loprest, P. & Brennan, K. (1998) 'State welfare-to-work policies for people with disabilities: changes since welfare reform', unpublished paper, Washington, DC, Urban Institute.

US General Accounting Office (1998) *Welfare Reform: Early Fiscal Effects of the TANF Block Grant,* Report No. GAO-AIMD 98-137, Washington, DC, US General Accounting Office.

Weil, A. (1997) *The New Children's Health Insurance Programme: Should States Expand Medicaid,* New Federalism: Issues and Options for States No. A-13, Washington, DC, Urban Institute.

Zedlewski, S., Holcomb, P. & Duke, A. E. (1998) *Cash Assistance in Transition: The Story of 13 States.* Assessing the New Federalism Occasional Paper No. 16, Washington, DC, Urban Institute, December.

13 To market to market to buy a...?? Social policy reform in Aotearoa/New Zealand, 1984–1998

Michael O'Brien

Introduction

Historically, Aotearoa/New Zealand[1] has prided itself on the development of its welfare state, a welfare state that has been described (erroneously) as providing 'cradle to the grave' welfare (Gustafson, 1986). A range of social policy legislation is associated with that development. That legislation has traversed areas as diverse as the creation of the first old-age pensions in 1898, the Industrial Conciliation and Arbitration Act in 1893, the Social Security Act of 1938 (which created free health care and extended social security coverage), the 1972 Accident Compensation legislation, the provision of free compulsory education, the universal national superannuation coverage of 1977, the 1984 Treaty of Waitangi Act – to name but some of the key legislative enactments. Alongside these legislative enactments was a critical state role in economic management, keeping unemployment historically at very low levels.

Furthermore, it was widely accepted, officially and publicly, that the welfare state had eliminated poverty. Events of the last fifteen years have turned much of this coverage around; the purpose of this chapter is to highlight key features of those changes, their characteristics and consequences.

It is not my intention here to regale all the details of the last fifteen years (interested readers should consult Sharp, 1994; Kelsey, 1995; Easton, 1997). Rather I want to draw out some themes which are important in Aotearoa/New Zealand but which also, hopefully, have salience when considered internationally. In particular, I want to concentrate on three major dimensions and their consequences: namely, the growth of income inequality and the associated unemployment and poverty; the 'remoralisation' of welfare through authoritarianism and surveillance; and third, the ways in which these two factors link to the retreating state and the associated emphasis on diversity and 'consumer choice'. This third theme is of particular relevance to the current social policy debates on difference and equality, debates which are drawn on in the chapter's conclusion. Maori and Pacific Islands communities have borne a heavy impact in the changes under consideration here. Hence, the position of these communities is a particular and specific consideration throughout the chapter.

The focus is on the period since the election of the fourth Labour government in 1984. It was that government which initiated many of the economic and social changes fundamental to the reordering of social policy in New Zealand, changes which the succeeding National governments, first elected in 1990, have continued and extended. The changes were not limited to social policy matters (using that term in its widest context), but our attention here is necessarily limited to such matters. I shall, however, use the term 'social policy' to refer to the structuring of inequality and the distributional consequences arising from those structures (Cheyne, 1997).

Inequality, unemployment and poverty

The historical development of the welfare state in Aotearoa/New Zealand was based around full male employment, in which it was expected that the worker would earn enough to support himself, his wife and two children (Castles, 1985). The economy was managed in such a way that official levels of unemployment were so low that the Minister of Labour is commonly reported to have commented in the late 1950s that there were five people unemployed and he knew them all! By the middle of 1984, 65,055 people were registered as unemployed. In 1998 unemployment stands officially at 144,000 or 7.7 per cent. The jobless figure is 226,500 (*The Jobs Letter*, 1999).[2] The official figure is predicted by the Treasury to rise a further 1 per cent in the next twelve months.[3] While the increases in the levels of unemployment have been extremely significant, this significance has been augmented by the changes in the pattern of employment. The labour market has been characterised by an increasing percentage of the workforce being located in part-time work. Over the decade between 1988 and 1998, there has been an increase of 11 per cent in the number of full-time employees compared with an increase of 36 per cent of part-time employees (Statistics New Zealand, 1998b). The relevance of these employment changes for our current purposes is that the shift in the nature and structure of employment and unemployment has been accompanied by the development of a range of income support and tax credit measures to supplement the incomes of those in paid work, measures which prior to 1984 were limited to tax exemptions and rebates of various kinds. For many, paid work cannot be guaranteed to provide adequate income.

Moreover, the economic and social costs of unemployment (frequently referred to by such euphemisms as 'downsizing' and 'restructuring') were not distributed equitably. The heaviest impact was in industries such as railways, forestry and meat processing, where Maori and Pacific Islands peoples were overrepresented. The impact of the change is starkly reflected in the recent review of the comparative position of Maori and Pakeha undertaken by Te Puni Kokiri, the Ministry of Maori Development (Te Puni Kokiri, 1998).[4] The report notes that before 1984 Maori were more likely to be found in employment than Pakeha.

As in other countries which have pursued the path of structural adjustment (Kelsey, 1995), the processes have resulted in substantial growth in inequality and poverty. In 1994 *The Economist* was to argue that, among the OECD countries, the growth of inequality in New Zealand was second only to the United Kingdom. Hills' (1995) work has pointed in the same direction. Reviewing income changes between 1982 and 1996, a recent report from Statistics New Zealand notes that: 'the increase in income inequality in New Zealand from 1982 to 1996 appears to have been as large as, or larger than, that in other countries for which similar data is available' (Statistics New Zealand, 1999, p95). The material widening of inequality has, then, been significant. Equally significant has been the political and ideological justification of the growing gap. Historically, New Zealand has prided itself as the country of equality. Irrespective of the empirical validity of this claim – and it was a claim that was as

important politically and rhetorically as it was substantively
(Pearson and Thorns, 1983) – recent political and ideological
responses have actively jettisoned not only the substance of the
claim, but also the desirability of the pursuit of equality as a goal.
Inequality is validated and lauded, reflected in the comment of the
Labour Prime Minister of 1987, who described inequality as the
engine which drove society (Lange, 1986) and the current (1999)
Finance Minister who responded to a recent economists' study
(Posser and Chatterjee, 1998) which showed growing income
inequality by asserting that this was desirable as it provided
evidence of reward for effort and qualification (*New Zealand
Herald,* 24 July 1998).

Growing unemployment has been an important feature
creating the greater inequality. So also have been the actions of
the state itself in its approach to disposable income distribution
through reducing taxes for higher-income earners and increasing
taxes for the poor through such mechanisms as user charges in
areas such as health and education and the introduction of an
almost universally applicable consumer tax, the Goods and
Services Tax in 1986.[5] The largest cuts in personal income taxes
have been given to the highest paid. Income taxes have been
reduced for higher-income earners from sixty-six cents in the
dollar on taxable income in excess of $38,000 in 1984 to thirty-
three cents in the dollar on income in excess of $38,000 in 1998,
while for those on lower incomes the rate has changed from
twenty cents in the dollar on taxable income below $6,000 in
1984 (thirty-three cents in the dollar for taxable income between
$6,000 and $25,000) to effectively fifteen cents in the dollar
below $9,500 and twenty-one cents in the dollar between $9,500
and $38,000.[6] Dalziel (1999) has calculated that in excess of one-
third of the income gains from the tax cuts of 1996 and 1998
have gone to those in the highest income quintile. The processes
and outcomes of change have represented significant redistribution, but in the opposite direction from that associated with the
welfare state. The state, directly and indirectly, has redistributed
both materially and ideologically from the poorer to the more
affluent.

This redistributive process is also reflected in the growth of
poverty in the last fifteen years. Again, rhetoric to the contrary,
poverty was apparent prior to 1984 (Easton, 1995). It has,
however, become much more pronounced since that time. In the
initial period following the 1984 election, the position of the
poorest improved in relation to the general pattern of income
distribution. These gains were short lived, and were more than
wiped out by the losses in the latter part of the 1980s (Martin,

1995; Johnstone and Pool, 1996). The disadvantages faced by low-income groups were dramatically augmented by the cuts to social security benefits that took effect in 1991, with the benefit for some lone parents (the Domestic Purposes Benefit) being reduced by almost 24 per cent. Benefits were cut for almost all beneficiaries with one significant exception, superannuitants. Initial attempts to turn this universal benefit into a means-tested payment were turned back, but a change is again under serious consideration. The cuts in entitlement have been matched by tightening of eligibility conditions through such measures as increasing the age of eligibility for unemployment and lone-parent benefits, and parental income assessment to determine eligibility for tertiary assistance allowance.

The result of these processes has been a significant increase in the numbers below the poverty line. Recent work by various authors (Easton, 1995; Krishnan, 995; Waldegrave *et al.*, 1996) demonstrates this growth, with current estimates giving a figure of approximately 30 per cent of children in poverty. Worst affected by the growing poverty are families with two or more children and lone parents. Among these groups, Maori and Pacific Islands families are significantly overrepresented, with Krishnan (1995) estimating that approximately twice as many Maori and Pacific Islands households were below the poverty line compared with their respective numbers in the population. Data from the 1996 census suggest that Asian families are also significantly overrepresented in the low-income groupings (Statistics New Zealand, 1998a).[7]

These quantitative data have been complemented and supplemented by a range of qualitative studies over the last fifteen years, highlighting the significant ways in which the processes and outcomes of social policy reform have impacted on lives, living standards and wellbeing (O'Brien, forthcoming). Basic areas such as access to food, clothing and shelter have become much more tenuous for many, while the diseases of poverty (tuberculosis, rheumatic fever and meningococcal meningitis) have reappeared. Foodbanks grew from sixteen in the Auckland region in 1990 to approximately 130 in 1994 (McKay, 1995), with an increasing proportion of users being in paid work (currently approximately 11 per cent in Auckland) (Auckland City Mission, 1998).[8]

Remoralising welfare

Thus far, I have highlighted some fundamental structural aspects and consequences of the social policy change programme that has occurred in New Zealand since 1984. The next section moves to a second key feature, namely the ideological forerunners and correlates. The move from citizenship rights to individual and familial obligations (including the rhetoric which focuses on replacement of the state by the market, voluntary charity and the family), the increasingly authoritarian nature of the state and its widening powers of surveillance, and the obsessional concentration on paid work as the replacement for state income support are critical features of these changes. While the structural changes identified above are critical in shaping the lives and opportunities of thousands of New Zealanders, particularly those who are the most impoverished and economically disadvantaged, the ideological changes reviewed here are equally critical in two fundamental senses.

First, they establish and sustain the climate within which the poor are required to manage their lives and the lives of their children. Increasingly, it is a climate which is cold and icy, with constant messages (subtle and not so subtle) about personal and family failure and attendant lack of responsibility, pejorative abuse for dependency, and a message that 'you are on your own and get cracking to sort your life out'. Recent changes to the provision of income support provide a good illustration of that climate; they were referred to by the Minister responsible as being based on 'hassling', a term also used by the Department of Social Welfare to describe elements of its approach to income support changes. ('Hassling' is described as solving the problem of welfare dependency by 'forcing a change in attitudes to work' (Department of Social Welfare, 1996, p26).)

Second, these ideological changes have a longer term significance in that they fundamentally alter the expectations about the nature of personal, family and social relations in ways which highlight individual and familial responsibility and minimise state responsibility. Over time, expectations of the rights of citizens in the nation state are replaced by the obligations of individuals and family members with an emphasis on caring for yourself and seeking assistance from voluntary charity for the desperate and unfortunate situations in which family cannot assist. Such a fundamental ideological shift represents a major change for social policy in New Zealand, representing a recommodification in place of the decommodification identified by Esping-Anderson (1990). Markets, including quasi-markets in areas such as health and education, replace the state. The accompanying political changes shift the balance of political forces with the result that re-establishing a fundamental place for the state in the shaping of the society becomes extremely difficult. Inequalities are cemented in; the focus moves from *how* can the state interact with civil society to provide greater opportunity for all to an active rejection of any notion that the state *should* attempt to create such a social framework. It is a change that is as pervasive as it is subtle, although it must be acknowledged that the processes have not always been subtle. In many instances they have been very direct and confrontational.

Two specific illustrations of the processes of transfer of responsibilities and the accompanying extension of surveillance and of punitive administrative oversight are provided by a proposed Code of Social and Family Responsibility and the changes to income support that took effect in October 1998. The Code was formally abandoned in October 1998, but some of the proposals within it, such as the workfare requirement, were adopted. Even more significant was its ideological impact, reinforcing a notion that the poor and beneficiaries were individually irresponsible.

The Code listed eleven specific items which were set out as expectations, each expectation being accompanied by a description of the sets of the individual and family behaviours which would reflect that expectation in operation. In addition, relevant current law was set out and there was a statement about 'how the government helps now'. The items included in the proposed Code covered such areas as getting children ready for school, sharing parenthood, training and learning for employment, keeping ourselves healthy, and managing money. Reflecting the critical and developing linkage between economics and the moralism of social policy, the Code was first formally announced in the 1997 budget statement. Focused initially on beneficiaries only, the proposed code was quickly extended to all New Zealanders. In the following year a booklet was sent to all households as a discussion document. Additional background information, labelled as 'fact sheets', was also available if requested. These fact sheets represented a very selective and, in some instances, inaccurate summary of empirical information on each item. For example, the fact sheet on managing money claimed that research showed that budgeting advice enabled people to improve their financial situation through improving their income and/or decreasing their expenditure. In fact the research report found that the most significant outcome for participants in the study was increasing income through paid work or taking in a boarder. Half of those coming to budget advice could not be assisted because their income was too low (Wilson *et al.*, 1995). In addition to commenting on each of the items, people were also asked to indicate what form the Code should take, that is, should it be legislated, used as a guide to legislation and policy, or published as a statement of government policy. An explicit option of rejecting it altogether was not included in the range of alternatives provided. Despite an extension of time, only approximately 95,000 responses were received; this represents less than a 6 per cent response rate. No work has been undertaken to identify the reasons for this low response rate.

The proposed Code was widely criticised, particularly, but not exclusively, by social services groups. Criticism focused on the statistically unrepresentative, unreliable and unmeasurable nature of the process, its selectiveness in that the emphasis was entirely on the responsibility of the individual and the family with no accompanying statement of state responsibility, and the punitiveness of the approach to the issues reviewed. The identification of possible sanctions for failure to meet expectations was one of the most significant aspects of the punitiveness which met with extensive opposition. For example, in an item entitled 'Keeping Children Healthy', one of the questions for discussion was: 'If parents have made an informed choice to have their children immunised, should up to date immunisations be required for entry to early childhood education services and schools?' Or, under an item called 'Getting Children to School Ready to Learn', one of the questions was: 'Should parents who receive a benefit be required, as a condition of benefit, to get their children to school?' (Department of Social Welfare, 1998). Similar illustrations could be provided from each of the other items. The responses were analysed by staff in the Social Policy Agency. The proposed release date was postponed twice. When finally formally abandoned, the Minister of Social Services commented that he had received a number of good ideas from the exercise. The proposal for the Code, its contents and its focus are highly illustrative, reflecting the emphasis on individual and family obligations and (by default) a reduced state, and locating this emphasis within a framework of obligations and sanctions – a framework which has become increasingly characteristic of social policy developments.

This emphasis on individual and family responsibility is also illustrated in the second specific example referred to above, namely the changes in the provision of income assistance. As noted earlier in this chapter, the levels of benefit were reduced in 1991; indeed, only in 1998 has the actual dollar amount for lone parents reached the level that existed before the cuts. Accompanying the cuts, and over the ensuing years, income support structures have been characterised by increased surveillance of beneficiaries and more recently by a clear shift of focus to obligation to work, failure to meet the requirement of which is heavily and punitively sanctioned. For example, failure to accept suitable employment leads to suspension of the benefit for one week on the first occasion and cancellation of the benefit on the second. The first failure to participate in organised activity leads to suspension until compliance is established, while a second failure leads to suspension of the benefit for a week and then continued suspension until compliance is obtained. A third failure leads to cancellation of the benefit. Failure to attend a mandatory interview results in a 20 per cent reduction of the benefit.

There is now an extensive network of connections between the Income Support service and other government departments such as Inland Revenue, Immigration, Employment, and Accident Compensation, with the stated aim of detecting fraud. The same connection does not operate for non-beneficiaries in areas such as tax evasion. Furthermore, the Income Support service regularly publishes figures purported to be benefit debt. However, the figures include such components as overpayments by a department and refundable advances made by the service. They are technically inaccurate as a measure of fraud but more importantly they are critical in creating a climate in which fraud is seen to be extensive, thereby facilitating and reinforcing criticisms of beneficiaries. Benefit payments are suspended while the investigation proceeds; in contrast to anywhere else in the legal system, guilty until proven innocent replaces innocent until proven guilty.

In October 1998 the former Income Support service and the Employment service were amalgamated in the symbolically entitled new Department of Work and Income (note the order of the words), established under the logo 'Our Future is Working'. The former Manager of Income Support was appointed as the chief executive of the new department. As part of the amalgamation, a range of former benefits (unemployment, sickness, training, fifty-five-plus benefit and young job-seekers allowance) were renamed as the community wage, and work assessment tests were introduced. In addition to the active attempts to place up to 65,000 unemployed in some form of work (with the requirement of working as a condition of continued receipt of income assistance), a fundamental feature of the new department is the introduction of a compulsory requirements for what is called 'organised activity'. This organised activity may include such elements as undertaking training, engaging in personal change (e.g. losing weight and changing appearance in order to be more 'presentable' to a potential employer), participation in an employment programme, seminar, scheme or specified activity, including community work or other experience activity, participation in training, or medical or psychological assessment. Failure to meet either the compulsory work or organised activity requirements produces substantial sanctions, such as loss of benefit for a second refusal of work and loss of up to 40 per cent of benefit for failure to comply with the organised activity requirements. The regulations surrounding the penalties for failure to comply with organised activity requirements are mandatory, and are established under regulation, not legislatively. The background notes accompanying the Work Test Bill were clear about the focus of the legislation, baldly asserting the key principle as: 'If you don't work, you don't get paid' (Social Security (Work Test) Amendment Bill, 1998, pii).

Targeting, choice and diversity

Two central themes have provided the ideological and political basis for the shape and direction of change, namely targeting and choice. Enunciated most clearly in the budget statement of 1991 (Shipley, 1991), these two themes (at times sloganised) have been persistently presented as both a critique of the inadequacies and failures of the Keynesian welfare state and the fundamental framework for the new shape of social policy and state involvement in social policy.[9] Although developed significantly in the previous five years (O'Brien and Wilkes, 1993), targeting had its most explicit articulation in the 1991 Budget.[10] 'Targeting resources to those in greatest need' was identified in that Budget as the first of the key elements governing state social policy. The Change Team established within the Prime Minister's Department in 1991 completed a review of issues surrounding targeting, a review in which the author strongly challenged the appropriateness of the emphasis on targeting (Mulgan, 1991). His challenges were, of course, largely ignored. Since that time it has continued to be the central theme, dominating all aspects of social policy (Birch, 1996; Shipley, 1998). It is not my intention to critique the general arguments in support of targeting here – others have done that very effectively (see e.g. Bosanquet, 1983; King, 1987; Chapple, 1996; Hyman, 1996; Stephens, 1996; Boston *et al.*, 1999).

In brief, the government and supporters of the neo-liberal agenda argue that the role of the state should be to ensure that individuals are able to exercise choice. Direct state intervention should be carefully targeted to those with greatest need, thus ensuring that resources are only provided for those who genuinely need them (a phrase used frequently) and by keeping the state out of people's lives so that they can exercise choice. In ensuring choice, the range of services available would most effectively meet the different needs of an increasingly diverse society. It is an argument in which there is a constant reiteration that individuals themselves are best able to exercise choice.

Health, education, social services and housing have all experienced extensive development of targeting as fundamental to the reshaping of social policy. For example, in health services, charges were introduced for public hospital care, care that was previously provided free at the point of use. Beneficiaries, low-income earners and some groups of superannuitants were provided with a Community Service Card, the level of assistance depending on income. This card is used, *inter alia,* to obtain prescriptions at lower costs, to reduce the cost of medical consultation and to reduce the cost of attendance at hospital outpatient services for those who fall within the income categories. A high-user card was also introduced for those who make frequent use of health services, e.g. more than twelve visits to a general practitioner in one year. In 1997, as part of the agreement that led to the formation of the coalition government in the previous year, visits to the doctor for children under six years became free. This policy development was strongly criticised both within the majority coalition party (National) and by the far-right party (ACT) because of its failure to target on the basis of income, criticism that has been sustained since its introduction. Nevertheless, following a recent review, the policy remains unchanged, despite the criticism.

In tertiary education, targeting has led to the introduction of significantly increased costs for many students, with student financial assistance provided through a mixture of *parental* income-tested student allowance and non-income-tested loans. (The means-tested allowance replaced a previous universal payment to students.) Eligibility for the student allowance uses a formula to test eligibility, with eligibility being based on assessment of the level of financial support the parent should provide, irrespective of whether the parent is contributing, and irrespective of whether the student is living with one or both parents. Students are now completing their study with substantial debts.

Targeting of income support has resulted in tightening of both eligibility for and entitlement to income support. For example, the ages of eligibility for superannuation, unemployment benefit and lone-parent benefit have been increased (the age of eligibility for superannuation is to continue to increase until 2001), benefit levels have been cut, assistance with childcare costs has been limited to those in work or study, and levels of compensation for loss as a result of an accident have been reduced.

Special needs grants (sng) and special benefit (sb) (two discretionary forms of income support assistance) are presented as providing the basis for meeting financial need.[11] The availability of these two forms of assistance is consistently and persistently referred to whenever areas of unmet or undermet need are identified, indicating that such assistance acts as the prevailing mechanism through which to meet poverty. These forms of assistance are both tightly constrained and administratively regulated. In 1988–89 77,289 sng grants were made, while in 1996–97 (the latest year for which figures are available) 84,535 grants were made. In 1988–89, 16,087 special benefit applications were granted, while in 1996/97 30,275 applications were granted. In addition, in the latter year 77,066 benefits in advance were approved compared with 38,416 in 1991–92 – the first year for which figures are available (Department of Social Welfare, 1997).

While these figures provide some illustration of the extent of the increasing use of these discretionary elements, they mask the ways in which tightening of eligibility conditions and of administrative practices actually reduce measures of need by reducing eligibility and by changing administrative practices. The impact of these changes is euphemistically illustrated by the following comment in a recent quarterly statistics report from Income Support, the agency responsible at that time for administering income support payments:

> Income Support has also changed its service delivery in ways that are designed to moderate demand for special needs grants. Customised service means that staff are encouraged to talk to beneficiaries about ways in which they can better manage their finances. The one-to-one contact also reduces the opportunity for exploitation of the programme. (Income Support, 1998, p 18).

While this targeted structure has been fundamental to social security provision historically, the component that is significantly different as a result of the reforms is that it is now firmly located within a framework of obligations and responsibilities rather than rights of citizenship. The persistent ideological expression of limiting assistance to those in greatest need has been accompanied by and reinforced the notion of a minimalist state, acting as an institution of last resort. Furthermore, consistent with the international experience with targeted social security systems (Bolderson and Mabbett, 1996), the levels of assistance have steadily eroded. For example, the real value of targeted family support for those in paid work has fallen since its introduction in 1988 (O'Brien, 1998).

While targeting has served as a means of reduce state assistance, universal assistance through family benefit and superannuation has not been immune from cuts. The universal family benefit was abolished in 1991, while a surtax on superannuitants' other income was introduced in 1988, extended in 1991 (following unsuccessful attempts to change superannuation to a targeted system – see St John (1999)) and abolished in 1998. There have been marked differences in public and political responses to these changes. For example, the proposed introduction of a means-tested framework for superannuation in 1991 was abandoned following extensive protest and there was significant protest at the 1998 reduction of the floor for superannuation payments. Conversely, there was virtually no resistance to the removal of the universal family benefit, although it must be said that abolition occurred alongside a range of other Draconian measures such as the benefit cuts, measures which tended to overshadow the end of the universal payment for children. Furthermore, and significantly, the extensive and sustained opposition to the cuts in benefit levels has not produced any policy changes and there are no signs that a change of government in 1999 will restore their spending levels. However, a change in government is likely to lead to a restoration of the value of national superannuation. The explanations for these different responses lie in the political power of elderly people, the shifting of financial responsibility for children to the family, and the studied neglect of family and beneficiary poverty.

Thus far the discussion of targeting has focused on the individual/family. The use of targeting in education demonstrates one other significant aspect of targeting, namely group targeting. Here I am using 'targeting' to refer to what might be described, albeit not totally adequately, as positive discrimination. Funding of schools is based on the school's decile rating, with schools ranked on a one-to-ten scale on a series of socio-economic characteristics such as ethnicity, proportion of beneficiaries in the school catchment area, levels of unemployment and levels of formal qualification. In an attempt to compensate for levels of economic and social disadvantage, schools in poorer areas (decile one) are funded at a higher per capita rate than their wealthier counterparts (decile ten). However, such measures do not compensate fully for disadvantage. Schools in more affluent areas, with more affluent parents are more easily able to obtain additional funds from the parents through such sources as direct contributions and levies, and indirectly through the provision of goods and services such as professional expertise. The effect is to retain and, in some instances, extend privilege, unequal opportunities and unequal outcomes for children (Nash, 1993). Nevertheless, targeting is used here as a means to provide additional resources to those groups, not to contain and constrain resource access – the basis of individual targeting.

Group targeting has also led to different forms of resource allocation and service provision to attempt to meet obligations arising out of the Treaty of Waitangi, the founding document of New Zealand which provides the basis for Maori and Pakeha relationships in this country. This allocation and provision takes such forms as, for example, specific allocation of resources for services to Maori by Maori in health and social services, funding of specific Maori initiatives in education and economic development, use of Maori delivery mechanisms in social services, and adoption of Maori institutional forms to respond to offending (Durie, 1998). Similarly, there has been some targeting as a basis for policy decisions and provisions for Pacific Islands peoples (education and health), women (health and education) and people with disability (education).

Concluding comments: reform, difference, inequality

In this final section I want to reflect briefly on the implications of the Aotearoa/New Zealand reform processes in the light of current social policy debates surrounding such central themes as difference and diversity, universality and particularism (Williams, 1992, 1994; Thompson and Hoggett, 1996; O'Brien and Penna, 1998; Ellison, 1999). One of the central considerations in those debates (and in the associated specific policy measures) is the development and provision of social policy in ways that reflect and reinforce identity and difference without losing (or worse abandoning) a commitment to social justice, however that term is understood. Policy makers have been at pains to emphasise the diversity of forms of provision and the equity inherent in formulae of resource allocation, almost universally eschewing any attention to 'social relations of power and inequality' (Williams, 1994, p70). It is a decontextualised, individualised choice (even when supported by limited group targeting) which defines the individual as a consumer. Diversity is provided for within a neo-liberal economic and political framework, overlain by liberal and neo-liberal notions of self-help at a group level.

The New Zealand changes have certainly given explicit emphasis to diversity and difference, an emphasis built on neo-liberal assumptions about the freely choosing individual. This individual is set against (in contrast to) the state, a state which is depicted as an overpowering, controlling, limiting institution, unable and unwilling to meet individually different needs. The role of the state is, then, limited to individually targeted provision, with the significant exception of group targeting discussed above. In the form developed in New Zealand, targeting links well with *choice* for *consumers* (Williams, 1994). Both words are deliberately emphasised because they represent two separate but linked dimensions. Citizens become reduced to 'consumers' who 'choose' the service which they require. In this process rights are replaced by individualised decisions which reflect the actions of buyers and sellers in the marketplace. Choice is reflected through those decisions. It is the neo-liberal framework at work; we are categorised and conceptualised as competitive unsocial individuals. In social policy it is clearly manifest in such specifics as the abolition of school zoning, with parents then (supposedly) able to choose where they will send their child. However, schools establish their own rules of admission, using such criteria as academic and sporting prowess as their yardstick. 'Choice' is limited to those who meet the established criteria, in some instances resulting in children being unable to attend their neighbourhood school. The diversified choice is markedly limited by economic and social inequalities that are inherent in the policy change project.

The context and framework within which targeting and choice have been developed need to be fully appreciated if the measures are to be evaluated and understood appropriately. The initiatives to facilitate Maori provision for Maori, and to provide frameworks for Maori and Pacific Islands responsiveness to their own communities have occurred in a context of growing and deepening poverty, growing and lengthening unemployment, growing underemployment, growing pressures on families, and dearer and less accessible housing. Individuals and communities are encouraged, often expected, to do more while resources decline.

Treaty of Waitangi obligations, historical injustices and the currently disadvantaged economic and social position of Maori (Te Puni Kokiri, 1998) are important forces driving Maori demands for the targeting responses referred to above. However, the economic and social context within which such responses are located means that there is less real choice for many, particularly the socially and economically excluded. The likelihood is that in such circumstances the excluded will be even further punished and penalised. After all, the argument will run (refrains are already beginning to appear), you had opportunities but you did not take them. In such circumstances, a thriving climate for hostile racism flourishes. The renewed moralism discussed above is also easily established, focusing on the immoral behaviour of those 'deviant' individuals and individual failures who did not succeed because they did not make the effort despite the opportunities made available to them.

Diversity and difference require equal attention to economic and social justices. The New Zealand experience indicates clearly that without attention to both, diversity becomes equated with consumer choice and develops alongside social and economic inequality. In such circumstances, diversity is a requisite component of widening inequalities. While the welfare state failed to adequately meet diverse and different needs, the unequal neo-liberal state is no solution. Indeed, as the New Zealand experience demonstrates, it offers much less.

As various commentators have noted internationally in their review of the politics of neo-liberalism, the free economy is matched by the strong state (Gamble, 1994). Liberalisation of the economy requires careful control and management of the poor and disadvantaged, legally, administratively and ideologically. The heralded new vision that was to be achieved through the economic and social reforms has proven to be something of a mirage. As the economic miracles have failed to materialise, there has been an increasing emphasis on targeting 'those in greatest need' and on the remoralisation of the social. The ideological and political emphasis has been placed on critique of the moral behaviour and standards, particularly of the poor but more generally also of families and users of state services. Built on an ideological construct which emphasises self and/or family responsibility, independence and self-reliance, the state has developed a more authoritarian style, emphasising administrative surveillance – a style and response which have become increasingly explicit over later years. Indeed, the most recent part of the period examined here might be characterised as the re-presentation of the morally authoritarian unequal state. Difference has provided a cloak in which inequality has flourished. In such circumstances there will inevitably be a close link between choice and location on the ladder of inequality.

Notes

1 'Aotearoa' is used here as the Maori name for the country internationally defined as 'New Zealand'. Literally the name translates as 'land of the long white cloud'. It is increasingly used within the country to refer to 'New Zealand'.

2 The former figure refers to those who are defined as actively seeking work, while the latter figure includes those who are unemployed but not actively seeking work.

3 In the period since 1984, a range of factors has made simple comparisons between the two time periods extremely difficult. In addition to the already incorporated elements, the comparative measure would need to include such factors as the number now involved in training programmes (non-existent in 1984), increased numbers in advanced secondary and tertiary study because employment is not available, older workers who have moved into transitional benefit prior to receiving national superannuation and discouraged workers who do not bother to register because there is no work available.

4 The term 'Pakeha' is widely used in New Zealand to refer particularly to New Zealanders of European descent.

5 The significant omissions were mortgages and rents. All basic commodities were included such as food, clothing and power. The regressive nature of the tax is indicated in Department of Statistics (1990, p87) and O'Brien and Wilkes (1993).

6 The word 'effectively' is used because of the way in which the low-income earner rebate affects the tax rate, lowering the effective tax rate for those earning less than $6,000.

7 The term 'Asian' is based on self-definition in the 1996 census.

8 Foodbanks are voluntary and church-operated social services which provide food parcels to individuals and families without sufficient food.

9 The other principles were identified as 'fairness', 'building opportunities', value for money', 'realism' and 'management of change' (Shipley, 1991).

10 It should be noted that social security provision has been built on a mixture of targeted and universal assistance since the first old-age pensions were introduced in 1898. The significant universal exception was family benefit, while income support for elderly people mixed the two, with a universal and a means-tested component. All benefits are and always have been taxpayer funded. The significant exception to the taxpayer model is provision of accident compensation following loss of income through injury, with payments related to previous levels of earnings, not to actual contributions.

11 The distinction between the two is that the former is a one-off payment for beneficiaries only, with annual capped limits for categories such as food and bedding. The payment is usually treated as a loan to be repaid from subsequent benefit payments. The latter is an ongoing payment, available to both beneficiaries and non-beneficiaries, and is paid on the basis of a formula applied to income and expenditure. It is not refundable.

References

Auckland City Mission (1998) 'Monthly statistics', unpublished document, December.

Birch, B. (1996) *Tax Reduction and Social Policy Programme Details,* Wellington, Treasury.

Bolderson, H. & Mabbett, D. (1996) 'Cost containment in complex social security systems: the limitations of targeting', *International Social Security Review,* vol. 49, pp3–18.

Bosanquet, N. (1983) *After The New Right,* London, Heinemann Education.

Boston, J., Dalziel, P. & St John, S. (1999) *Redesigning the Welfare State in New Zealand,* Oxford Univesity Press, Auckland.

Castles, F. (1985) *The Working Class and Welfare: Reflections on the Political Development of the Welfare State in Australia and New Zealand,* Sydney, Allen & Unwin/Port Nicholson Press.

Chapple, S. (1996) 'From welfare state to welfare society by David C. Green – a review', *Social Policy Journal of New Zealand,* issue 6, pp231–235.

Cheyne, C., O'Brien, M. & Belgrave, M. (1997) *Social Policy in Aotearoa New Zealand: A Critical Introduction,* Auckland, Oxford University Press.

Dalziel, P. (1999) 'Macroeconomic constraints', in J. Boston, P. Dalziel &S. St John (eds) *Redesigning the New Zealand Welfare State,* Auckland, Oxford University Press.

Department of Social Welfare (1996) *Social Welfare in New Zealand – Strategic Directions,* Ministerial Briefing Papers, Wellington, Department of Social Welfare.

Department of Social Welfare (1997) *Statistics Report,* Wellington, Department of Social Welfare.

Department of Social Welfare (1998) *Towards A Code of Social and Family Responsibility,* Wellington, Department of Social Weffare.

Department of Statistics (1990) *The Fiscal Impact of Income Distnbution,* Wellington, Government Printer.

Durie, M. (1998) *Te Mana, Te Kawanatanga,* Auckland, Oxford University Press.

Easton, B. (1995) 'Poverty in New Zealand: 1981–1993', *New Zealand Sociology,* vol. 10, no. 2, pp181–213.

Easton, B. (1997) *The Commercialisation of New Zealand,* Auckland, Auckland University Press.

Ellison, N. (1999) 'Beyond universalism and particularism. Rethinking contemporary welfare theory', *Critical Social Policy,* vol. 19, no. 1, issue 19, pp57–85.

Esping-Anderson, C. (1990) *The Three Worlds of Welfare Capitalism,* Cambridge, Polity Press.

Gamble, A. (1994) *The Free Economy and the Strong State: The Politics of Thatcherism,* Basingstoke, Macmillan.

Gustafson, B. (1986) *From the Cradle to the Grave,* Auckland, Penguin.

Hills, J. (1995) *Inquiry into Income and Wealth,* York, Joseph Rowntree Foundation.

Hyman, P. (1996) 'From welfare state to welfare society by David C. Green – a review', *Social Policy Journal of New Zealand,* issue 6, pp228–230.

Income Support (1998) *Quarterly Review of Benefit Trends, Period Ended 30 June 1998,* Wellington, Income Support Service.

Johnstone, K. & Pool, I. (1996) 'New Zealand families: size, income and labour force participation', *Social Policy Journal of New Zealand,* issue 7, pp143–173.

Kelsey, J. (1995) *The New Zealand Experiment,* Auckland, Auckland University Press.

King, D. (1987) *The New Right: Politics, Markets and Citizenship,* Basingstoke, Macmillan Education.

Krishnan, V. (1995) 'Modest but adequate: an appraisal of changing household income circumstances in New Zealand', *Social Policy Journal of New Zealand,* issue 4, pp76–97.

Lange, D. (1986) *The Mackintosh Lecture: The Future of The Welfare State,* Wellington, Government Printer.

Martin, B. (1995) *The New Zealand Family and Economic Restructuring in the 1980s,* Hamilton, Population Studies Centre, University of Waikato.

McKay, R. (1995) 'Foodbank demand and supplementary assistance programmes: a research and policy case study', *Social Policy Journal of New Zealand,* issue 5, pp129–141.

Mulgan, R. (1991) 'Targeting the welfare state – a theoretical overview', Report Prepared for the Change Team on Targeting Social Assistance, Wellington.

Nash, R. (1993) *Succeeding Generations: Family Resources and Access to Education in New Zealand,* Auckland, Oxford University Press.

O'Brien, M. (1998) 'Changes in social security and pension provision in New Zealand', unpublished background paper prepared for ISSA.

O'Brien, M. (forthcoming) *Incomes, Poverty and Social Security in New Zealand – What Do We Know?,* Social Policy Research Centre Monograph, Massey University.

O'Brien, M. & Penna, S. (1998) *Theorising Welfare. Enlightenment and Modern Society,* London, Sage.

O'Brien, M. & Wilkes, C. (1993) *The Tragedy of the Market,* Palmerston North, Dunmore Press.

Pearson, D. & Thorns, D. (1983) *The Eclipse of Equality,* Sydney, Allen & Unwin.

Posser, S. & Chatterjee, S. (1998) *Sharing the National Cake in Post Reform New Zealand: Income Inequality Trends in Terms of Income Sources,* Palmerston North, Social Policy Research Centre.

Sharp, A. (1994) *Leap Into the Dark,* Auckland, Auckland University Press.

Shipley, J. (1991) *Social Assistance. Welfare That Works,* Wellington, GP Print.

Shipley, J. (1998) *Prime Minister's Statement,* 17 February, Wellington, New Zealand Government.

Statistics New Zealand (1998a) *Families and Households,* Wellington, Statistics New Zealand.

Statistics New Zealand (1998b) *Key Statistics.* Wellington, Statistics New Zealand.

Statistics New Zealand (1999) *New Zealand Now. Incomes,* Wellington, Statistics New Zealand.

Stephens, R. (1996) 'From welfare state to welfare society by David C. Green – a review', *Social Policy Journal of New Zealand,* issue 6, pp236–138.

St John, S. (1999) 'Superannuation in the 1990s: where angels fear to tread', in J. Boston, P. Dalziel & S. St John (eds) *Redesigning the New Zealand Welfare State,* Auckland, Oxford University Press.

Te Puni Kokiri (1998) *Progress Towards Closing Social and Economic Gaps Between Maori and Non-Maori,* Wellington, Te Puni Kokiri.

The Economist (1994) 'Inequality – for richer or poorer', The Economist, no. 333, pp. 13-14; 19-23.

The Jobs Letter (1998) No. 90, New Plymouth.

The Jobs Letter (1999) No. 94, New Plymouth.

Thompson, S. & Hoggett, P. (1996) 'Universalism, selectivism and particularism: towards a postmodern social policy', *Critical Social Policy,* vol. 16, no. 1, pp21–43.

Waldegrave, C., Stephens, R. & Frater, P. (1996) 'Most recent findings in the New Zealand poverty measurement project', *Social Work Review,* vol. 8, no. 3, pp22–24.

Williams, F. (1992) 'Somewhere over the rainbow: universality and diversity', in N. Manning & R. Page (eds) *Social Policy Review 4,* Canterbury, Social Policy Association.

Williams, F. (1994) 'Social relations and welfare', in R. Burrowes & B. Loader (ed.) *Towards A Post-Fordist Welfare State?,* London, Routledge.

Wilson, A., Houghton, R. & Piper, R. (1995) *Budgeting Assistance and Low-income Families: A Survey of Patterns of Income and Expenditure of New Zealand Federation of Family Budgeting Service Clients,* Wellington, Social Policy Agency.

14 The future of work and welfare in Germany and the UK: prospects for transitional labour markets

Jacqueline O'Reilly and
Günther Schmid

Introduction

This chapter sets out to examine contemporary problems facing welfare reform associated with a restructuring of employment in Germany and the UK. A long tradition of comparative research on the two countries has highlighted the very different principles underlying the organisation of work and welfare in these societies. For example, in Germany Bismarkian principles of social insurance are in sharp contrast to the more universalist, but minimalist 'safety net' system of the Beveridge model found in the UK. Additionally, the world of work in the German model of a social market economy has given greater importance to the role of labour market policy to facilitate adjustment than has been the case in the UK, where more liberal market principles have been the basis of adaptation. These institutional differences, alongside the more developed dual training system in Germany, have been cited as reasons why Germany has achieved a high skill–high wage equilibrium. The UK has been criticised for perpetuating an unsuccessful low wage–low skill employment system (Finegold and Soskice, 1988).

Since the 1970s the employment performance of these two societies has varied considerably. The phenomenally high rates of unemployment in the immediate post-war period in West Germany were drastically reduced by the late 1950s and throughout the 1960s. Although Britain traditionally had lower levels of unemployment in this earlier period, the numbers began to soar well above the German rate during the late 1970s and 1980s. However, since German unification unemployment rates have risen to their post-war level, with nearly four million unemployed at the end of the 1990s. At the same time that British unemployment was showing signs of falling, in Germany there were no immediate signs of abating the upward rise. This persistent growth in unemployment has raised questions about whether the German model of a social market economy is sustainable, especially since reunification. Considerable debate has taken place on whether deregulation along the lines of the Anglo-Saxon model would improve the current employment problems. Opponents have argued that it would only result in a more polarised income distribution, higher levels of poverty and a higher proportion of households without work, effectively undermining the very basis of the post-war success of the German model.

In this chapter we provide an overview of employment trends in the two countries. In particular we look at the impact of labour flexibility and non-standard employment on these very different policy regimes. These developments illustrate the problems facing policy makers in each country and the extent to which they represent a challenge to the post-war social and gender contracts in both societies. We use these developments to provide a critical analysis of welfare regime theory and to inform a discussion of gender relations. Finally, we assess the potential offered by the concept of transitional labour markets to provide a new model for reconceptualising active labour market policy that prevents the tendencies to social exclusion which are present in both countries, albeit in quite different ways.

Employment trends

Labour force participation and unemployment

The importance of the proportion of the population in paid employment is very significant for the development of social policy. This is because many systems have been set up with an expected ratio between those paying social contributions to finance welfare services and those benefiting from them. Looking first at levels of labour force participation (i.e. the proportion of the population working or looking for work) since the 1960s, data from the OECD and Eurostat[1] indicate that participation rates have been higher in the UK than in Germany. In the 1960s nearly 70 per cent of the population aged 15–64 years was in paid work, or registered unemployed, in both countries. Participation rates have fallen in Germany, so that in 1996 64 per cent compared with 71 per cent in the UK were actively employed or looking for work.

However, these general figures hide more than they reveal, in particular in relation to the differences in male and female participation rates. Between 1960 and 1996 male participation in Germany declined from 94 to 80 per cent, compared with a fall from 99 to 86 per cent in the UK, i.e. a higher proportion of German males are no longer actively involved in work than is the case in the UK. This is in part due to labour market policies encouraging early retirement for older workers, as well as younger people spending longer in education and training. Women's participation patterns show a contrasting trend. Since the 1960s we have seen a substantial increase in female labour force participation in these two countries. For example, in Germany female participation increased from 49 per cent in 1960 to 60 per cent in 1996, compared with an increase from 46 to 68 per cent in the UK over the same period. The unification with East Germany also contributed to the increasing levels of female participation rates, as well as a growing trend for younger West German women to seek paid employment and work continuously (Holst and Schupp, 1996). Nevertheless, British women are slightly more likely than German women to be found in paid employment in the late 1990s.

The growth in unemployment has been the major challenge for policy makers, as well as a key election issue, in both countries. Since the 1960s the UK has had higher levels of unemployment than Germany, particularly during the 1980s. Since 1994 male unemployment in the UK has declined substantially, although it is still somewhat higher than in Germany, where it has continued to rise. Women's unemployment in the UK fell significantly during the mid-1980s and again from 1994 onwards. The low level of female unemployment in the UK is an exception in European terms in that it is much lower than for men. (There is considerable debate about whether this is the result of a discouraged worker effect, the influence of the benefits system or the growth of underemployment in the form of part-time work.) Female unemployment in Germany is much higher. It has continued to increase especially since reunification, as women from the New Länder appear to be reluctant to withdraw from the labour market to levels comparable with West Germany. (These trends can be seen in Figure 1.)

Figure 1 Male and Female Unemployment 1960-96

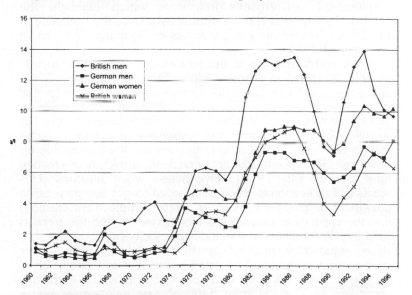

Overall, we can identify a number of similarities in employment trends in both countries, with a fall in male partici-pation rates and a rise in female rates. However, differences between the countries indicate that overall higher levels of employment are found in the UK. A much higher level of female unemployment is visible in Germany. Nevertheless, changing employment patterns and the differences between the loss and growth in male and female jobs add a more significant dimension to the type of problems resulting from labour market restruc-turing. To assess the implications of this for social policy we turn to examine where the growth in new jobs has taken place.

Table 1: Employment growth in UK and Germany

	1983–93	1994	1995	1996	1997
D[a]	0.7	–1.8	–0.3	–1.2	–0.9
UK	0.6	1.2	0.8	0.5	1.3

[a]Until 1993 West Germany only.
Source: OECD 1998.

Job growth

The reason for revived interest in the UK is partly attributable to employment performance indicators which highlight the continued job growth in the UK, especially since the beginning of the 1990s, in contrast with job losses in Germany. This can be seen from Table 1.

Econometric analysis of the relationship between economic growth, measured in terms of Gross Domestic Product (GDP), and employment has shown that Germany needs a higher level of GDP growth than the UK to benefit from an increase in employment (see also Walwei, 1998). Employment in the UK seems to be more dynamic and responsive to economic cycles than in Germany. However, in both countries the threshold levels of where GDP growth has an impact on employment creation have risen since the 1960s. Nevertheless, when this threshold is reached, less economic growth is needed to get one percentage growth of employment. In other words, employment elasticity (i.e. the capacity to create jobs) has increased, and this trend is valid for almost all other post-industrial societies. Thus there is a strong argument for qualified growth strategies in growing sectors such as services through increasing investment and innovation. If we take a closer look at the distribution of employment in the two countries, we can see from Table 2 that it is service sector occupations which are accounting for an increasing proportion of jobs, notably in the UK.

In both countries more jobs are found in the service sector than in manufacturing or agriculture. Within services, both high- and low-skill areas are marked by substantial higher employment intensity. Among the low-skill branches, retailing, hotel and restaurant services are more developed in the UK than in Germany. High-skill services found in business services, financing and banking, information and communications, education and health imply new requirements of skills and competencies, challenging the educational and training systems of both countries.

Table 2: Distribution of employment in services, 1996 (as % of the working population aged 15–64)

	Germany	UK
Agriculture, industry	23.9	20.7
Total services	37.7	48.2
Distribution	8.9	10.8
Retail	5.7	7.2
Hotels, restaurants	2.0	3.1
Transport, communications	3.4	4.3
Banking, financial services	1.6	2.7
Business services	4.0	6.6
Public administration	5.5	4.2
Education	3.3	5.4
Health, social services	5.8	7.5
Other services	3.2	3.6
Leisure, cultural	0.9	1.9
Employment in households	0.?	0.4
Total employment	61.6	68.9

Source: Employment In Europe, 1997, p97.

In this context the role of a highly trained and skilled labour force has a significant influence on the types of jobs which will be developed by employers (Quack et al., 1995). A key element which distinguishes the two countries is the importance of training. The dual system in Germany, where young people are encouraged to take up an apprenticeship programme which combines practical knowledge within the firm with theoretical knowledge learnt in training schools, has provided employers with a highly skilled and comparatively cheaper young workforce. In the UK, despite attempts to improve the educational and training standards with the introduction of National Vocational Qualifications (NVQs), Balls (1993, p27) points out that

> only 27 per cent of 16 year olds reach the equivalent of GCSE grade A–C in maths, English and a science, compared with 62 per cent in Germany and 65 per cent in France.

These simple figures highlight the extent of the problem facing policy makers and employers in the UK. There remains a considerable underinvestment in training and in particular a growing number of unskilled, inactive men unable to find employment in the UK. The focus of government policy since 1997 on welfare to work sets out to address these problems (for a critical review see Jordan (1998) and Chapters 2 and 6 above). In Germany the debates over the training system revolve around the falling number of places for apprentices and the need to adapt the system to be more innovative and up to date, but the basic skills deficit is by no means as severe as in the UK.

More recent debate has focused around an alternative, or complementary, approach to training policies. This has emphasised the need to encourage the growth of low-skilled jobs, which are usually associated with low pay. Encouraging the growth of low-skilled jobs depends on the wages and earnings structure in a given country. Considerable debate has focused on high-wage and non-wage costs in Germany as a barrier to the growth of low-paid jobs. Looking at Table 3, we can see how the cost of labour and non-wage costs (i.e. social contributions, e.g. for pensions and health care) are much lower in the UK. The first row compares hourly wage costs in manufacturing in 1994 (measured in DMs); these were nearly twice as high as in the UK. Measured over time, the second row shows how between 1980 and 1994 labour costs increased by 102.4 per cent in Germany compared with an equivalent rise of 63.1 per cent in the UK. Additionally non-wage costs were also double that of the UK (column three). Nevertheless, the last row shows the differences in unit labour costs. This can be interpreted as a measure of productivity, in that it presents the costs of labour divided by employees' output, to indicate how much it costs to produce one unit of production. Here Germany has a slightly more favourable position, indicating that unit labour costs are higher in the UK and productivity is lower.

Table 3: Labour costs in manufacturing in UK and Germany

	Germany	UK
Level in DM, 1994	43.97	22.06
% change in labour costs, 1980–94	102.4	63.1
Non-wage costs (%)[a]	82	40
Labour costs[b]	100	50
Unit labour costs	100	106

[a]Indirect labour costs as a percentage of direct labour costs.
[b]Germany= 100 index total labour costs per hour in manufacturing.
Source: Visser and Hemerijck, 1997, p27.

Apart from the cost of labour, it has also been argued that higher wage differentials and growing income inequality encourage demand for services from high-income groups that create employment usually associated with low-paid jobs. To some extent this has also been used to account for the more limited growth of service employment in Germany, and the more expanded development in the UK and the USA. Earnings inequalities across the employed population rose much more sharply in the UK between 1982 and 1995. In Germany they declined during this period (Roorda and Vogels, 1997).

Gregg and Wadsworth (1997) have drawn attention to the relationship between income polarisation, the take-up of new jobs and the growth of workless households. They point out that the take-up of new forms of employment, such as part-time work, has been from people in households which already have a full-time employed person; unemployment in the UK is increasingly concentrated in particular types of 'work-poor' households, where no one has a job. One of the key issues surrounding welfare reform in relation to labour market restructuring revolves around the types of new jobs that are being created. Are these jobs covered by social insurance contributions and entitlements, and if not, who can afford to take them? To understand the types of problems this raises for policy makers we need to examine the relationship between standard and marginal employment (Rubery, 1998).

Standard and marginal employment

One of the characteristics distinguishing the UK and Germany in the past has been the relationship between marginal and standard employment. Standard employment refers to employees who work full-time and benefit from a range of employment protection measures and financial and career benefits within the firms in which they are employed. Marginal or peripheral workers are those who are usually found outside the internal labour market structure; they have more precarious, disadvantaged forms of employment, with limited, if any, career mobility chances (Doeringer and Piore, 1971). Considerable debate over the growth of labour market flexibility has taken place since the 1980s. In particular, growing concern with the development of part-time and temporary employment has been seen as potentially undermining the benefits and rights of core groups of employees, or standard employment.

However, in the UK the concept of a standard worker, or standard employment contract, is much weaker than in other European countries (O'Reilly and Spee, 1998). This is partly due to different ideologically embedded concepts around citizenship in the workplace. Whereas more continental republican traditions emphasise the importance of solidarity, the liberal tradition in the UK has given more weight to the idea of libertarianism. In this sense citizens and workers are seen as individuals with very different preferences, which should not be constrained by statutory regulation. In a more republican tradition, best symbolised by France, all workers and citizens should be treated the same and the state has responsibility to ensure this (Silver, 1994). To some extent Germany is closer to this republican tradition than the UK, albeit that this is heavily influenced by more conservative and corporatist elements (Crouch, 1993). To illustrate how these differences impact on the organisation of work in the two countries, we draw on developments in working time patterns to highlight how labour market restructuring has affected the balance between full-time and marginal part-time jobs.

In Germany the trend, since the mid-1980s, has been for a reduction in normal full-time working hours. Through a bitter trade union struggle in the mid-1980s, IG Metall, one of the biggest trade unions in Germany, succeeded in negotiating the introduction of a 35-hour week (Bosch, 1990). Subsequent reductions have occurred in other sectors outside the metal industry. Over this period Germany has seen a progressive reduction of standard working time. This is in sharp contrast to the patterns found in the UK. Working time patterns are not concentrated around a 'norm', but are more widely distributed between those working very long or very short hours (Fagan, 1997; Anxo and O'Reilly, forthcoming). This polarisation of working time in the UK has also been related to the higher rates of part-time employment and very-short-hour jobs. Although the introduction of the new European Working Time Directive and improvement of part-timers' conditions may curtail this distribution at the extremes, it is unlikely to result in the establishment of a norm comparable to that found in other European countries (*European Industrial Relations and Reports,* 1998). In contrast, the importance of working time as a tool to reduce or redistribute employment plays a key role in German debates on solutions to unemployment.

Despite these differences, labour market restructuring has resulted in a significant decline in the number of standard employees and the growth of non-standard employment in Germany. The proportion of part-time employees working less than 15 hours a week, and exempt from social contributions, has increased since 1991 from 10 per cent of all part-timers to over

25 per cent by 1995. The UK has continued to have nearly a third of all part-timers working very short hours over the same period (O'Reilly and Bothfeld, forthcoming). Marginal employment ('geringfügige Beschäftigung'), defined as those earning less than 630DM per month and usually working short hours, accounted for nearly four million jobs, approximately 10 per cent of all employment in Germany (Schupp *et al.,* 1997).

As in the UK, there are incentives for employers to offer marginal employment which falls below social insurance thresholds. In the UK the New Labour government has attempted to address the question of marginalised low-paid workers through the introduction of a minimum wage which is likely to affect three million part-timers. They have additionally raised the level of income, from £62 per week to £81, before social insurance contributions are made (Taylor, 1998). This may help reduce the very large proportion of part-timers found in low-income households as the thresholds are similar to those in Germany. However, although this policy aims to remove high rates of marginal taxation from those at the lower end of the earnings distribution, it still perpetuates, as in Germany, incentives for employers to create low-hour jobs which fall below insurance thresholds.

These thresholds can have an adverse affect on labour market transitions and policies designed to meet the needs of the registered unemployed. If employers are encouraged to offer marginal forms of part-time work it is unlikely to be seen as an attractive alternative to the unemployed, who may not be able to earn enough from such jobs to compensate for their loss of benefits. The implications of encouraging the growth of short-hour, and by default low-income, jobs is that in order to take up these jobs the unemployed will need to be offered some kind of assurance that they will not be financially worse off from working. This implies that welfare subsidies, or in-work benefits, will continue to be required, effectively acting as a subsidy to employers offering low-paid jobs (Rubery, 1998). This seems to stand in stark contradiction to the aims of the current Labour government's goals of breaking a welfare dependency culture and of making work pay, notably through the introduction of a Working Families Tax Credit (see Chapter 7 above), an adapted form of the American Earned Income Tax Credit (see Chapter 12 above). The assumption behind recent changes is based on the idea that once in work people will be able to move to longer hours and better-paying jobs. However, in the case of Germany, where higher earnings thresholds already exist, the most noticeable growth in part-time work has been in short-hour jobs, and it is not the unemployed who are taking these (Holst and Schupp, 1997; Doudeijns, 1998; Walwei, 1998). The development of marginal employment, commonly taken up by non-employed women rather than unemployed men, highlights the centrality of the workwelfare nexus for future reform in both societies.

The work–welfare nexus: a social or a gender contract?

The future of welfare provision and social security regulation is closely bound to the historical principles on which existing systems have been built. Comparative research on welfare states has highlighted the diversity of these systems, ranging from minimalist universal entitlement to insurance-based systems which currently exist within the European community (Bundesministerium für Arbeit und Sozialordnung, 1996; Schmid *et al.*, 1996).

One of the most notable, and much discussed, contributions to this field has been the work of Esping-Andersen (1990). He argues that welfare states can be examined in terms of liberal, conservative and social democratic types. The basis for his classification rests on three key concepts: the degree of decommodification, the principles of stratification and the nature of state–market relations. Decommodification accounts for the cash–wage nexus, i.e. the extent to which the state intervenes in the class system so that 'a person can maintain a livelihood without reliance on the market' (Esping-Andersen, 1990, pp21–22). He argues that these different welfare state regimes are 'unique configurations' which refute both Marxist and modernisation theses on convergence.

These regimes have differential labour market effects, in particular for women. For example, social-democratic states (e.g. Sweden) have a stronger commitment to providing public childcare services than liberal states (e.g. the USA and UK), and in doing so create a larger demand for women's labour as public sector employees. In countries with a stronger reliance on private rather than public provision, service sector job opportunities will develop in the market sphere. In more conservative regimes, where female labour force participation is lower, these services are provided unpaid within the household.

The future work opportunities generated by these systems will also affect the principles of stratification and the basis of the social contract established in these regimes. Where full employment in the 1960s led to a renegotiation of the immediate post-war social contract, the current phase of persistently high levels of unemployment and the growth of marginal jobs is likely to create pressures for further reform.

According to Esping-Andersen, each regime created different types of social stratification, in terms of who was included or excluded from paid work. Competitive economic pressures create 'new axes of social conflict'. The social-democratic regime with high levels of occupational segregation between men and women is likely to create conflict between private and public sector wage claims. The conservative regime clearly distinguishes between 'insiders' with jobs and unemployed or inactive 'outsiders'; and in liberal regimes, relative deprivation will be experienced by those left out of the system as some disadvantaged groups, such as women and blacks, secure individual success and integration.

Critiques of this approach have argued that the post-war settlement in the UK resulted in a greater decommodification for men than for women. McLaughlin (1995, p294) argues that

> Working-class men in particular had a strong interest in, and influence over, the development of social rights to weaken their dependency on the labour market, which meant employment legislation and cash social security provision, not care services, since these were already available to them through marriage.

Orloff (1993, 1996) suggests that Esping-Andersen's framework needs to be reformulated to examine how far the state guarantees women's access to paid work or the 'right to be commodified', and how far it enables women to form autonomous households. Feminist critiques have also questioned whether family and gender relations can be adequately examined with concepts deriving from a narrow understanding of political economy, where state–market relations are the key focus (Daly, 1997).

Alternative approaches have focused on the ideological basis of the welfare system (Mósesdóttir, 1995; Pfau-Effinger, 1998). Sainsbury (1994, 1996) argues that differences in the contribution to, the entitlement to and receipt of benefits affects the distribution of both financial resources and power among family members. Other approaches have distinguished between the way the different roles for women as workers, mothers or wives are treated in such systems. For example, Lewis and Ostner categorise social policy regimes in terms of strong, moderate or weak 'breadwinner' systems (Lewis, 1992). Thery distinguish regimes according to the extent to which systems of taxation and social transfers are based on the principle of households composed of a single, full-time employed, male earner with inactive dependants; women are generally treated as dependent on male earners in strong breadwinner systems, rather than as individuals. This creates a different clustering to that suggested by

Esping-Andersen: Britain, Germany and the Netherlands are strong breadwinner societies; France is a moderate breadwinner society because, while women are encouraged to work full-time, family policy is also supportive of family-centred motherhood. Weak breadwinner states such as Sweden and Denmark have high levels of female labour force participation, with a public social infrastructure to support motherhood. The key indicator for allocating countries to these types is based on assessing the extent to which the welfare state supports the traditionally gendered division of labour.

However, this provides no perception of the prevalence of the male breadwinner model in practice (Sainsbury, 1996). Daly (1997) argues in favour of developing more sophisticated conceptualisation of household types. Alongside the traditional male earner model, we need to distinguish between dual earners, one-and-a-half earners (where the woman works part-time) and long-term no-earner households (Gregg and Wadsworth, 1995), as well as single parent households and other minority constellations.

Sainsbury (1996) argues that the concepts of 'decommodification' and 'breadwinner' are too simplistic to capture the complexity and paradoxes found within welfare regimes. She argues that welfare states operate on several principles simultaneously. She identifies five such principles: maintenance (which privileges the traditional marriage model), care (where carers receive benefits in their own right), citizenship, need, and labour market performance or status. Such principles make it more difficult to arrange countries into regime types. Daly (1997) raises the question of whether we should analyse welfare states in terms of 'types' at all. Only the USA and Sweden really fit unproblematically into the regime types; the Netherlands, Italy, Germany, France, the UK, Ireland and Australia are all more problematic and contradictory than this simple classification can allow for.

We would argue that the evidence from these debates indicates that the future reform and regulation of welfare systems is likely to develop contrasting trajectories. This has implications for the future organisation of work, the characteristics of social divisions and how policies are developed, or not, to generate social cohesion in different countries (Silver, 1994). We would argue further that the future organisation of work and welfare in contemporary society would emerge from the conflict between two inherent tensions in the principles of organisation found in the sphere of public production and private reproduction. Weber (1978) argued that the public sphere is organised on the principle of individual political citizenship and employment contracts.

Women's entry into waged employment produces a growing 'contradiction of equality' as they are increasingly involved in competitive relations based on the principle of individual merit and citizenship, which is largely defined with reference to institutionalised male norms. The 'conflict of difference' arises because women realise that this individualised, public role stands in sharp contradiction to the family responsibilities and dependencies in the sphere of social reproduction. These tensions produce a renegotiation of the gender contract, which is more to do with changes in social practices and particular institutional reform rather than explicit and open political negotiation (Hirdman, 1988).

The tensions which result can provide a catalyst for change by challenging the status quo. As a result, a new or revised gender contract may emerge in the subsequent process of negotiation and compromise. The constellation of conditions which challenged the existing gender relations in the 1960s and 1970s included: the availability of more reliable contraception; the expansion of women's access to higher education; and the tension between the 'rhetoric of equality and the practice of sexual oppression' experienced by women involved in the civil rights movements (Connell, 1987, p160). Certain groups will have more resources and incentives to challenge the dominant gender culture. This may be seen at the individual level, where professional qualifications raise women's employment aspirations and opportunities. Similarly, the resources to rebel may come via collective action with other women and coalitions with supportive men, for example when implementing equal opportunities at the workplace (Cockburn, 1991), and in the development of trade union policies in connection with equality and distribution issues.

The key point is that particular institutional arrangements and gender contracts give rise to particular forms of gender relations, and inherent tensions can be identified within a given society. Part of the dynamic comes simply from women and men responding to economic restructuring and changes in their material conditions, in the light of their resources and values, and the constraints that they face. Another important dynamic in modern states is organised political action premised on notions of citizenship, so that gender relations in any society are a form of 'gender compromise' in the sense that they have resulted from coalitions of interests supporting, or opposing, a more equal treatment of men and women in the workplace and the household at particular historical periods. Different forms of political alliances have had a marked impact on the welfare state regime which emerged and its future development (Mósesdóttir, 1995).

What comparative research on the work–welfare nexus has revealed is that there has been a reconceptualisation of the nature of risk, social exclusion and citizenship in modern societies (Beck, 1986). Earlier concepts saw welfare as a means to integrate either the working class or the bourgeoisie in building national forms of social cohesion. Today these factors have been decoupled from traditional forms of class stratification that shaped the basis of the traditional welfare state. New risk groups are emerging from those outside the workforce, e.g. single mothers, the long-term unemployed, the old and the ill. Recent comparative research on poverty dynamics has also shown how the risks of entering poverty have increased. Leisering and Walker (1998) have argued

Figure 2: Labour Market policy as a Strategy of Transitional Labour Markets

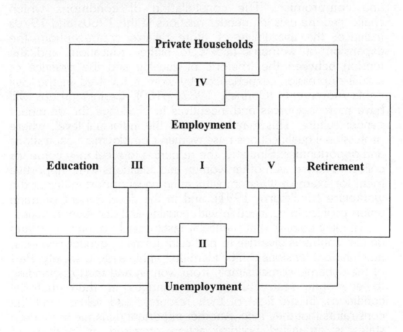

I   Transitional arrangements between short-time working and full-time
     employment or between dependent work and self-employment
II   Transitional arrangements between unemployment and employment
III Transitional arrangements between education and employment
IV   Transitional arrangements between private domestic activities and employment
V   Transitional arrangements between employment and retirement

that policy needs to be targeted to specific transitions over the life cycle. The transitional labour market approach is an attempt to move in this direction.

The potential for transitional labour markets to offer a new employment strategy

Both countries are faced with the question of whether there are approaches to the distribution of work that do not threaten productivity and competitiveness in the long term and encourage better social integration in the labour market. One answer to this question might lie in the stronger institutionalisation of *transitional labour markets* (Schmid, 1993). In metaphorical terms, these are institutional 'bridges' between unemployment and the regular labour market that allow a choice permanently to be made between various employment forms. They build on the concept of a target-oriented approach to labour market policy making (Schmid-*et al.*, 1996); and they represent a choice of policies which seek to adjust to market and policy failures in the past (see Figure ?)

Current trends in labour market restructuring require a rethinking of the traditional social contract underpinning the social security system. To provide continuous, full-time employment for all – in the past self-evidently male – heads of households would not only be an unrealistically utopian goal, but also backward looking. A 30-hour week for all, men and women alike, would be a more realistic target figure. However, in view of the changed economic and social conditions, this would have to be an average figure achieved over the course of the working life. Actual working time would fluctuate widely around the 30-hour mark, depending on the phase of the life cycle and economic needs. In extreme cases, this model would allow for periods of transitional unemployment as well as periods of extremely intensive work; even in normal cases, however, increasing use would be made of hybrid employment forms combining part-time work and training or dependent employment and self-employment.

Transitional labour markets are characterised by the following principles:

- in *organisational terms*, by a combination of wage work with other socially useful activities, such as further training, retraining, child-rearing, creative or cultural work, political activity, voluntary work or self-employment;
- in *terms of income policy,* by a combination of earned income with transfer payments from social security funds or tax credits, or with income from self-employment and assets;

- in *social policy terms,* by the acquisition of entitlement to the periodic use of institutionalised 'bridges', under conditions that are laid down in company or collective agreements or in legislation and are therefore enforceable;
- in *fiscal policy terms,* by the financing of employment or other useful activity with money that would otherwise be used to support the unemployed.

There is space here merely to indicate, with the aid of a few examples, the ways in which a cooperative rather than an interventionist long-term active labour market policy might support such transitional labour markets in the future:

1. Instead of redundancies, company agreements providing for fixed-term part-time work for all or a large share of the employees, possibly combined with further training, could be concluded; the 4-day week at Volkswagen in Germany is an example. These types of policies facilitate job maintenance and employment continuity. Under certain conditions, unemployment or employment insurance could pay partial unemployment benefits during this time.
2. The employment of unemployed people in socially important areas, such as environmental, social and infrastructure activities, could be encouraged by long-term, degressive wage subsidies. Generous support for those setting up on their own who then go on to develop their businesses into small firms is also part of such a policy of structural wage subsidies. The regional authorities should have a great deal of latitude in defining those employment structures worth supporting, and they would step in as co-financiers of such programmes. This would facilitate integration paths, as exemplified by the European programme New Opportunities for Women.
3. Large-scale 'rotation' models along Danish and Swedish lines could be promoted, in which employees on training leave are replaced by unemployed people hired on fixed-term contracts; also, apprenticeship training for long-term unemployed as well as for low-skilled people in immediate risk of becoming unemployed could be introduced. This would further facilitate integration and maintenance transitions. It has the advantage of improving on the existing labour force skills as well as allowing outsiders access to paid employment and work experience.
4. The right to take sabbaticals could be established in collective agreements or in law, as in Denmark. During such sabbaticals, cost-neutral wage replacement payments could be made if unemployed people filled the temporary vacancies. Alternatively sabbaticals could also be financed by savings on wages, along the lines of the Berlin system of sabbaticals for teachers.[2]

5. Phased early retirement systems could be implemented on a wider scale; in other words, part-time working for older workers could be encouraged instead of full early retirement, which is socially questionable and economically very costly. IG Metall in Germany has already taken this up as a negotiating issue.

The aim of the transitional labour market approach[3] is to target particular problems and identify potential policy bridges, to facilitate social integration, or maintenance transitions which ensure continuity of employment. This approach seeks to show how adapting to labour market restructuring does not necessarily imply that particular groups need be socially excluded. Further, there already exists a number of potential policies which could be taken up and developed to meet these goals.

Conclusions

In this chapter we have sought to compare and contrast the implications of labour market restructuring for policy makers in Germany and the UK. The differences between the two countries provides a particularly interesting contrast on this issue. In the German social market regime, the state and the social partners are (or at least have been) committed to full employment (see Schmid and Gazier, forthcoming). The right to work is reflected in the strong role of active labour market policy complemented by an aggressive work sharing or working time reduction policy of the trade unions, and in the tradition of a high-skill equilibrium that favours adjustment to globalisation by quality competition. Germany is considered as a coordinated employment system in which the social partners play a dominant role both in terms of wage setting and vocational training. This produces a system with lower wage differentials and leads to a broader range of medium- and highly skilled workers. However, for women the German labour market shows stronger signs of gender segregation, and the integration of women in this society is increasingly taking the form of marginal part-time employment, with important consequences for the financing of welfare.

In contrast, in the British liberal market regime, neither the state, particularly during the Thatcher period, nor the social partners were committed to full employment. The right to work has been left to the regulation of market prices, and according to the tradition of a low-skill equilibrium. Price competition and increasing wage differentials have been used to fight the challenge of globalisation. In terms of wage setting and training arrangements, the UK is seen as an uncoordinated employment system where voluntarism and free collective bargaining have played a key role in industrial relations. Such a regime tends to lead to high wage differentials and unequal provision of education and vocational training. Additionally, this form of polarisation also affects the female labour market: although more British women are likely to be in paid employment, the large number of short-hour jobs means that they are more likely to be in marginalised occupations.

The implications for the future of work where deregulation is occurring in response to high levels of unemployment and the political quest for more flexible labour markets may be to generate further levels of marginalisation. Those women and men who are able to do so will avoid non-standard forms of employment, contributing to a polarisation of employment conditions and standards of living between the sexes and between households. Alternatively, where policies are being developed to modernise rather than dilute labour market standards as an explicit response to accommodate or encourage flexibility, then the quality of this non-standard work is likely to increase and become normalised. The terms of the post-war social contract are being challenged, and in some cases eroded or reformed, in all European countries.

This comparison of Germany and the UK highlights the similarities and differences in the issues at stake within these debates. The challenge for the future will be to establish new social and gender contracts in the sphere of labour and social welfare regulation. As in the past these sought to integrate members of a nation, the future will require us to develop new forms of social cohesion and solidarity between the generations, the sexes, the working poor and the rich. The implications of these changes are likely to lead to a new, or at least revised, form of gender contract, specifying the relations and rights between men and women in society. But the progressive nature of this will depend on the degree to which citizenship rights for equality are extended to the private as well as the public sphere.

The concept of transitional labour markets is an example of how this may materialise. The recent dynamics of change within these two countries highlight the problems associated with trying to reduce high levels of unemployment and the simultaneous development of new, flexible forms of employment. What these trends indicate is the need for reform within the existing welfare system; current arrangements reflect the friction between a system based on a concept of social and gender contracts that is now out of date. If these societies are to take on the advantages of flexibility, this will require reconceptualising and reorganising the labour market to build policy bridges along the lines suggested by the transitional labour markets approach.

Notes

1 OECD Historical Statistics, 1960–93; Eurostat Employment in Europe, 1997; European Commission.
2 This scheme involves teachers having the right to one year off work over a five-year period. Throughout this time they receive 80 per cent of their salary.
3 For a more detailed study of the theory and practice of transitional labour markets in the Federal Republic of Germany, see Schmid (1998, 1995).

References

Anxo, D. & O'Reilly, J. (forthcoming) 'Working time regimes and transitions in comparative perspective', in J. O'Reilly, I. Cebrián & M. Lallement (eds) *Working Time Changes: Social Integration through Transitional Labour Markets,* Cheltenham, Edward Elgar.
Balls, E. (1993) 'Danger: men not at work. Unemployment and non-employment in the UK and beyond', In E. Balls & P. Gregg *Work and Welfare: Tackling the Jobs Deficit,* London, Institute for Public Policy Research, The Commission on Social Justice.
Beck, U. (1986) *Risikogesellschaft: Auf dem Weg in eine andere Moderne,* Frankfurt, editions suhrkamp.
Bosch, G. (1990) 'From 40 to 35 hours: reduction and flexibilisation of the working week in the Federal Republic of Germany', *International Labour Review,* vol. 129, no. 5, pp611–627.
Bundesministerium für Arbeit und Sozialordnung (1996) *Euro Atlas. Soziale Sicherheit im Vergleich,* Bonn, Bundesministerium für Arbeit und Sozialordnung, also available under http://www.de/eu_atlas/index.html.
Cockburn, C. (1991) *In the Way of Women: Men's Resistance to Sex Equality in Organizations,* London, Macmillan.
Connell, R. W. (1987) *Gender and Power,* Cambridge, Polity.
Crouch, C. (1993) *Industrial Relations and European State Transitions,* Oxford, Clarendon Press.
Daly, M. (1997) 'The case of welfare state change and transition: some feminist approaches reviewed', paper presented to the 33rd World Congress of Sociology, 7–11 July, University of Cologne.
Doeringer, P. & Piore, M. (1971) *Internal Labour Market and Manpower Analysis,* Massachusetts, Lexington Books.
Doudeijns, M. (1998) 'Are benefits a disincentive to work part-time?', in J. O'Reilly & C. Fagan (eds) *Part-time Prospects,* London, Routledge.
Employment in Europe (1997), Brussels, Commission of the European Communities.
European Industrial Relations and Reports (1998), 'New working-time legislation' *European Industrial Relations and Reports,* no. 297, pp24–27.
Esping-Andersen, G. (1990) *The Three Worlds of Welfare Capitalism,* Cambridge, Polity.

Fagan, C. (1997) 'Absent men and juggling women: gender, households and working time schedules in Britain', unpublished D.Phil Thesis submitted to the Faculty of Economics and Social Studies, Manchester University.

Finegold, D. & Soskice, D. (1988) 'The failure of training in Britain: analysis and prescription', *Oxford Review of Economic Policy*, vol. 4, no. 3, pp21–53.

Gregg, P. & Wadsworth, J. (1995) 'Gender, households and access to employment', in J. Humphries & J. Rubery (eds) *The Economics of Equal Opportunities*, Manchester, Equal Opportunities Commission.

Gregg, B. & Wadsworth, J. (1997) 'A year in the labour market', in *Employment Audit*, London, Employment Policy Institute and Institute of Personnel and Development.

Hirdman, Y. (1988) 'Genussystemet – reflexioner kring kvinnors sociala underordning', *Kvinnovetenskaplig Tidskrift*, vol. 3, pp46–63. An English language summary is provided by Rantalaihio, L. (1993) 'The gender contract', in Vasa, H. (ed.) *Shaping Structural Change in Finland: the Role of Women*, Helsinki, Ministry of Social Affairs and Health, Equality Publications.

Holst, E. & Schupp, J. (1996) 'Erwerbstätigkeit von Frauen in Ost- und Westdeutschland weiterhin von steigender Bedeutung', *Wochenbericht des DIW*, No. 28/96, http://www.diw-berlin.de/diwwbd/96–281.html.

Holst, E. & Schupp, J. (1997) 'Hohe Fluktuation in der Stillen Reserve', *Wochenbericht des DIW*, No. 47/97, http://www.diw-berlin.de/diwwbd/97–47.html.

Jordan, B. (1998) *The New Politics of Welfare*, London, Sage.

Leisering, L. & Walker, R. (1998) *The Dynamics of Modern Society: Poverty, Policy and Welfare*, Bristol, The Policy Press.

Lewis, J. (ed.) (1992) *Women and Social Policy in Europe*, Aldershot, Edward Elgar.

McLaughlin, E. (1995) 'Gender and egalitarianism in the British welfare state', in J. Humphries & J. Rubery (eds) *The Economics of Equal Opportunities*, Manchester, EOC.

Mósesdóttir, L. (1995) 'The state and the egalitarian, ecclesiastical and liberal regimes of gender relations', *British Journal of Sociology*, vol. 46, no. 4, pp623–642.

OECD (1998) *Employment Outlook*, June, Paris, OECD

O'Reilly, J. & Bothfeld, S. (forthcoming) 'For better or worse? Part-time work in Germany and the UK. A comparison of the British Household Panel Survey and the German Social Economic Panel', *Cambridge Journal of Economics*.

O'Reilly, J. & Spee, C. (1998) 'Regulating work and welfare of the future: towards a new social and gender contract?', *European Journal of Industrial Relations*, vol. 4, no. 3, pp259–281.

Orloff, A. (1993) 'Gender and the social rights of citizenship: the comparative analysis of gender relations and welfare states', *American Sociological Review*, vol. 58, no. 3, pp303–328.

Orloff, A. (1996) 'Gender in the welfare state', *American Review of Sociology*, vol. 22, pp51–78.

Pfau-Effinger, B. (1998) 'Culture or structure as explanations for differences in part-time work in Germany, Finland and the Netherlands?', in J. O'Reilly & C. Fagan (eds) *Part-time Prospects,* London, Routledge.

Quack, S., O'Reilly, J. & Hilderbrandt, S.(1995) 'Structuring change: recruitment and training in retail banking in Germany, Britain and France', *International Journal of Human Resource Management,* vol. 6, no. 4, pp759–794.

Roorda, W.B. & Vogels, E.H.W.M. (1997) 'Arbeidsmarkt, bescherming en prestaties', *Economisch Statistische Berichten,* 26 March, pp245–248.

Rubery, J. (1998) 'Part-time work: a threat to Labour standards?', in J. O'Reilly & C. Fagan (eds) *Part-time Prospects,* London, Routledge.

Sainsbury, D. (1996) *Gender Equality and Welfare States,* Cambridge, Cambridge University Press.

Schmid, G. (1993) *Übergänge in die Vollbeschäftigung: Formen und Finanzierung einer zukunftsgerechten Arbeitsmarktpolitik,* WZB Discussion Paper FS 1 93-208, Berlin, WZB, http://www.wz-berlin.de/amb/dp/amb93208.de.html.

Schmid, G. (1995) 'Is full employment still possible? Transitional Labour markets as a new strategy of Labour market policy', *Economic and Industrial Policy,* no. 16, pp429–456.

Schmid, G. (1998) *Transitional Labour Markets: a New European Employment Strategy,* WZB Discussion Paper FS I 98-206, Berlin, Wissenschaftszentrum Berlin.

Schmid, G. & Gazier, B. (forthcoming) *The Dynamics of Full Employment: Social Integration by Transitional Labour Markets,* Cheltenham, Elgar.

Schmid, G., O'Reilly, J. & Schömann, K. (1996) *International Handbook of Labour Market Policy and Evaluation,* Cheltenham, Edward Elgar.

Schupp, J., Schwarze, J. & Wagner, G. (1997) 'Erwerbsstatistik unterschätzt Beschäftigung um 2 Millionen Personen', *DIW Wochenbericht,* 38/97, http://www.diw-berlin.de/diwwbd/ 97-3 8-2. html.

Silver, H. (1994) 'Social exclusion and social solidarity: three paradigms', *International Labour Review,* vol. 133, no. 5/6, pp531–578.

Taylor, M. (1998) *The Modernisation of Britain's Tax and Benefit System,* London, HMSO, http://www.hm-treasury.gov.uk/ pub/html/ budget98/taylor.pdf.

Visser, J. & Hemerijck, A. (1997) *'A Dutch miracle': Job growth, welfare reform and corporatism in the Netherlands,* Amsterdam, Amsterdam University Press.

Walwei, U. (1998) 'Are part-time jobs better than no jobs?', In J. O'Reilly & C. Fagan (eds) *Part-time Prospects,* London, Routledge.

Weber, M. (1978) *Economy and Society: an Outline of Interpretive Sociology,* vol. 1, Berkeley, CA, University of California Press.

Social Policy Review 10

Edited by Edward Brunsdon, Hartley Dean and Roberta Woods